Macs For Dummies,® 9th Edition

S0-AEV-404

How Windows and Macs See Things

Windows Term	Rough Mac Equivalent
Accessories	Dashboard widgets, Utilities, Applications
Alt key	Option key
Control key	⌘ (Command) key
Control panel	System Preferences
Device Manager	System Profiler
Exit	Quit
My Computer	Desktop
My Pictures	Pictures folder
Program Files	Applications folder
Properties	Get Info
Recycle Bin	Trash
Shortcut	Alias
Start menu and taskbar	Dock
Windows Explorer	Finder

Common Keyboard Shortcuts

Command	Shortcut
New Finder Window	⌘+N
New Folder	Shift+⌘+N
New Smart Folder	Option+⌘+N
Open	⌘+O
Close Window	⌘+W
Get Info	⌘+I
Duplicate	⌘+D
Make Alias	⌘+L
Show Original	⌘+R
Add to Sidebar	⌘+T
Eject	⌘+E
Find	⌘+F

For Dummies: Bestselling Book Series for Beginners

Macs For Dummies,®
9th Edition

Quick Escapes from Computer Hell

Use Force Quit when an application is unresponsive: On the menu, choose Force Quit (or press ⌘+Option+Esc). Click the name of the deviant application (it probably has *not responding* next to its name). You typically won't have to reboot.

Restart. If Force Quit doesn't bail you out, try rebooting the computer. If a frozen Mac prevents you from clicking the Restart command on the menu, hold down the power button for several seconds or press Control+⌘ and then press the power button. If all else fails, pull the plug, but remember that powering down without logging out should be used only as a last resort.

Restart in Safe Mode. Press the power button to turn on your computer, and then press and hold the Shift key the instant you hear the welcome chime. Release Shift when the Apple logo appears. The words *Safe Boot* appear in Tiger's login window. In Safe mode, the Mac unleashes a series of troubleshooting steps designed to return the computer to good health. If Safe Boot resolved the issue, restart the Mac normally the next time.

Five Reasons Macs Kick Butt

They play chess. Challenge the computer or watch the computer challenge itself (Applications).

They're multilingual. Display menus and dialog boxes in 15 foreign languages. (Choose International in System Preferences.)

They recognize speech. Use your voice to open applications, choose menu items, and send e-mail. (Choose Speech in System Preferences.)

They enable you to use parental controls. Specify Web sites your kids can visit, people they can e-mail or chat with, and applications they can run. (Choose Accounts in System Preferences.)

They allow video conferencing. Hold a video conference with up to three people through iChat AV (Applications).

For Dummies: Bestselling Book Series for Beginners

Macs
FOR
DUMMIES®
9TH EDITION

by Edward C. Baig

USA TODAY's Personal Technology columnist

Wiley Publishing, Inc.

Macs For Dummies®, 9th Edition

Published by
Wiley Publishing, Inc.
111 River Street
Hoboken, NJ 07030-5774
www.wiley.com

For general information on our other products and services, please contact our Customer Care Department within the U.S. at 800-762-2974, outside the U.S. at 317-572-3993, or fax 317-572-4002.

For technical support, please visit www.wiley.com/techsupport.

Wiley also publishes its books in a variety of electronic formats. Some content that appears in print may not be available in electronic books.

Library of Congress Control Number: 2006926376

ISBN-13: 978-0-470-04849-8

ISBN-10: 0-470-04849-2

Manufactured in the United States of America

10 9 8 7 6 5 4 3 2

9B/RS/QZ/QW/IN

WILEY

Dedication

I dedicate this book with love to the ladies in my life, my beautiful wife, Janie, for putting up with my messy office and inspiring me daily to do better things, and my adorable daughter, Sydney, for recognizing (I think) the phrase "daddy is working" and for lighting up any room she walks into. This book is also dedicated to my canine "son," Eddie, for reminding me through his barks that it is I who live and work in *his* house.

Author's Acknowledgments

No book is written in a vacuum; a lot of people are responsible for making it happen. Let me start by thanking my agent, Matt Wagner, for bringing this project to me in the first place.

I'd like to thank Project Editor Susan Pink, Acquisitions Manager Bob Woerner, and Technical Editor Clint McCarty for watching my back and guiding this first-time *For Dummies* author through the process.

A special word of thanks and respect for the terrific *For Dummies* writers who have come before me and set such a high bar for excellence, including David Pogue and Dan Gookin.

I'd like to thank Jim Henderson and the rest of my *USA TODAY* colleagues for being supportive and putting the newspaper's stamp of approval on this project.

Last but not least, I'm appreciative of friends and family members who not only encouraged me to take on this book but forgave me for not being exactly swift in initiating or returning phone calls and e-mails. Now I have no more excuses.

Publisher's Acknowledgments

We're proud of this book; please send us your comments through our online registration form located at www.dummies.com/register/.

Some of the people who helped bring this book to market include the following:

Acquisitions, Editorial, and Media Development

Project Editor: Susan Pink

Acquisitions Editor: Bob Woerner

Technical Editor: Clint McCarty

Editorial Manager: Jodi Jensen

Media Development Manager: Laura VanWinkle

Editorial Assistant: Amanda Foxworth

Sr. Editorial Assistant: Cherie Case

Cartoons: Rich Tennant (www.the5thwave.com)

Composition

Project Coordinator: Tera Knapp

Layout and Graphics: Carl Byers, Denny Hager, Lynsey Osborn, Alicia B. South

Proofreaders: John Greenough, Jessica Kramer, Techbooks

Indexer: Techbooks

Publishing and Editorial for Technology Dummies

  Richard Swadley, Vice President and Executive Group Publisher

  Andy Cummings, Vice President and Publisher

  Mary Bednarek, Executive Acquisitions Director

  Mary C. Corder, Editorial Director

Publishing for Consumer Dummies

  Diane Graves Steele, Vice President and Publisher

  Joyce Pepple, Acquisitions Director

Composition Services

  Gerry Fahey, Vice President of Production Services

  Debbie Stailey, Director of Composition Services

Contents at a Glance

Table of Contents

Introduction

· ·

*W*hat an amazing time to get to know the Mac. For years these elegantly designed computers have been a model of simplicity and virus-free stability. Now Macs are undergoing stunning changes that make these machines even harder to resist.

Apple's seismic embrace of Intel means you, Mr. or Ms. Computer Buyer, can have your cake *and* eat it too. (I love a good cliché when you need it.) You can benefit from what remains the best marriage in personal computing (the blessed union between Mac hardware and Mac software). But you no longer have to ditch the Microsoft Windows–based software you currently use out of habit, business obligations, or because you don't know any better.

Indeed, this book is partially targeted at Windows vets who are at least thinking about defecting to the Mac. It is also squarely aimed at people who are new to computers — and the Internet — period.

And though this is primarily a book for beginners, I trust people who have already dabbled with computers in general and Macs in particular will also find it useful.

About This Book

A word about the *For Dummies* franchise I'm now proud to be a part of. These books are built around the idea that all of us feel like dopes whenever we tackle something new, especially when the subject at hand (technology) reeks of a jargon-y stench.

I happen to know you don't have a dummy bone in your body, and the publishers at Wiley know it too. *Au contraire*. (How dumb can you be if you speak French?) If anything, you've already demonstrated smarts by purchasing this book. You're ready to plunge into the best computing environment I know of.

Because you're so intelligent, you're probably wondering "who is this guy asking me for 400 pages or so of my time?" Go ahead and read my bio, which appears just before the Table of Contents.

What you won't find there is this: I'm a relative latecomer to the Mac. I grew up on MS-DOS computing and then migrated like most of the rest of the world into Windows. I still use Windows machines every day.

But I've since become a devoted Mac convert and I use my various Apples every day too. (No snide remarks, please; I find time for other pursuits.)

When writing this book, I vowed to keep the geek-speak to a minimum. I couldn't eliminate it entirely and, to be honest, wouldn't want to. Here's why:

✓ You may come across some of these absurdly complicated terms in advertisements and on the Web. So it's helpful to have at least a passing familiarity with some of them.

✓ Nothing says we can't poke a little fun now and then at the nerds who drummed up this stuff.

Conventions Used in This Book

Anyone who has skimmed the pages of this or other *For Dummies* books knows they're not exactly *War and Peace*. Come to think of it, it's too bad Tolstoy got to that name first. Would have made a great title when the definitive account of the Apple-Intel alliance is written.

Macs For Dummies makes generous use of numbered and bulleted lists, and screen grabs captured, by the way, using a handy little freebie Mac utility (invaluable to writers of books like this) called *Grab*. See, you haven't even escaped the introduction, and I threw in your first Mac lesson, just like that.

You'll also note several sidebars in the book, containing material that's not part of the required syllabus (well, nothing is really required). I hope you'll read them anyhow. Some sidebars are technical in nature, and some provide a little historical perspective.

How This Book Is Organized

The beauty of the *For Dummies* format is that you can jump around and read any section you want. You are not obliged to follow a linear structure. Need to solve a problem? Head straight to the troubleshooting section (Chapter 20) and do not pass Go. Want to start putting a coffee table photo book together? Meet me in Chapter 15. You bring the coffee.

An organizing principle *is* at work here. This edition of *Macs For Dummies* is split into a half-dozen parts. If you're new to computing, you might want to digest this book from start to finish.

Part I: Freshman Year at Drag-and-Drop Tech

In Part I, I lay out the groundwork for your Mac education: from turning the machine on to navigating the Mac desktop. You are introduced to ports and connectors, the dock, freebie programs, and the various Macs models.

Part II: Mac Daily Dealings

If Part I was mainly for seminars and lectures, Part II is where you get to do lab work. You find out how to process words and print and how to start taming the Tiger operating system.

Part III: Rocketing into Cyberspace

Part III covers all things Internet. You find out how to get connected, conduct online research, shop, and send e-mail. I also introduce .Mac, Apple's fee-based online club.

Part IV: Getting an iLife

In Part IV you really move into the fun stuff, the programs that may have driven you to purchase a Mac in the first place: iTunes, iPhoto, iMovie HD, iDVD, GarageBand, and iWeb.

Part V: The Creepy Geeky Section

Part V is the part of this computer book that you might imagine is most, well, like a computer book. Don't worry, you can read the chapters in this section without being branded a nerd. In any event, it's chock-full of practical information on networking and diagnosing problems.

Part VI: The Part of Tens

Listmania is a *For Dummies* trademark. Check out Part VI for ten Mac-flavored Web sites, ten dashboard widgets, plus ten more nifty things a Mac can do, from playing chess to telling a joke.

Icons Used in This Book

Sprinkled through the margins of these pages are round little pictures, or icons. I could have easily mentioned icons in the "Conventions Used in This Book" section, because icons are *For Dummies* conventions too, not to mention essential ingredients in today's computers. I use four of them throughout this book.

I present the tip icon when a shortcut or recommendation might make the task at hand faster or simpler.

This icon is my way of saying pay heed to this passage and proceed gingerly, lest you wreak the kind of havoc that can cause real and possibly permanent damage to your computer and (by extension) your wallet.

Some percentage of *For Dummies* readers will get so hooked on computing they will become the geeks of tomorrow. These are the people who will welcome the presence of these pointy-faced little icons. Others among you would rather swallow turpentine than read an overly technical passage. You can safely ignore this material. (Still, won't you be the least bit curious about what it is you might be missing?)

A remember icon means a point of *emphasis* is here. So along with remembering where you put the house keys and your spouse's birthday, you might want to retain some of this stuff.

Where to Go from Here

I've made every effort to get things right and present them in a coherent manner. But if I've erred in any way, confused you, made you mad, whatever, drop me an e-mail at baigdummies@aol.com. I truly welcome your comments and suggestions, and I'll do my best to respond to reasonable queries in a timely fashion. Mac people aren't shy about voicing their opinions. Oh, and since all writers have fragile egos, feel free to send *nice* e-mails my way too.

Above all, I hope you have fun reading the book and, more importantly, a grand ole time with your Mac. Thanks for buying the book.

Part I
Freshman Year at Drag-and-Drop Tech

The 5th Wave   By Rich Tennant

In this part . . .

Even at a party school, you have to enroll in a few academic classes. In these early chapters, the coursework provides you with your first glimpse at the tools and programs that make Macs so appealing. Plus, the homework is light.

You've chosen an excellent major.

Chapter 1

Adventuring into the Mac World

*F*orgive me for getting too personal right off the bat, but next to your spouse or significant other, is there anyone or anything you touch more often than a computer keyboard? Or gaze at more intensely than a monitor?

If this is your initial dalliance with a Macintosh, you are probably already smitten. And quite possibly at the start of a lifelong affair.

Despite its good looks, the Mac is much more than a trophy computer. You can admire the machine for flaunting intelligent design, versatility, and toughness. A Mac can take care of itself. As of this writing, the Mac has avoided the scourge of viruses that plague PCs based on Microsoft Windows. Apple's darlings are a lot more stable too, so they crash and burn less often.

Mac-Spectacular Computing

You shouldn't be alarmed that far fewer people own Macs compared with PCs. That's like saying more people drive Chevy's than Ferraris. By my way of thinking, strength in numbers is overrated.

Besides, as a new member of the Mac community consider the company you are about to keep. Mac owners tend to belong to the cool crowd: artists, designers, performers, and (can't resist this one) writers.

For sure, these same people can be smug at times. I've had Mac mavens go ballistic on me for penning *positive* reviews that were not flattering enough. Or for even daring to suggest that Macs aren't always perfect.

The machines come pretty darn close, though, so if you're new to the Mac you're in for a treat. It has been suggested that most Windows users go to their computers to complete the task at hand and be done with it. The Mac owner also gets things done, of course. The difference is that machines branded with the Apple logo tend to be a labor of love. Moreover, now that Intel is inside newer Macs, Apple's computer can double as a pretty darn effective Windows machine.

Oh, and you will always remember the first time.

Checking out shapes and sizes

When people speak of the Mac, they may refer to both the physical machine or hardware and the *operating system* software that makes it all tick. One is worthless without the other. On a Mac, the operating system is called *OS X* (pronounced oh-S-ten). The latest version also carries a ferocious moniker, Tiger (see Chapter 6 for more on the operating system), with Leopard poised to follow.

Apple Computer has a tremendous advantage over the companies promoting Windows PCs because it is the single entity responsible for producing not only the computer itself but also the important software that choreographs the way the system behaves. Everything is simpatico.

That's in stark contrast to the way of the PC world. Companies such as Dell and Hewlett-Packard manufacture hardware. Microsoft produces the Windows software that fuels the machines. Sure these companies maintain close relationships. They just don't share Apple's blood relationships.

You will find a variety of Macintoshes meant to sit on top of your desk, thus the term *desktop computer.* These are discussed in greater detail in Chapter 4. Just know for now that the main examples of the breed are the iMac, the Mac Mini, and the Power Mac.

Mac *laptops,* so named because they rest on your lap and are portable, include the MacBook and the MacBook Pro. They are sometimes referred to as *notebook computers* or just plain *notebooks.* As with spiral notebooks, they can fit into a briefcase.

Seeing what they do best

Like any computer that's been around since the Middle Ages (or at least the latter stages of the twentieth century), the Mac is adept at handling mundane tasks, from crunching numbers to processing words. Where Apples truly shine, though, is in making your pictures, music, and videos come alive.

You need not run out to purchase a lot of excess software, either (though there's plenty of dandy programs to be had). That's because you can do so much with the software already on hand.

Matching a Mac to your needs

Haven't settled on which Mac to buy? This book provides assistance. Cheap advice: If you can eyeball the computers in person, by all means do so. Apple operates more than 100 retail stores in North America, plus outlets in the United Kingdom and Japan. Trolling through these high-tech candy stores is a delight. Of course, you can also buy Macs on the Internet or in traditional "brick and mortar" computer stores.

Just be prepared to part with some loot. Although the gap between the cost of PCs and Macs is narrowing, you will typically pay more for a Mac versus a comparable unit on the PC side.

(Uh oh! The Mac diehards are boiling at that remark: I can practically see their heads exploding as they rant: "There is no such thing as a *comparable* Windows machine.")

Keep in mind that students are often eligible for discounts on computers. Check with your college or university bookstore. Apple also gives breaks to faculty, administrators, and K-12 teachers.

Selecting handy peripherals

As you might imagine, Macs complement the full range of peripherals. Although much of what you create in *bits* and *bytes,* to put it in computer-speak, stays in that electronic form, at some point you're probably going to want to print your work. On old-fashioned paper, no less. Fortunately, a number of excellent printers work with Macs. I provide details in Chapter 8.

You may also choose a *scanner,* which in some respects is the opposite of a printer. That's because you start with an image that's already in paper form, and scan, or translate, it into a form your computer can understand and display.

Some machines combine printing and scanning functions, often with copier and fax capabilities as well. These are called *multifunction* or all-in-one devices.

Hooking Up Is a Snap

Connecting electronics gear is often a frightening experience. For example, figuring out the cords and cables in a home theater system is a bit like solving a challenging SAT problem. No wonder so many folks are willing to pay some brainy technician a small ransom to do the deed for them. Or else they're practically begging the nerdy neighbor across the street to lend a helping hand.

Relax. You won't need the smarts of a Nobel laureate to hook up a Mac. As you'll see in the Chapter 2, even a kid who has barely learned to ride a bike can do it. Come to think of it, that kid may need this book a lot less than you do.

Communicating with Your Mac

The Mac isn't at all standoffish like some human objects of affection. It is friendly and approachable. In this section, I tell you how.

It's a GUI

Every mainstream computer in operation today employs what's called a *graphical user interface,* or GUI. The Mac's GUI is arguably the most inviting of all. It consists of colorful objects or pictures on your screen, plus windows and menus (Chapter 3). You interact with these (using a computer *mouse*) to tell your machine and its various programs how to behave. Sure beats typing instructions as arcane commands or taking a crash course in programming.

Even though GUI is pronounced "gooey," there's nothing remotely yucky about it.

With great tools for you

Given its versatility, I've often thought a Mac would make a terrific product to peddle on one of those late-night infomercials. *"It slices, it dices. Why it even does more than a Ginsu Knife or Popeil Pocket Fisherman!"*

Indeed, have you ever paused to consider what a computer is anyhow? Let's consider a few of its most primitive (albeit handy) functions. A Mac can

- ✔ Tell time
- ✔ Display family portraits
- ✔ Solve arithmetic
- ✔ Play movies
- ✔ Let you chat with friends

I dare say you didn't surrender a grand or two for a simple clock, photo album, calculator, DVD player, or telephone. But it's sure nice having all those capabilities in one place, and as that TV announcer might bark, *"that's not all folks."*

I can't possibly rattle off all the nifty things a Mac can do in this one section (besides, I encourage you to read the rest of the book). But whether you bought or intend to buy a Mac for work, play, or more likely some combination of the two, some little birdie tells me the contents of the Mac's tool chest will surpass your expectations.

And output, too

I'm quite confident that you will spend many pleasurable hours in front of your computer. At the end of the day, though, you're going to want to show other people how productive and clever you've been. So whether you produce documents for a legal brief, spiffy newsletters for the PTA, or music CDs to serve as the soundtrack to your fraternity's big bash, the Mac will again make you proud.

Living the iLife

All the latest Macs are loaded with a terrific suite of software programs called iLife to help you master the digital lifestyle you are about to become accustomed to. (On older systems, you can purchase the upgraded iLife suite of programs.) I dig deeper into the various iLife components throughout Part IV. Here's a sneak preview:

- ✔ **iPhoto:** The great photographer Ansel Adams would have had a field day with iPhoto. This software lets you organize and share your best pictures and place them in calendars and coffee table books.

- ✔ **iMovie HD:** Can an Academy Award be far behind? iMovie is all about applying cinematic effects to turn your video into a piece of high-minded art that would make Martin Scorsese proud. (Or maybe the kind of Hollywood fluff that generates a box-office bonanza.) Who knows, maybe Apple boss Steve Jobs will find work for you at Disney or Pixar.

- ✔ **iDVD:** Use this program to create DVDs with chapters like the films you rent at the video store.

- ✔ **GarageBand:** Did somebody mention groupies? GarageBand lets you make music using "virtual" software instruments. The latest version also can help you create online radio shows, or *podcasts*.

- ✔ **iWeb:** The newest member of the iLife troupe is all about helping you create your own Web site.

Reaching Outside the Box

The modern computing experience extends well beyond the inner workings of the physical contraption on your desk. Computing is more about what occurs in the magical kingdom of cyberspace, better known to the public as the Internet.

Getting online

In Chapter 9, you discover all there is to know about finding your way to the Internet, and the many paths you can take once you get there. The Mac comes with the software you need to get started and (depending on your model) the circuitry required to connect online through fast broadband methods. Older machines may still dial up the Internet.

Networking with or without wires

Ask a few people to explain what networking is all about and they'll probably utter something about trying to meet and cozy up to influential people who might help them advance their careers or social lives.

A Mac can help with such things, too, but that's not the kind of networking I have in mind. Computer networks are about having two or more machines communicate with one another to share files, pictures, music and, most importantly, a connection to various online outposts. Even on a Mac, this networking business can get kind of geeky, though Apple does as well as anyone in helping to simplify the process. You can network by connecting certain cords and cables. The preferred method is do so without wires. This is all explained in Chapter 18.

Staying Safe and Trouble-Free

As noted, the Mac has historically been able to avoid the nasty viruses and other malevolent programs that give Windows owners the heebie-jeebies. In the nastiest scenarios, those Windows machines (or certain programs) are shut down, and personal information is surreptitiously lifted.

In this day and age, not even Mac owners should let their guard down. (And remember, in some instances the Mac can become a Windows machine.) Chapter 13 offers counsel on avoiding online dangers.

No matter how much care and feeding went into producing these beautiful computers, when all is said and done we are talking about physical contraptions filled with circuits and silicon. Machines do break, or at the very least get cranky like your 2-year-old. So drop by Chapter 20 as well, where I outline common troubleshooting steps you can take to ensure that you and your computer develop your relationship gracefully. Consider it the high-tech alternative to couple's counseling.

Chapter 2

The Nuts and Bolts of Your Mac

*H*ave you taken the plunge and purchased the computer? If so, you've made a fabulous decision.

I bet you're dying to get started. You may even have gotten going without reading these initial instructions. Fine with me. No offense taken. The Mac is intuitive, after all, and the title on this cover notwithstanding, you're no dummy. I know because you had the good sense to buy a Macintosh — and this book. Besides, what would it say about Apple's product designers if they couldn't make you understand how to turn on the computer?

If you didn't jump the gun, that's cool too. That's why your humble servant, um, author, is here.

Turning On and Tuning In Your Mac

To borrow a line from a famous musical, "Let's start at the very beginning, a very good place to start . . ." In the *Do-Re-Mi*'s of Macintosh computing, plugging the computer in the wall is a very good place to start. It doesn't get a whole lot more complicated from there.

The on button

Take a second to locate the round on, or power, button (Figure 2-1). Where it resides depends on the Mac model you purchased, but finding it shouldn't be too taxing. I'll even give away the secret on recently issued models. On the latest iMac, the on button is on the lower-left back panel of the monitor. On MacBook Pro laptops, the button is to the right of the keyboard.

Go ahead and press it now. Explosive things are about to happen. Not those kinds of explosives; it's just that igniting your first session on the Mac makes you *da bomb* (translation: college slang for awesome or cool).

To let you know all is peachy (or should I say Apple-y), you hear a musical chime (see the sidebar) while the Apple logo briefly shows up on the screen in front of a gray background.

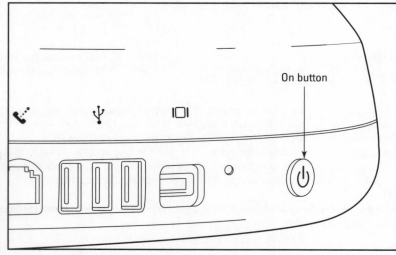

On button

Figure 2-1:
The on button is where it all starts.

Getting credentials

Powering up a new Mac for the first time may make you feel like you're entering the United Nations. After the Apple logo disappears, a lengthy interrogation process commences.

You are kindly instructed to pledge allegiance to a particular language. *Deutsch als Standardsprache verwenden* and *Gebruik Nederlands als hoofdtaal* are among the 15 choices in a drop-down menu. If you don't know what either of these means, you probably ought to make another choice. In any case, choose your selection by clicking with the mouse (see details later in this chapter) or pressing Enter or Return on the keyboard.

If you select *Use English as the main language* (as I did), you're treated to a short movie welcoming you in several different languages to OS X Tiger, the Mac's *operating system* software. Next, you get to tell your nosy computer your country or region (United States, Canada, United Kingdom, Australia, New Zealand, Ireland, and so on). There's no need to whip out a passport.

At this stage you have the option to *hear* instructions for setting up your Mac. To do so, press the Escape key.

If you happen to own another Mac, you can then transfer network settings, user accounts, documents, applications, files, e-mail, and various preferences from that other computer to this one. The process involves connecting a *FireWire* cable, which you discover more about later in this chapter.

You also are presented with the option to transfer information from another *partition* on this Mac. That's a geeky term we'll skip for now.

Of course, if this is your maiden voyage on the SS Macintosh, the previous choices are unimportant. Instead, select the box "Do not transfer my information" and click Continue.

As the cross-examination goes on, you get to choose a keyboard layout and then select any available wireless Internet service to use.

The next step is to enter your Apple ID, assuming you have one. Such credentials let you buy stuff later.

The Fab Four chime?

That musical chord you hear just after pressing the on button may sound vaguely familiar. For a long time I thought it was the same chime that ends the Beatles' *A Day In The Life*. I was mistaken. Former hippies, flower children, baby boomers, and just about everyone else conscious during the 1960s may wish it were so. For one thing, Macs are sold with iLife software. Wouldn't it be groovy to make a nexus between iLife and the Beatle's *Life?* Moreover, John, Paul, George, and Ringo famously recorded on the Apple record label. (Anyone remember records?) I've read that's one reason Beatles fan and Apple cofounder Steve Jobs chose Eve's forbidden fruit as a name for his upstart company. Even if the Beatles connection is bunk, it makes a good story. The sad reality is that the Beatles' Apple Corps has a history of suing Apple Computer over trademark issues. So much for giving peace a chance.

Before completing this drill, you are also asked to reveal your name, address, phone number, and (again if you have one) e-mail address. You can't say no, (though I suppose you can fib).

Distrustful types can click to read Apple's privacy policy. Best I can tell, no one will ask for your social security number or driver's license.

Still, the prying goes on. Apple next wants to know what you do for a living ("Other" is a safe choice in the drop-down menu) and where you will primarily use the computer. You also get to tell Apple whether to keep you abreast on company news, software updates, and the latest products and services. Opting-in is entirely up to you. Just be aware that you have to remove the check mark in the box to opt-out.

Creating an identity

You're almost ready to begin touring the computer. But not quite. An important step remains. You must choose an identity, or *user account*. This tells the Mac that you are the Grand Poobah of this particular computer. As this almighty administrator, you and you alone can subsequently add accounts for other members of your family or workplace, each with a password that keeps them from snooping into one another's computing workspace (Chapter 5).

Type the name of the account holder (for example, *Cookie Monster*), the short name (*Cookie*), the password (*chocolatechip* or better yet something that's harder to guess), and to verify the password (*chocolatechip* or whatever again). You are also asked to type a password hint (*yummy flavor*) as a gentle reminder should you ever forget your password. Failing to remember things may not happen to you, but it sure happens to me.

On newer models with a built-in camera you will also be asked at this stage to choose an account picture. Better not be camera-shy, because this too you can't refuse.

Time is on your side

Because it probably already seems like day is turning into night, this is as appropriate a time as any to, well, select your time zone by clicking near where you live on the world map that appears. If you're connected to the Internet, the computer already knows the date and time. If not, you can enter them now.

Registering your Mac

When all is said and done, the nice folks at Apple would also like you to register the Mac. You can put this off till later or forever. Letting Apple know who you are gives the company the opportunity to flood you with promotional e-mail. That too is up to you.

Making acquaintances

The *welcome screen* lists all the people on the computer with a user account, each with a personal mug shot or other graphical thumbnail next to their names. Click the name or picture next to the miniature picture or thumbnail. You're asked to enter your password (assuming you have one). Type it properly, and you are transported to the main working area, or *desktop*.

The desktop I am referring to here is the *interface* you see on the computer display, not to be confused with a desktop-type machine.

Shutting down

We began this chapter with a noble discussion of how to turn on the Mac. (Humor me if you didn't think the discussion was even remotely noble.) So even though you barely have your feet wet, I'm going to tell you how to turn the dang thing off. Don't you just hate people who not only give away the ending (it's the butler) but also tell you to do something and then tell you why you shouldn't have done it?

Okay. Ready? Sayonara time.

Using the arrow-shaped *cursor,* which you control with your mouse, stab the small logo found at the upper-left corner of the screen. Click once and a drop-down menu appears. Move the cursor down until the Shut Down entry is highlighted. You know a command or entry is highlighted because a blue strip appears over its name.

Pressing Enter on the keyboard or clicking Shut Down brings up what's called a *dialog box* (see Figure 2-2). I'm no shrink, but it's obvious based on the question the computer asks inside this box that it suffers from separation anxiety. "Are you *sure* you want to shut down your computer now?"

Figure 2-2:
Are you
sure you
want to shut
down?

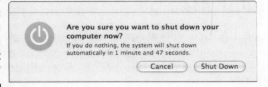

Do nothing, and the machine will indeed turn itself off in two minutes. If you want to say so long immediately, click the button labeled Shut Down.

Having second thoughts? Click Cancel.

Giving your Mac a nap

Apart from guilt, why not shut down? The main reason is that you can let the computer catch a few Zs without turning it off. A sleeping Mac consumes far less energy than one that's in a conscious state. Mac's don't snore, but you know they're alive because of a dim blinking light. As it turns out, your machine is a light sleeper. You can wake it up right away by pressing any key on the keyboard. Best of all, whatever you happened to be working on is just where you left it. You have to begin from scratch when you restart a Mac that you had completely shut down.

If you're going to leave the Mac on for an extended period of time, make sure it's plugged in to a surge protector that can protect the machine from lightning.

You can make a Mac laptop go to sleep immediately by shutting its cover. To make a desktop machine go to sleep, click the Sleep command on the menu.

Mousing Around the Interface

By now you're catching on to the idea that this computing business requires a lot more clicking than Dorothy had to do to get back to Kansas. She used ruby slippers. You get to use a mouse.

A computer mouse is generally less frightening than that other kind of critter. In keeping with this *Wizard of Oz* comparison, not even the Cowardly Lion would be scared of it. And though your high-tech rodent can get finicky at times, you're unlikely to set traps to bring about its demise.

Some mice connect to the computer through cords. Some are wireless. Either way, they're called *pointing devices* because — brace yourself for this advanced concept — they're devices that sort of point.

I'll explain. You roll the mouse across a flat surface (typically your desk, perhaps a specialized mouse pad). As you do so, a cursor, or insertion point, on the screen miraculously apes the movement of your hand gliding the mouse. (Note to self: The mixed metaphor police, a.k.a. my editor, must love mention of a mouse and a monkey in the same breath. Or perhaps not.) If the mouse loses touch with the surface of your desk, the cursor will no longer move.

When you place the cursor precisely where you want it, you're ready for the clicking part. Place your index finger on the upper-left portion of the mouse, press down quickly, and let go. You'll hear a clicking sound, and in some cases your entire body will tingle with satisfaction. You have indeed mastered the fine art of clicking.

Don't get too cocky. Now try *double-clicking,* an action often required to get something accomplished. You're pretty much repeating the preceding exercise, only now you're clicking twice in rapid succession while keeping the cursor in the same location. It may take a little practice. But you'll get it.

Left- and right-clicking

If you've been using a Windows computer, you're accustomed to working with a mouse that has two or more buttons. More times than not you click, or double-click, using the upper-left button. That's where the remarkably unoriginal name of *left-clicking* comes from. Left-clicking usually serves the purpose of selecting things on the screen. By contrast, the opposite action, *right-clicking,* brings up a menu of shortcut commands.

Until recently, the typical Apple mouse had just one button, the functional equivalent of the left button on a Windows mouse. (Apple's programmable Mighty Mouse, included with recent Macs, can behave like a multibutton mouse.) Having just one button on a Mac is less of a big deal than some think. That's because you can effectively right-click, or bring up a shortcut menu, with a one-button Mac mouse anyway. To accomplish this great feat, press Control on the keyboard while you click.

Pointing and clicking on a laptop

You can attach a regular mouse to any Mac laptop, but it is not always convenient to use one when you're on a 747 or working in tight quarters.

Fortunately, Mac portables have something called a *trackpad,* a smooth area just below the keyboard. You glide your finger on the trackpad to choreograph the movement of the cursor. The button just below the trackpad handles clicking chores.

What a drag

The mouse is responsible for at least one other important bit of business: *dragging.* Position the cursor on top of the symbol or icon you want to drag. Then hold down the mouse button and roll the mouse across your desk. As you do so, the icon moves to a new location on the screen.

Knowing What's Handy about the Keyboard

As with any computer — or an old-fashioned typewriter for that matter — the Mac keyboard is laid out *QWERTY* style, meaning the top row of letters starts out with *Q, W, E, R, T,* and *Y.* But a computer keyboard also contains a bunch of specialized keys that the inventors of the typewriter wouldn't have dreamed of.

Apple sells localized versions of its keyboards for use in different parts of the world. In North America, the keyboard standard is known as *ANSI,* in Japan it's *JIS,* and in Europe, *ISO.*

Finding the major functions

The top row of the Mac keyboard carries a bunch of keys with the letter *F* followed a number. From left to right, you go from F1, F2, F3, all the way out (in some cases) to F16. These are your loyal *function keys,* and their particular marching orders vary among Mac models. Depending on your setup, pressing certain F keys has no effect at all.

The F9, F10, F11, and F12 may all relate to a Mac feature called *Exposé,* which I explain in Chapter 5.

On Mac laptops, the F1 and F2 keys can raise or lower the brightness of your screen. On other types of Macs, F14 and F15 perform those functions.

The keys you use every day

Quick quiz? Guess which keys you employ most often? Too easy. The keys you use every day are the ones representing vowels and letters with low point values in *Scrabble*.

Naturally, these aren't the only keys that work overtime. The space bar, comma, and period are darn busy. If you're into hyperbole, the exclamation mark key puts in an honest day's effort too. Don't let me shortchange Shift or Return. And I know you accountants in the crowd spend a lot of time hammering away at all those number keys.

More keys to success

You'll find these other keys extremely useful:

- **esc:** The great Escape key. The equivalent of clicking Cancel in a dialog box.

- 🔉 🔊 🔈 **:** These lower, raise, or mute the volume of the computer's speakers, though in laptops certain function keys perform these duties.

- ⏏: No doubt this is James Bond's favorite key. Press it, and one of two things is supposed to happen. On most newer Macs, a CD or DVD loaded inside the guts of the computer spits out of a hidden slot. On other models, the tray holding the disc slides out.

- **Delete, delete:** You are not reading double. There are two delete keys on some Mac keyboards, each with different assignments. Regular delete is your backspace key. Press it, and it erases the character directly to the left of the cursor. The second delete key, which sometimes appears as Del and sometimes as delete accompanied by an x inside a small pentagon is the forward delete key. It wipes out the character to right of the cursor. Confusingly, on some laptops you can purge the letter to the right of the cursor by pressing fn and delete at the same time.

- **Home, End:** The jumpiest keys you will come across. Press Home and you're instantly vaulted to the top of the document or Web page window in which you are working. Press End, and the opposite occurs; you plunge to the bottom.

- **Page Up, Page Down:** A mouse alternative for moving up or down one huge gulp or screenful at a time.

- **Option:** Pressing Option (labeled Alt Option on some keyboards) at the same time that you press another specific key generates symbols. You can't possibly recall them all, though over time, you'll learn the key combinations for symbols you regularly call upon. For example, press Option and 2 for ™, Option and V for √, and Option and R for ®. Feel free to play around with other combinations.

✔ **Control:** The Control key and the mouse click make a powerful combination. Control-clicking yields pop-up *contextual menus* that only make sense in the moment. For example, control-clicking a term inside the Microsoft Word word processing program brings up a menu that lets you find a synonym for that word, among other options. Because finding a synonym doesn't make a lot of sense when you control-click a picture inside iPhoto (Chapter 15), the action opens up different possibilities, including editing, rotating, and duplicating an image.

✔ **⌘:** Pressing this cloverleaf key at the same time you press another keyboard character creates keyboard shortcuts, a subject worthy of its own topic (see the next section).

Taking a shortcut

If you hold the mouse in high regard, you may want to give the little fellow time off now and then. (Just don't tell him that you can sometimes move much faster without him.) That's the beauty of keyboard shortcuts. When you simultaneously press ⌘ and a given key, stuff happens. You just have to remember which combination of keys to use under which circumstances.

To understand how such shortcuts work, consider the popular act of copying material from one program and reproducing it in another. You are about to practice *copy-and-paste* surgery.

I present two ways to do this. One leaves pretty much everything up to your mouse. The other, while still using a mouse a little, mainly exploits keyboard shortcuts.

Using the first option:

1. **Use the mouse to highlight, or select, the passage you want to copy.**

2. **On the menu bar at the top of the screen, choose Edit⇨Copy.**

3. **Move the mouse and click to place your mouse at the point where you want to paste the text.**

4. **Choose Edit⇨Paste.**

   The copied material magically appears at its new destination.

Here is the keyboard shortcut method:

1. **Highlight the text you want to copy.**
2. **Hold down the ⌘ key while you press the C key.**

   The result is the same as if you clicked Edit and Copy.

3. **Move the mouse and click to place the mouse at the point where you want to paste.**
4. **Press ⌘ and the V key.**

   You just pasted the text.

Many clickable menu items have keyboard equivalents. These shortcuts are displayed in the various menus to the right of their associated commands, as shown in Figure 2-3. Notice that some keyboard shortcuts shown in the menu appear dimmed. That's because the commands can't be used at this particular point.

Figure 2-3:
To use a keyboard shortcut or not to? That is the question.

Keyboard shortcuts

Storing Stuff on the Hard Drive

You keep lots of things on a computer. Software you've added. Photos, songs, movies. Your graduate thesis examining Simon Cowell's grip on young American divas. What's more, before you even arrived on the scene, your friends at Apple left a lot of stuff behind too, mainly the files and programs that make your Mac special.

The bottom line: Computers are a lot like houses. The longer you stick around, the more clutter you accumulate. And despite your best rainy day intentions, you almost never seem to get rid of the junk.

Besides, you have plenty of treasures worth holding on to, and you need a place to store them. The great storage closet on your computer is called the *hard drive,* and just as with a physical closet, the bigger it is, the better. You may even choose to eventually add a new closet or second hard drive. (Some people add a second disk drive when they buy a new computer.) You can almost always take advantage of the extra storage. Plus, you can use an additional hard drive to *back up,* or keep a copy of, your most precious digital keepsakes. Hard drives can be fragile.

Indeed, this is a point I cannot ram into your heads hard enough: Back up, back up, back up. I warn you about this again in Chapter 20.

Memory Essentials, or RAM On

Notice my not-so-subtle use of the word *ram* in the preceding section? That's to get you thinking about the other kind of *RAM.* It stands for *Random Access Memory,* or, mercifully, just memory for short. (I can't help but think that accessing my own memory is random, which may explain why I can recall things from the third grade but not yesterday.) Just as you want as capacious a hard drive as possible, you want to load as much RAM into your system as you can possibly afford.

Here's why. The hard drive is the place for your long-term storage requirements. RAM is *temporary storage,* and having lots of RAM on hand helps when you open several programs at once and work with large documents. You may be editing videos, listening to music, and crunching numbers, all while pausing your work to defend the planet by deep-sixing evil aliens. Dude, you are doing some serious high-tech juggling, otherwise known as *multitasking.* Multitaskers guzzle up RAM.

 Geeks refer to the amount of memory and hard drive space you have in terms of *bits* and *bytes.* The itsy-bitsy bit (short for binary digit) is the tiniest unit of information handled by a computer. Eight bits make up a byte, and a byte typically represents a letter, a punctuation mark, or a digit on your screen. I know. That's an awful lot to chew, um, byte on.

You'll typically see measurements in *kilobytes,* or KB (actually 1,024 bytes), *megabytes,* or MB (1,048,576 bytes), and *gigabytes,* or GB (1,073,741,824 bytes). To provide a little perspective, at the time of this writing, the least expensive iMac model comes with a 160GB hard drive and 512MB of RAM.

Locating the Common Port and Connectors

Industry standard jacks, holes, and connectors on the back or side of your Mac (depending on whether you have a desktop or laptop) may look funky. But you can't live without (most) of them. They are your bridge to the gaggle of devices and peripherals that want to have a relationship with your computer (see Figure 2-4).

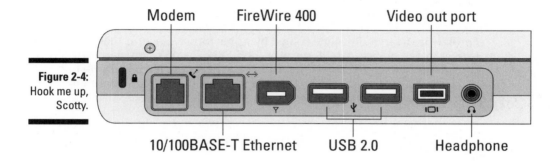

Figure 2-4: Hook me up, Scotty.

Modem   FireWire 400   Video out port

10/100BASE-T Ethernet   USB 2.0   Headphone

Peripherally speaking: USB versus FireWire

Ralph Kramden presumably never drove a *Universal Serial Bus.* But you will take the USB route quite often. That's because USB (pronounced "you-S-bee") connects printers, scanners, digital cameras, webcams, iPods, joysticks, speakers, keychain disk drives, piano keyboards, and even your mouse and computer keyboard.

Plugging in a USB device is as simple as, well, plugging it in (though sometimes you have to load software first). You can often remove USB devices from the computer without causing harm by merely pulling the cable out of the jack.

Sometimes, however, the Mac prefers that you let it know before pulling out the cable. To remove an iPod connected by USB, for example, your Mac wants you to click a tiny little icon in the iTunes software source list, next to the name you've assigned the portable music player. Failure to click the icon can cause unpleasant consequences. (For complete details on iPods and iTunes, let me refer you to Chapter 14.)

USB generally works like a charm. But like most things in life, there are occasional drawbacks. For one, given all the devices that love USB, you may run out of available ports. In that case, you can buy a USB *expansion hub*. If you do so, I recommend a hub that you can plug into an electrical outlet.

Many USB devices don't require any kind of electrical outlet because they draw power from the Mac itself. You can recharge an iPod, for example, by plugging it into a Mac's USB port. That's the good news. But some available USB ports, typically those that reside on the keyboard, are relative weaklings. They work fine with low-power devices such as your mouse but not with, say, a power-thirsty digital camera. If you plug a USB device into a port in the keyboard and it doesn't work, try plugging it into a USB port directly on the back or side of the computer.

FireWire is the friendly name coined by Apple for a connector that is also known by the unfortunate descriptor IEEE 1394. (I won't bore you with an explanation except to say it's the reason engineers are engineers and not marketers.) FireWire is a speedy connector often used with digital camcorders. But it also connects iPods and external hard drives.

FireWire comes in two flavors, the older *FireWire 400* specification and its faster cousin, *FireWire 800*. Only certain Macs can handle the speedier guy.

Two of a kind: The phone jack and Ethernet

The phone jack on some Macs is identical to the wall outlet where you plug in a regular phone. You connect a phone line to this jack to take advantage of a dial-up modem to the Internet (Chapter 9). Now that we've entered the speedy broadband era, dial-up modems are yesterday's news, which is why Apple no longer considers them standard issue on newer Macs. That's unfortunate because you may still encounter situations where dial-up is your only option. Apple sells optional USB dial-up modems for just that situation.

The end of the cable that plugs into an *Ethernet* jack looks just like a phone jack on steroids. In fact, Ethernet and phone cords are easily mistaken. Ethernet's main purpose in life is to provide a fast outlet to the Internet or your office computer network.

Jacks of all trades

The following connectors are used less often:

- ✔ **Video output jack:** This connects a Mac to an external monitor for, say, giving classroom presentations.

- ✔ **External Apple monitor:** Apple's own proprietary jack for connecting one of its own monitors.

- ✔ **Lock:** Found on laptops, this tiny hole is where you fit in a Kensington Security lock cable. With one end securely attached to the computer, you loop a Kensington cable around the leg of a heavy desk or other immovable object. The hope is that you'll prevent a thief from walking off with your notebook. The laptop cable is similar to a bicycle lock and cable that you wrap around the wheel and a pole to prevent a heist.

- ✔ **Headphones:** For playing games or taking in tunes without bothering your next-door neighbor or cubby mate.

- ✔ **S-video:** A special cable for connecting the computer to a TV, DVD player, or projector hooks up here. That way, you can watch a DVD in your Mac on a large screen. You can add an inexpensive S-video adapter to models that don't include this connector.

- ✔ **ExpressCard slot:** The slot (for adding memory card readers or TV tuners) is a relatively new standard that has started to replace the PC Card slot you find on older Mac notebooks.

Making the right connections on your computer, as in life, can take you a long way.

Chapter 3

Getting to the Core of the Apple

A lthough I'm quite positive he never used a personal computer a day in his life, the wise Chinese philosopher Confucius could have had the Mac in mind when he said, "If you enjoy what you do, you'll never work another day in your life." People surely enjoy their Macs, even when they are doing *work* on the machine. Before you can totally whoop it up, however, it is helpful to get down a few more basics. That way you'll better appreciate why this particular Apple is so yummy.

Navigating the Mac Desktop

All roads lead to and depart from the computer's *desktop,* a confusing name if ever there was one. In this context, I do not mean the physical hardware that might sit on top of, say, a mahogany desktop. I also don't mean the kind of desktop you might buy instead of a laptop.

Rather, this is the desktop that takes over the whole of your computer screen. On a PC, this is known as the Windows desktop. On a Macintosh, it is the Mac desktop or (as a homage to the machine's operating system) the Tiger desktop.

There's yet another name, *Finder,* because as Apple's own marketers put it, "Everything you need, just a click away."

Indeed, the desktop, or Finder, is a launch pad for all that you may do on your computer. It is the scenic landscape upon which you organize and store things.

Have a peek at Figure 3-1, which shows a typical Mac desktop layout. The background is blue by default. You can alter that and make other cosmetic changes (see Chapter 5). The time is displayed near the upper-right corner of the screen, and there's a trash can at the bottom right. Look around and you'll see other funky looking graphical *icons* on the screen.

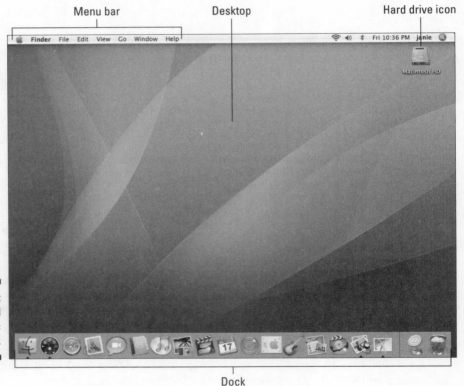

Menu bar   Desktop   Hard drive icon

Figure 3-1: The typical Mac desktop.

Dock

Let me try this comparison. A Major League ballpark always has foul lines, bases 90 feet apart, and a pitcher's rubber 60 feet and 6 inches from home plate. These are standard rules to be followed. But outfield dimensions and seating capacities vary dramatically. So do dugouts, bullpens, and stadium architecture.

Certain conventions apply to the Mac desktop too; then you can deviate from those conventions. So in the end, everyone's Mac desktop will look different, a subject treated in Chapter 4. For now, I address some of the main conventions.

Clicking the Menu Bar

See the narrow strip extending across the entire top of the desktop screen? Yes, the one with the little picture of an Apple at the extreme left side, and words such as File, Edit, and View to its right? This is your *menu bar*, so-named because clicking the Apple — or any of the words in the strip — brings up a *menu,* or list, of commands. (Sorry, it's not that kind of menu. You can't order cocktails.)

Single-click the Apple, and a menu pops up with some important functions. Readers of Chapter 2 are already familiar with the Sleep and Shut Down commands. You will also find Software Update, System Preferences, Force Quit, and other commands I revisit throughout this book. Suffice to say, the Apple menu is so relevant that it is always available from whichever application you're working in.

Now click the top item under the menu, About This Mac. The *window* that appears lets you know the version of the Mac OS X operating system software you're running (see Chapter 6), the kind of *processor,* or main chip, that the system is operating on, and the amount of memory onboard.

Click More Info in the same window, and the *System Profiler* appears (Figure 3-2). Among other things, you can find your machine's serial number, darn useful information if you are ever captured by the enemy. I trust you already know your name and rank. (According to the Geneva Conventions, that's all you need to reveal to Microsoft.)

Most of the rest of the stuff, frankly, is a lot of technical mumbo-jumbo presented in list form. However, some information is worth knowing, including a quick peek at your system power settings.

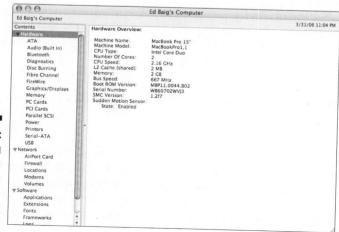

Figure 3-2:
Profiling
your Mac
through the
System
Profiler.

Understanding Icons, Folders, and Windows

You've already been introduced to *icons,* the cutesy pictures that miraculously cause things to happen when you double-click them. That you need not give a moment's thought to the heavy machinations taking place under the hood after you click an icon is the beauty of graphical computing.

Try double-clicking the icon labeled Macintosh HD. It stands for hard drive and appears (by default) near the upper-right corner of the desktop. A window containing more icons appears. These represent the various software applications loaded on your hard drive, plus *folders* stuffed with files and documents.

Now try this one out for size. Double-click the Users folder. See whether you can locate your *home folder.* Giveaway hint: It's the one with a picture of a house and your name. Double-click the home folder, and yet another window jumps to the forefront. It contains *subfolders* for the documents you have created, plus movies, music, and pictures.

You can double-click under Users to see home folders for other people with user accounts on your system. But the tiny red circles with a white line through them tell you that the contents of these respective subfolders are private or restricted. I call the little red circles *Back off, Bud* symbols. If you do boldly click a *BoB,* you will be gently scolded with a note that says "you do not have sufficient access privileges."

Windows dressing

The mere mention of windows may make some of you skittish. It might conjure up thoughts about a certain vision of computing propagated by that really rich fellow hanging out in the Seattle outskirts. But I'm not speaking of Microsoft or Bill Gates. The windows under discussion here start with a lowercase "dubya."

There's nothing small about these windows' capabilities. Just as opening windows in your house can let in fresh air, opening and closing Mac windows can do so too, at least metaphorically.

Of course, the windows on the Mac can do a heck of a lot more than your typical windows at home, unless you live with Willy Wonka. These windows can be stretched, dragged to a new locale on the desktop, and laid one on top of another.

To help you understand these windows, check out Figure 3-3.

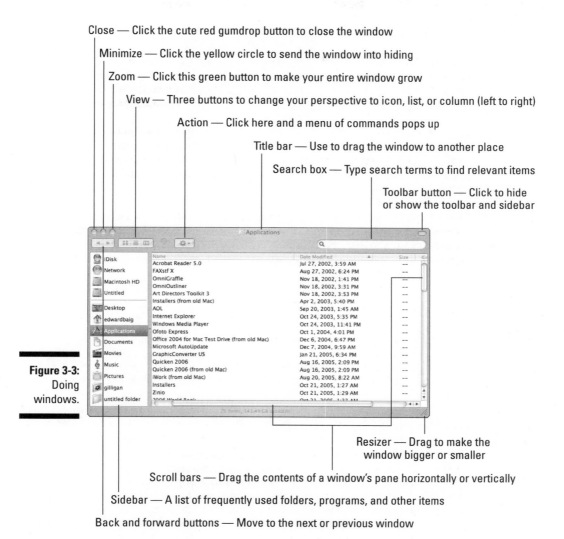

Close — Click the cute red gumdrop button to close the window

Minimize — Click the yellow circle to send the window into hiding

Zoom — Click this green button to make your entire window grow

View — Three buttons to change your perspective to icon, list, or column (left to right)

Action — Click here and a menu of commands pops up

Title bar — Use to drag the window to another place

Search box — Type search terms to find relevant items

Toolbar button — Click to hide or show the toolbar and sidebar

Figure 3-3:
Doing
windows.

Resizer — Drag to make the window bigger or smaller

Scroll bars — Drag the contents of a window's pane horizontally or vertically

Sidebar — A list of frequently used folders, programs, and other items

Back and forward buttons — Move to the next or previous window

A stunning view

The Mac graciously lets you peek at information from three main perspectives. Open the View menu in the menu bar and choose As icons, As list, or As columns. Alternatively, click the appropriate button, as shown in Figure 3-4. Let's zoom in for a close-up of these views.

Icon view

List view

Column view

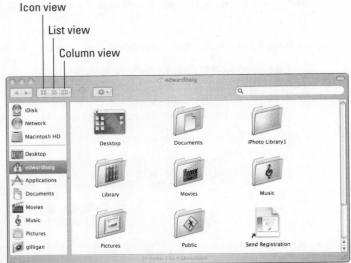

Figure 3-4:
An icon
view of the
home folder.

By icon

In the example in Figure 3-4, we explored the home folder window through what's known as the *icon view* because the windows are populated by those pretty little pictures. You know the Music subfolder by its icon of a musical note. And you know the Movies subfolder by the small picture of a movie clapper.

If you are in a playful mood (or have nothing better to do), you can change the size of the icons by choosing View➪Show View and moving the Icon size slider from left to right.

By accessing View Options under the View menu, you can alter the position of an icon label (by clicking the Bottom or Right radio button). You can change the color of the window background or use one of your own images as the background. You can also arrange the order of icons by the date they were modified, the date they were created, size, kind, or label.

By list

Look on the View menu, and note the check mark next to As Icons. Now click the As List item, and the check mark moves there. The icons shrink dramatically, and the subfolders in the home folder appear, well, as a list. Thus, you are living in *List view* land, shown in Figure 3-5. A lot more info is displayed in this view, including the date and time a file was modified, its size, and the type of file (such as application or folder). And by clicking a column heading, you can sort the list anyway you see fit, without having to choose View➪Arrange By, which is the method for sorting in Icon view.

Click heading to sort

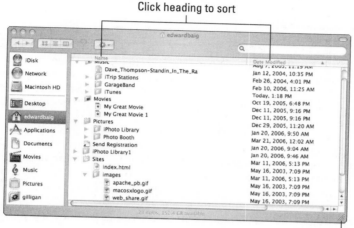

Figure 3-5: The list view.

Drag to change the window's size

Suppose you're looking for a file in your Documents folder. You can't remember the name of the file, but you can remember the month and day you worked on it. Click the Date Modified heading, and subfolders and files are now listed chronically, oldest or newest first, depending on the direction of the tiny triangle next to the heading. Click the Date Modified heading again to change the order from most recent to oldest or vice versa.

If size matters (and doesn't it always?), click the Size heading to display the list from the biggest file size to the smallest or smallest to biggest. Again, clicking the little triangle changes the order.

If you would rather organize the list by type of file (such as text or folder), click the Kind column heading to clump together like-minded entries.

While in list view, you may notice right-pointing triangles next to some of the names. This tells you that a particular listing contains subfolders or files. To see what they are, click the triangle. The little symbol points in a downward direction, and any subfolders and files associated with the original folder are now revealed, in some cases with a little triangle of their own.

Sometimes you can't see all the headings because the window isn't large enough. You have a few options. Drag a column heading to the right or left to reorder the columns so the one you want to see appears. You can drag the slider bar at the bottom of the screen to view headings without rearranging the order. Or grab the handle at the bottom-right corner of the window to increase the size of the entire window.

By columns

Next, choose View⇨As Columns. Again, the check mark moves, altering your perspective. Several vertical panes appear inside one large window. These smaller windows within windows show a progression. At the far left is a pane called the *sidebar,* a regular hangout for your network, hard disk, home folder, applications, documents, movies, and more. The sidebar appears in the same place in every Finder window.

Now suppose that the home folder is highlighted in the sidebar. The pane to its immediate right displays its contents. Highlight an item in that pane, and the folder to its immediate right reveals its contents. Each time you highlight an entry in a particular pane, a new pane appears to its right.

Again, you can resize a column pane by dragging the handle at the bottom of the pane, as shown in Figure 3-6. To resize all the columns simultaneously, press the Option key while dragging. You can expand the entire window by dragging its handle at the bottom right.

Figure 3-6:
When in Rome try the column view.

Drag a handle to change a column's size

What's Up, Dock?

Your eyes can't help but be drawn to the colorful bar at the bottom of the screen (see Figure 3-7). This is your *dock,* and it may comfort those familiar with Microsoft's way of designing a computer interface to think of the dock as a rough cross between the Windows taskbar and the Start menu. In my humble opinion, it's more attractive than the Windows taskbar. More fun too.

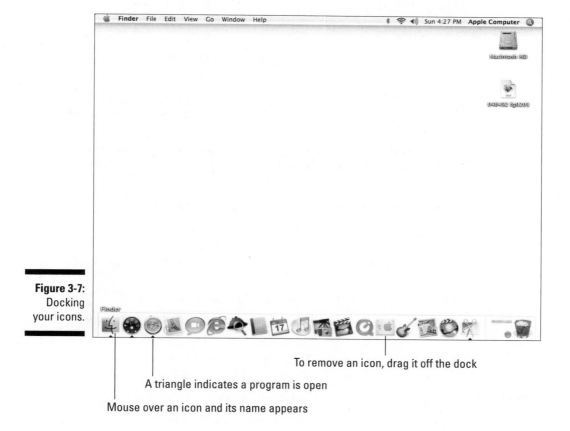

Figure 3-7:
Docking
your icons.

To remove an icon, drag it off the dock

A triangle indicates a program is open

Mouse over an icon and its name appears

Try single-clicking an icon in the dock. The little picture bobs up and down like a school kid desperate to get the teacher's attention so he can safely make it to the bathroom.

What you'll find on the dock

The dock is divided by a thin black line into two parts. To the left of the line are programs. To the right are any open files and folders, plus the trash can. Keep in mind that the mere act of single-clicking a dock icon launches a program or other activity. In most other places on a Mac, you have to double-click an icon to make it get off its derrière.

If a tiny up-pointing triangle appears below a dock icon, that means the program is open. When you mouse over a dock icon, the title of the appropriate application appears.

On newer Macs, the following icons appear by default on the left side of the dock:

- **Finder:** With a goofy face on top of a square, the Finder icon looks like it belongs in a *SpongeBob SquarePants* cartoon. Single-clicking here brings up the main Finder window.

- **Dashboard:** The round gauge is the front end for clever little applications called widgets (see Chapters 6 and 21 for more information).

- **Safari:** The Mac's fine Web browser (Chapter 9).

- **Mail:** Yes, Apple has a built-in e-mail program (Chapter 10).

- **iChat:** Part instant messenger, part audio and video chat program (Chapter 11).

- **Address book:** The place for phone numbers and e-mail addresses (more later in the chapter).

- **iTunes:** Apple's renowned musical jukebox (Chapter 14).

- **iPhoto:** The shoebox for storing and touching up digital images (Chapter 15).

- **iMovie HD:** The place to edit videos (Chapter 16).

- **iCal:** A built-in calendar (more later in this chapter).

- **QuickTime Player:** Multimedia audio/video player (later in this chapter).

- **System Preferences:** Having it your way (Chapter 5).

- **GarageBand:** This is where you can launch your musical career (Chapter 17).

- **iWeb:** Lets you creating personal Web sites, blogs, and podcasts (Chapter 12).

- **iDVD:** Burn movies onto a disk (Chapter 16).

And these appear on the right bank:

✔ **Apple — Mac OS X:** Clicking here launches Safari to take you to the OS X portion of Apple's Web site.

✔ **Trash:** Hey, even computer garbage has to go somewhere (Chapter 7).

Loading up the dock

Adding favorite items to the dock is as simple as dragging and dropping them there. Of course, the more icons that get dropped in the dock, the more congested the joint gets. Even icons deserve breathing room. To remove items, just drag them outside the dock. The icon disappears behind a little white cloud.

Here's another neat stunt:

1. **Open the Apple menu.**

2. **Choose Dock⇨Turn Magnification On.**

   Now as your cursor runs over the icons, the little pictures blow up like bubble gum.

If you're into resizing dock icons, choose Dock⇨Dock Preferences. Make sure the Magnification box is selected and drag the Magnification slider from left (Min) to right (Max) depending upon your fancy. A separate slider lets you alter the dock size.

Docking the dock

The very first time you notice the dock, it appears at the bottom of your screen. Apple doesn't make you keep it there. The dock can move to the left or right flank of the screen, depending, I suppose, on your political persuasion.

Again, choose the Dock command from the menu. Choose either Position on Left or Position on Right. Pardon the pun, but your dock is now dockside.

If you find that the dock is getting in the way no matter where you put it, you can make it disappear altogether, at least until you need it again. Choose ⇨ Dock⇨Turn Hiding On.

When Hiding is On, drag the cursor to the bottom (or sides) of the screen where the dock would have otherwise been visible. It magically glides into view. The dock retreats to its cave when you glide the cursor away. If you find you miss the dock after all, repeat the earlier steps, but now choose Turn Hiding Off.

A minimizing effect

The dock isn't the only thing you'd like to nudge out of the way from time to time. Sometimes entire windows take up too much screen real estate or cover up other windows you want to see. You can close the objectionable window altogether, but that is sometimes a Draconian maneuver, especially if you intend to work in the window again a moment or so later.

You can minimize the window instead. Move the mouse to the upper-left corner of your open window and find the tiny yellow droplet flanked by tiny red and green droplets. (That is, they are red, yellow, and green by default.) I'd show you a picture, but this book is in black-and-white. I'd say leave it to your imagination, but something tells me you're already familiar with this red, yellow, and green idea. In any case, if you single-click the yellow circle in the upper-left corner of a window, the entire thing shrivels up and lands safely on the right side of the dock (assuming you've stuck with Minimize using Genie Effect inside Dock preferences).

To restore the window to its full and (presumably) upright position, single-click its newly created dock icon.

Be careful not to click the tiny red circle instead. That closes the window instead of minimizing it.

Clicking the green circle maximizes the window to its full potential.

If one of the circles appears with no color, it means that particular function is currently unavailable.

Quitting time

It's 5 p.m. (or in my world, hours later), so it's quitting time. Here's how to punch out of a specific application. Just to the right of the menu, you see the name of the program you're currently working in. Suppose it's Safari. Single-click the Safari name and choose Quit Safari from the drop-down menu. Or if you had been working in, say, Word, you'd choose Quit Word from the drop-down menu.

Here's a quickie keyboard alternative: Press ⌘+Q and choose the program you're in from the drop-down menu.

A Gaggle of Freebie Programs

A major fringe benefit of Mac ownership is all the nifty software you get gratis. Many of these freebie programs, notably those that are part of iLife, are such a big deal that they deserve entire chapters onto themselves.

In this section, I discuss programs of smaller stature. I'm not demeaning them; in fact, a number of these *bundled* programs are quite handy to have around.

You'll find some of the programs I am about to mention in the dock. But another good place to look is the *Applications folder,* which is accessible in three ways:

 ✔ Click Applications in the sidebar.

 ✔ Choose Go⇨Applications.

 ✔ Press the keyboard shortcut Shift+⌘+A.

Staying organized

Not all of us have the luxury of hiring a secretary or assistant to keep our life in some semblance of order or to just provide a jolt of caffeine when we need it. I sure don't (sigh).

Regrettably, a Mac still can't make coffee. (Although I wouldn't bet against the ultrasecretive programmers inside Apple figuring out how to brew a cup inside the machine.) But it is reassuring that the computer can simplify other administrative chores. Check out the applications in this section:

Address Book

You just met an attractive stranger on the way to the Apple store? The Address Book, accessed through the Applications folder or by clicking its dock icon, is a handy repository for addresses, phone numbers, and e-mail address. You can also add a picture and note about the person ("awfully cute; owns a Mac").

After opening the program, here's how to add an address book entry:

1. **Under the column marked Name, click the + sign (shown if Figure 3-8).**

   You can alternatively open the Address Book and choose File⇨New Card.

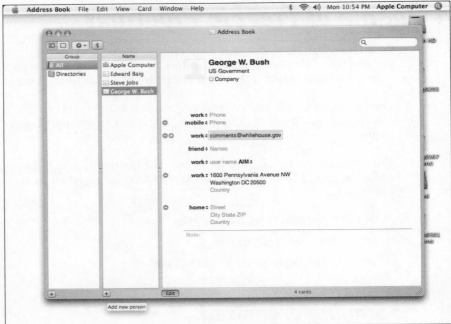

Figure 3-8:
Adding an
entry in the
Address
Book.

2. **Type the person's first and last names, company, phone number, and other information in their appropriate fields.**

   Press the tab key to move from one field to the next. You can skip fields if you don't have information and add others as need be. For example, to add space for a new mobile phone number entry, click the + next to the field name.

3. **Close the Address Book.**

If someone sends you a virtual address card (known as a *vCard*), just drag it into the Address Book window. If you already have an entry for the person, you'll have the option to blend the new data with the old.

As you might imagine, Address Book has close ties to a bunch of other Mac applications that I discuss later in this book, most notably Mail and iChat.

Creating Smart Groups

Now suppose a whole bunch of people in your Address Book have something in common. Maybe you all play softball on weekends. (That's a good thing. Break away. Have fun. Limber up. Your computer will be waiting for you when you get back.) A *Smart Group* is a terrific way to manage information in Address Book on all your teammates.

The key is to add a descriptive word that lumps you all together in the Notes field. Something, like, voila, softball. So whenever a new contact comes along and you type in the word "softball," he or she will become part of your Smart Group.

To create a Smart Group from scratch, follow these steps:

1. **Choose File⇨New Smart Group.**

2. **In the Smart Group Name field, type a name for your group.**

   I typed Weekend Athletes.

3. **Click the + and specify the group criteria using drop-down menus, as shown in Figure 3-9.**

4. **If you want to know when a new slugger has been added to the roster, make sure the Highlight Group When Updated Option is selected.**

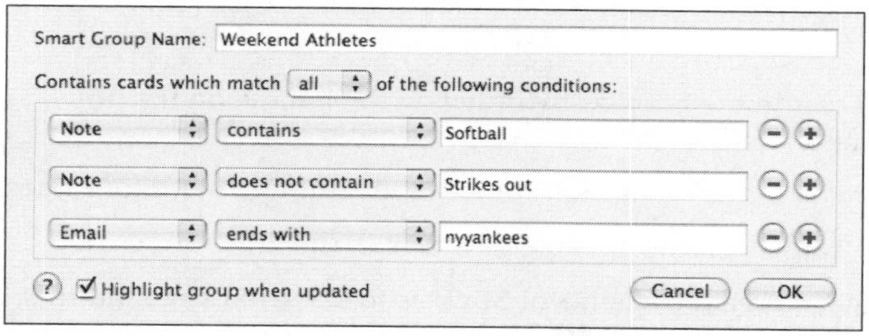

Figure 3-9:
Creating a
Smart
Group.

iCal

It's swell that all your friends want to join the team. But good luck figuring out a time when everybody can play.

For assistance, consult the Mac's personal calendar application, iCal. It lets you share your calendar with people on the same computer or "publish" a calendar over the Internet to share with others, perhaps by subscribing to *.Mac.* (pronounced "dot Mac"), to which I devote Chapter 12.

iCal also lets you subscribe to public calendars over the Internet (sports teams, movie openings, and so on). As you might imagine, it can also show the birthday of folks residing in your Address Book.

iSync

Many of you use more than one computer (you should be so lucky if you have more than one Mac). You probably also have a cell phone, a personal digital assistant (PDA), and an iPod. Through iSync, you can keep your calendar, Address Book, and Internet bookmarks synchronized across multiple devices. If you change an e-mail address on your cell phone, you can connect the device to the Mac (even wirelessly through technology known as *Bluetooth*) and have the number automatically updated in the computer's Address Book.

Stickies

Walk around your office and I'll lay odds that at least some of your colleagues have yellow Post-it notes attached to their computer monitors. You too, huh? They're a great way to make your supervisor think you're really busy.

The Mac provides an electronic version called *Stickies*. Just like the gluey paper kind, electronic notes let you jot down those quickie shopping lists, phone numbers, and To-Dos.

But virtual Stickies have it all over their paper counterparts. Consider these stunts:

- You can resize Stickies by dragging the handle on the note's lower-right corner.
- You can import text or graphics, and alter fonts and font sizes.
- You can check the spelling of words in the note.
- You can create translucent Stickies to see what's behind them.
- You can delete a note without crumpling it or crossing out its contents.
- You won't clutter up your good-looking Macintosh computer. (You will have to concoct another scheme to convince your boss how hard you are working.)

Creating a new Stickie doesn't count as work. After opening the app, choose File⇨New Note. Then start scribbling, um, typing away.

Tooling around for a reference

A lot of what people do on a computer is look things up, mainly through Internet search engines (Chapter 9) and other online tools (Chapter 11). There's help closer at hand — in the Applications Folder.

Dictionary

Finding the meaning of words or phrases is as simple as typing them in a search box. Finding the meaning of life is something else altogether. The Mac supplies versions of the *New Oxford American Dictionary* and *Oxford American Writer's Thesaurus*. The computer can even read a dictionary entry out loud.

TextEdit

TextEdit is a freebie word processor. Although it offers nowhere near the flexibility of an industrial-strength word processor such as Microsoft Word (Chapter 7), it's no slouch either. You can create tables and lists, and apply a bunch of formatting tricks. And it can accommodate Word documents (if someone sends you one). Truth is, most Word users exploit only a narrow subset of features anyway. I'm not urging you to steer clear of Word. Just know that you already have a decent little word processor onboard.

Calculator

Hey if all of us could do math in our heads, we wouldn't need a calculator. In fact, the Mac supplies three on-screen calculators: Basic, Scientific, and Programmer. Choose the one you need from the calculator's View menu.

The Basic calculator is for people like me who find the need to perform simple arithmetic here and there. You can use the numeric keypad on your keyboard or use the mouse to click the calculator's keypad.

The Scientific version adds square root, sin, cos, and other keys whose mere thought causes me to break out in hives. (Don't count on seeing me as a future author of *Math For Dummies*.)

The Programmer calculator is even more intimidating. It has keys labeled Hide Binary, Byte Flip, Unicode, RoL, and RoR. You earn extra credit if you know what all these do.

The Mac calculator is capable of tricks that blow away even the fanciest pocket calculator, such as going online to fetch the latest currency exchange rates.

QuickTime in the nick of time

QuickTime, the Mac's free multimedia player comes to the rescue when you want to watch a movie (but not a DVD), play sounds, or display pictures. QuickTime typically pops up as needed.

If you want to edit movies or have other bold ambitions (that is, full-screen playback), consider springing for a $30 version of the program called QuickTime Pro.

Previewing Preview

Preview is a versatile program that lets you view graphics files, faxes, take screen shots or screen captures, and peek at PDFs. (That's shorthand for Adobe's *portable document format.*) It typically loads automatically as needed. For example, if you double-click a PDF file someone sent you, Preview is probably the program that lets you read it. You can use Preview to rotate, resize, and crop images in one of the many file types it recognizes.

Chapter 4

Here a Mac, There a Mac, Everywhere a Mac Mac

hich of the following describes you?

> ✔ Based on what you already know (or gleaned from this book), you are on the righteous path toward purchasing a Macintosh computer. *The challenge now is figuring out which model makes the most sense.*
>
> ✔ You already own a Mac and are looking to add a second or even third machine to your arsenal. *The challenge now is figuring out which model makes the most sense.*
>
> ✔ You received this book as a gift and have no intention of buying any computer. The challenge now is explaining to the person who gave it to you why no model makes sense (without hurting his or her feelings).

Regrettably, I can't help anyone in the third group. Feel free to tag along anyway. Hey, you might want to hear about how all these Macs are getting brain transplants.

Intel's Inside?

The computer industry creates strange bedfellows sometimes, maybe none stranger than the apparently blissful union between Apple and Intel. To veteran Mac diehards, placing Intel *processors* (or chips) inside their beloved computers is a scandal analogous to an intimate liaison between George Jetson and Wilma Flintstone.

Intel was the enemy, after all. Its processors belonged inside Windows computers, not Apple's, hence the derided (from a Mac point of view) moniker Win-tel. Suffice to say, Apple's head honcho Steve Jobs blew a few minds when he broke the news that the company was jilting long-fancied *PowerPC G4* and *G5* processors produced by IBM and going with chips made by Intel.

Apple announced it would overhaul its entire hardware lineup with Intel chips throughout 2006, a process well underway as this book went to press.

So what is a processor anyway? Put simply, it is the brains behind your computer.

Two chips are better than one

Most Macs reborn with Intel processors actually have two chips engineered on a single slab of silicon. These *Core Duo* chips, as they are known, boast twice the computational horsepower of a more traditional single chip design. The idea is that the two chips can team up and share resources as needed but also conserve power if one of the Cores is not needed for a particular function.

But are you giving up something to get something?

The burning issue for Mac loyalists is whether the presence of Intel would somehow mess things up. For the most part, the answer is a resounding no. Intel-based machines still look like Macs, quack like Macs and behave like Macs. I explain the exceptions in the "Leave it to Rosetta" sidebar.

Leave it to Rosetta

To help you deal with the Mac's brain transplant, Apple and its industry pals started designing so-called *Universal* software applications. These programs are meant to run *natively* on both G4/G5 machines and Intel-based Macs. In other words, they rock either place. You know you've bought a Universal application because the box carries the logo shown here. Not surprisingly, the iLife software already loaded on your computer also receives the Universal seal of approval.

Universal

But what about older software you may have lying around? Will those programs make nice with Intel? Most will, thanks to behind-the-scenes technology known as *Rosetta*. (I will resist a joke about Apple leaving no stone unturned.) You don't have to actively mouse around to wake up Rosetta. Quietly and invisibly, it does its thing, which basically involves translating software code to ensure that (for now) non-Universal programs such as Microsoft Office and Adobe Photoshop will work, if not up to their maximum potential.

Ancient programs won't work at all on "Mactel" machines. These include the Classic apps that predate OS X.

Big Mac or Little Mac? The Laptop versus Desktop Decision

Desktop? Laptop? Or notebook? Okay, that was a bit of a trick question because people use notebook and laptop to refer to the same thing. So it's really desktop versus laptop/notebook.

The choice comes down to lifestyle, economics, and what you do for a living. If you burn lots of frequent-flier miles, chances are you'll gravitate to a laptop. If you tend to be home- or office-bound, a desktop might be more suitable.

Because you're getting a Mac whichever way you go, take solace in the fact that the system comes preloaded with the OS X Tiger operating system and other software goodies I expound on in other chapters.

Let's give each side their due. The typical trade-offs follow. Here are the reasons for buying a Mac desktop:

- ✔ You generally get more computing bang for the buck.
- ✔ Larger hard drives.

✔ Bigger displays.

✔ Extra jacks and connectors.

✔ Easier to upgrade.

✔ You won't slow anyone down checking in at airport security.

✔ The machine looks cool in your home or office.

And here's why you would want to buy a Mac laptop:

✔ Light and portable.

✔ Appealing if you work or live in cramped quarters.

✔ Runs off battery or AC power.

✔ You can impress your seatmate on an airplane.

If a Desktop Is Your Poison

In most instances, buying an Apple desktop computer does not mean you have to start rearranging or buying new furniture. Sure Mac desktops generally take up more space than Mac notebooks. But the machines are no larger than they have to be, and in some cases are so good-looking you want to show them off anyway.

iMac

As shown in Figure 4-1, the *iMac* is the most elegantly designed desktop computer on the planet.

Now that I've said that, let me mention a proviso: The iMac is the most elegantly designed desktop computer on the day that I write this. Apple wouldn't be Apple without surprises. By the time this book gets to you, the gang inside the company's Cupertino, California, headquarters may well have one-upped themselves. (I'm not ready to predict that anybody outside Cupertino will come up with a bolder design than Jobs & Co.)

Now that that lawyerly comment is out of the way, back to the captivating charmer at hand. The innards of the system — Intel Core Duo processor, memory, hard drive, CD/DVD player, and more — are concealed inside a 2-inch-thin flat-screen monitor. You can't help wonder where the rest of the computer is, especially if you're accustomed to seeing a more traditional tower-type PC design.

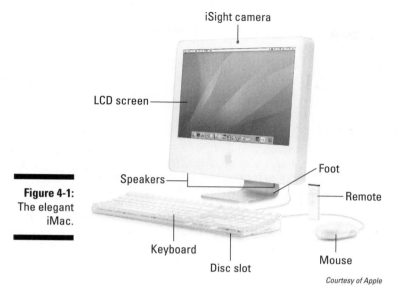

iSight camera

LCD screen

Speakers

Foot

Figure 4-1:
The elegant
iMac.

Remote

Keyboard

Mouse

Disc slot

Courtesy of Apple

When you place a CD or DVD in the slot on the iMac's right side, the disc gets sucked inside the machine like a dollar in a vending machine's bill changer.

The small square peephole at the top of the monitor covers up a built-in *iSight* video camera (I bring up possible uses in Chapters 5 and 11). The computer also comes with a Bic-lighter–sized Apple remote used to control music, videos, and other media through Apple's slick alternative full-screen *Front Row* software interface, for launching the music, photos, DVDs, and videos that reside on your Mac, especially when you're not quite sitting on top of the computer.

Mac Mini

Is the *Mac Mini* shown in Figure 4-2 really a desktop? After all, Mac Mini is easily mistaken for a bread box or coaster on steroids. But the petite 2-inch tall, 6.5-inch square aluminum contraption is indeed Apple's crazy (and cozy) notion of what a budget desktop computer is all about. At less than 3 pounds, Mac Mini is portable, but not in the same sense as a notebook you would fly with cross-country. (Carting this computer from room to room is more like it.)

Figure 4-2:
Mini's
favorite
Macintosh.

Courtesy of Apple

Models start at just $599, but keep in mind that this is a BYOB computer — as in bring your own keyboard, mouse, and monitor. (The assumption is that you have these already, but if not, Apple will happily sell them to you.) Hey, at least the Apple remote is supplied. Given its size and price, Mac Mini might make an ideal second or third computer and is a perfect dorm room companion.

Because Mac Mini has Front Row and a collection of video connectors, you can also hook it up to a big screen TV or take advantage of a superior speaker system. And Mini includes the smarts to play back music or videos stored on other computers in your house, including Windows systems.

Mac Pro

I don't really expect many readers of this book to run out and buy the Mac Pro. It may seem tempting to own the machine Apple billed as the "fastest Mac ever" when it was introduced in August 2006. But there's a reason the word *Pro* is included in the name of this desktop machine — it's not a computer aimed at the masses. Instead, this machine is intended for professionals facing demanding graphics and other computing tasks. The computer is noteworthy for another reason: Its arrival completed the transition of the Mac line to Intel processors.

A standard Mac Pro configuration fetches $2499 and includes two 2.66 GHz Dual-Core Intel Xeon processors, plus a 250GB hard drive. But this Mac is meant to be the ultimate built-to-order computer. Apple says there are up to 4.9 *million* possible configurations, and you can build a Mac Pro that costs well north of $10,000.

Going Mobile

You don't have to be a traditional road warrior to crave a notebook these days. You might just need something to schlep from lecture hall to lecture hall, your home to your office, or maybe just from the basement to the bedroom.

In choosing any laptop, take into account its *traveling weight*. Besides the weight of the machine itself, consider the heft of the AC power cord and possibly a spare battery. None of the Mac laptops are killers as far as weight is concerned, but some are lighter than others.

One of the first decisions you have to make is how big a screen you want. Bigger displays are nice, of course, but they weigh and cost more. And you may be sacrificing some battery life. Hmm, are you getting the sense that this battery business is a big deal? It can be, which is why I offer tips on how to stay juiced, at the end of the chapter.

As part of its migration to Intel processors, Apple retired two longtime members of its laptop lineup in 2006, the ivory white iBook (popular with students) and the silver PowerBook. Here's a brief look at their Intel-inside replacements, the MacBook and MacBook Pro.

MacBook Pro

The successor to the PowerBook is *MacBook Pro,* shown in Figure 4-3. It will set you back $1999 or more. MacBook Pro resembles the PowerBook on the outside, but it's a lot different on the inside. That's because it's the first of the Mac-tel notebooks. The inch-thin machine runs Core Duo processors. It has a brighter (15.4-inch) screen than its predecessors, plus one of those inconspicuous iSight cameras. (There's also a $2799 17-inch model.) MacBook Pros also come with the Apple remote and Front Row.

Figure 4-3:
The handsome MacBook Pro.

Courtesy of Apple

MacBook Pro did relinquish some features found on PowerBooks, such as fewer ports and connectors. The absence of a standard dialup modem for connecting to the Internet in hotels and elsewhere is an annoying and silly omission. You can purchase an external modem that will connect to one of the computer's USB ports for $50.

Apple also replaced a standard PC Card–type slot for adding such things as memory card readers and cellular modems with a new-generation slot called ExpressCard. Many of those type cards are still being developed.

On the plus side, ambient sensors can illuminate the keyboard when the cabin lights are dimmed on an airplane. If that doesn't create a mood and show the cute passenger in 12C how resourceful you are, nothing will. Meanwhile, if you drop the machine, and trust me it happens, built-in sensors instantly park the hard drive to reduce the damage.

The next neat feature, called MagSafe, may not win brownie points with strangers on a plane. But it just might earn you raves at home. To find out about it, see the "Cord tripping" sidebar.

Cord tripping

Has your dog or kid ever come barreling into a room and tripped over the power cord connected to your laptop? The machine goes flying off your desk, and you scramble to assess the damage. Have you no shame? Tend to your kid first.

Apple had this scenario in mind when it designed the MagSafe connector, a nifty innovation that debuted on the MacBook Pro. Instead of physically inserting the power cord to a connector as on previous Mac laptops, you adhere the MagSafe magnetically.

So the next time your adolescents (canine or human) come running in and trip the wire, the cord should easily yank free, presumably without harming the Mac or your first born. One downside: The *power brick* in the middle of the new cord is bulkier than cords used on previous models.

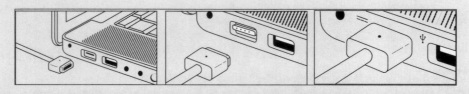

MacBook

Despite a lower price — they start at $1099 for a white model and $1499 for a version in black — the MacBook shares some of the features of its Pro cousin, including the built-in iSight camera, Front Row, the Apple remote, and MagSafe. The main difference is the 5.2-pound nearly inch-thick MacBook has a smaller (13.3-inch wide) screen and not quite the robust graphics capabilities for running high-end photography programs such as Aperture. As with the iBook it supplants, it should find a home on college campuses.

Taming the Trackpad

In Chapter 2, I introduce the trackpad, the smooth rectangular finger-licking surface below the keyboard that's your laptop's answer to using a mouse. You can still use a regular mouse with a laptop, of course, and may prefer to do so if you're sitting at your regular desk. If you're sitting in coach instead, the mouse is an unwelcome companion, critter, especially to the passenger sitting next to you. Don't be surprised if he or she calls an exterminator (or at least the flight attendant).

TIP

A trackpad (and the human beings who control it) has its own annoying idiosyncrasies. It may refuse to cooperate if you touch it coming out of the shower. Hand-lotions are also a no-no. A trackpad loathes moisture and humidity. If it does get wet, gently wipe it with a clean cloth. Do not use any kind of household cleaning solution.

The best place to train a trackpad is in Keyboard and Mouse preferences. Choose ⌘⇨System Preferences. Under Keyboard and Mouse preferences, click Trackpad. The window in Figure 4-4 appears.

Here are some of the things you can do:

✔ Drag the Tracking Speed slider to change how fast the pointer moves and the Double-Click Speed slider to set how fast *you* have to double-click.

✔ If you want to click by tapping the trackpad surface, without having to press the trackpad button, select the Clicking option.

✔ You can drag an item by tapping it twice, without having to hold down the button, by selecting the Dragging option.

✔ Using two fingers on the trackpad surface will not move the cursor when you select the Ignore accidental trackpad input option.

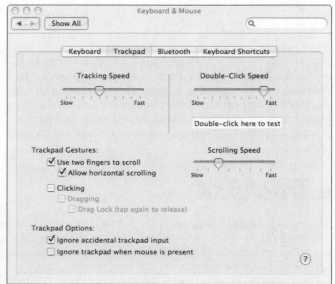

Figure 4-4:
The key to
taming your
trackpad.

- ✔ If you plan on using a regular mouse, select the Ignore trackpad when mouse is present option.

- ✔ Two-finger scrolling is a recent trackpad function not included on older models.

Keeping Your Notebook Juiced

Sooner or later, especially if Murphy (the fellow behind that nasty Law) has any say in the manner, your battery will lose its charge. At precisely the worst possible moment. Like when your professor is prepping you for a final exam. Or you are about to discover whodunit while watching a DVD on an overseas flight. I hasten to point out that watching a movie will drain your battery a lot quicker than working on a spreadsheet.

A tiny gauge on the menu bar, as shown in Figure 4-5, gives you a decent measurement of how long you can work before your battery peters out. You can display this gauge by time or percentage. Just click the menu bar icon, choose Show, and then choose Icon Only, Time, or Percentage.

The battery life cited by manufacturers has a lot in common with the miles per gallon estimates quoted by automakers. Your actual battery life will vary, depending on how you drive your computer. Expect the total to be less than the manufacturer's claim.

Battery gauge

You may routinely keep the computer plugged to recharge the battery. Still, Apple recommends pulling the plug periodically to keep the juices flowing. If you don't plan on using the computer for six months or more (and why the heck not?), remove the battery and store it with about a 50% charge. You may not be able to resuscitate a fully discharged battery that has been kept on the sidelines too long.

Rechargeable batteries have a finite number of charging cycles, so even with the best feed and caring they have to be replaced eventually. It is quite evident when it's time to put the battery out to pasture because it will no longer hold a charge. Remember to give it an environmentally correct burial.

Don't give up the fight just yet. You can take steps to boost your battery's longevity. Your computer is smart about conservation. When plugged in, it feels free to let loose. That means the hard drive will spin around to its heart's content, and the display can be turned up to maximum brightness settings.

You can tell a Mac how to behave when it is unplugged:

✔ **Dim the screen.** There's nothing your laptop battery likes better than mood lighting. Press F1 on the keyboard to turn down the brightness.

✔ **Open** *Energy Saver* (see Figure 4-6) by single-clicking the battery gauge in the menu bar and then selecting Open Energy Saver. Alternatively, choose ⌘⇨System Preferences, and double-click Energy Saver. Near the top of the window, choose Better Battery Life from the Optimization list. You will notice other options in Energy Saver, including a slider to put the computer to sleep when it's not used for a certain period, plus a slider to put the display asleep after the machine is inactive. Make sure the option to Put the Hard Disk(s) to Sleep When Possible is checked.

✔ Shut down the *AirPort* wireless networking feature (Chapter 18) if you are not surfing the Internet. AirPort hogs power. And you shouldn't be using it anyway if you're traveling on an airplane.

✔ Likewise, turn off the wireless settings for Bluetooth if you're on a plane or if you just want to save some juice.

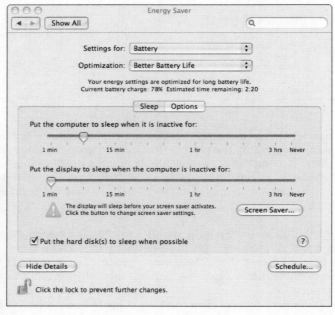

Figure 4-6:
Mac
conser-
vation.
Inside the
Energy
Saver.

After all, given all your aspirations with your computer, the last thing you want to have happen is to run out of power.

Part II
Mac Daily Dealings

The 5th Wave   By Rich Tennant

"Oh, Anthony loves working with Mac OS X. He customized all our Word documents with a sound file so they all close with a 'Bada Bing!'"

In this part . . .

*I*sn't it about time to do some honest-to-goodness *computing?* Roll up your sleeves. You're about to personalize the Mac to your taste and styles, dig into System Preferences, go on lively search expeditions using Spotlight, and create and print documents. And take on the warm and fuzzy feeling that comes when you've accomplished what you've set out to do.

Chapter 5

Making the Mac Your Own

*Y*ou adore your family and friends to death, but you have to admit that they can get under your skin from time to time. They know how to push your buttons, and you sure know how to push theirs. People are fussy about certain things, and that includes you (and me).

So it goes with your Macintosh. The presumption is that you and your Mac are going to cohabit well into the future. Still, it can't hurt to get off on the right foot and set up the machine so that it matches your personal preferences and expectations, and not some programmer's at Apple. No two Macs ever end up the same. The software you load on your system differs from the programs your best buddies install on their computers. You tolerate dozens of icons on the Mac desktop, they prefer a less cluttered screen. You choose a blown-up picture of Homer Simpson for your desktop background; your pals go with a screen-size poster of Jessica Simpson.

Establishing User Accounts

As much as the computer staring you in the face is your very own Mac, chances are you'll be sharing it with someone else: your spouse and kids, perhaps, if not your students and co-workers. I know you generously thought about buying each of them a computer. But then your little one needs braces, you've been eyeing a new set of golf clubs and, the truth is, your largesse has limits. So you'll be sharing the computer, all right, at least for awhile. The challenge now is avoiding chaos and all-out civil war.

The Mac helps keep the peace by giving everyone their own user accounts, which are separate areas to hang out in that are password protected to prevent intrusions. (There's not much the folks at Apple can do to avert fights over *when* people use the computer.)

In Chapter 2, I explain how you create your own user account as part of the initial computer setup. Not all user accounts are created equal, and yours is extra special. That's because as the owner of the machine, you're the head honcho, the Big Cheese, or in the bureaucracy of your computer, the *administrator*.

Being the Big Cheese doesn't earn you an expense account or a plush corner office with a view of the lakefront. It does, however, carry executive privileges. You get to lord over not only who else can use the machine but who, if anyone, gets the same administrative rights you have.

Think long and hard before you grant anyone else these dictatorial powers. Only an administrator can install new programs in the Applications folder, choose which files to share among all users, or muck around with such system settings such as Date & Time and Energy Saver. And only an administrator can effectively hire and fire, by creating or eliminating other user accounts.

To create a new account for one of your coworkers, say, follow the steps below:

1. **Choose ⌘⇨System Preferences, and then click the Accounts icon.**

   Alternatively, click your user name on the upper-right corner of the screen, mouse down to Accounts Preferences, and click. In both instances, you end up in Accounts Preferences.

   It's worth remembering how you get to System Preferences because you'll be spending quite a bit of time there in this chapter. The Accounts window that appears is shown in Figure 5-1.

2. **If the Password tab isn't highlighted, click it.**

3. **Click the + below the list of names on the right.**

   If the + appears dimmed, you have to click the padlock at the bottom of the screen and enter your name and password to proceed. (You'll encounter this padlock throughout System Preferences and must click it and enter an administrative password before being allowed to make changes.)

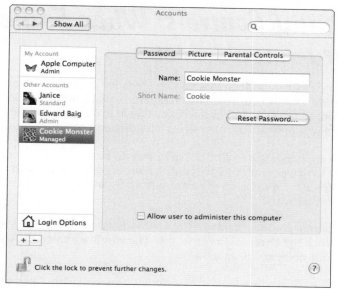

Figure 5-1:
Change
preferences
here.

4. **Enter a name, a short name, a password, the password verification, and (if you chose) a password hint.**

   This is the same drill you went through to create your own account. Unless you have a good reason to do otherwise, leave the Allow user to administer this computer option unchecked. (Of course, you may want to give a coworker or other person sharing an account the ability to enter his or her own password and user name.)

5. **Click the Picture tab.**

6. **Select the small image that will be displayed next to the user name when the account holder logs on to the computer. (Again, you may allow the other person to choose his or her own picture.)**

   You can click the bowling pins, gingerbread cookie, or other goofy iconic images presented by Apple in the Accounts window. But account holders may well want to choose one of their own images. To do so, open OS X's default navigational window Finder (by clicking the Finder dock icon) and then click Pictures. Drag an image into the little picture box next to the word *Edit* in the Accounts window. Alternatively, click the Edit button and then click Choose, which puts the user back in the Finder.

Check out the "Entering the photo booth" sidebar for another, more enjoyable way to create an account picture.

Using Parental Controls: When Father (or Mother) Knows Best

Suppose one of the new accounts you create is for your impressionable offspring Cookie Monster. As a responsible parent, you want to set limits to keep him out of trouble. And as a responsible Mac owner, you want to keep him from unwittingly or (or otherwise) inflicting damage on the computer.

It's time to apply *parental controls.* When you do so, Cookie's account goes from being a regular standard account to a *managed account,* with you as the manager. You have quite a bit of say about what your youngster can and cannot get away with.

In the Accounts window, highlight Cookie Monster's name in the list on the left. Then click the Parental Controls tab. The window shown in Figure 5-2 appears. Your choices are as follows:

- **Mail:** Specifies who your kid can exchange e-mail with. Click to select the Mail option. A separate window opens. (If the option is already selected, click Configure instead.) Click the Add (+) button in that window and type an acceptable e-mail address. Separately enter your own e-mail address in the "Send Permission Emails To" box at the bottom of the window to approve any requests from Cookie Monster to correspond with a person not already on the approved list.

- **Finder & System:** Provides various options for what Cookie Monster can do on the computer. You find out more about these in a moment.

- **iChat:** Spells out who Cookie Monster can hold chats with through instant messages.

- **Safari:** Requires you, the administrator, to log in as Cookie Monster and launch the Safari Web browser (Chapter 9). You can then add the sites you deem kosher for your little guy.

- **Dictionary:** Keeps Cookie Monster from looking up certain four-letter words.

Now let's explore Finder & System parental control options. Click the Configure for Finder & System button, and the screen shown in Figure 5-3 appears. Select the Some Limits option. Here's where you get to decide whether Cookie Monster will be able to administer printers, modify the dock, burn CDs and DVDs, or open all System Preferences by selecting the corresponding check boxes. You can also specify which applications he can open.

Figure 5-2:
Parental controls may protect your kid and your computer.

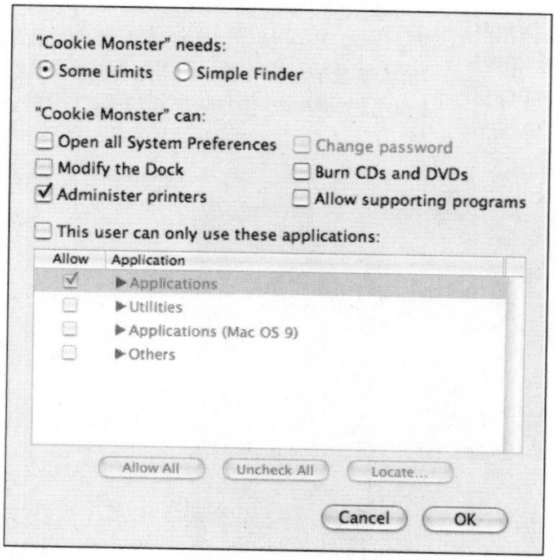

Figure 5-3:
Placing stringent limits on junior.

Entering the photo booth

Remember when you and your high school sweetheart slipped into one of those coin-operated photo booths at the Five and Dime? Don't worry, I'm not telling what went on behind that curtain. You probably confiscated the evidence years ago, a strip with all those silly poses.

Silly poses are back in vogue. Apple is supplying its own photo booth of sorts as a built-in software feature on recent Macs with integrated iSight cameras. You can produce an acceptable account picture to use when exchanging instant messages (Chapter 11).

The Apple Photo Booth and the photo booth of yesteryear have some major differences. For starters, you don't have to surrender any loose change. What's more, there's no curtain to hide behind (which is kind of too bad), though there is a picture of a curtain in the Photo Booth icon.

Still, Apple's Photo Booth application is practically guaranteed to provide you hours of unbridled pleasure thanks mostly to the warped things you can do to doctor up images. You have

not lived until you've seen a picture of your face morph into a light tunnel.

Open Photo Booth by clicking its name in the Applications folder. Then, to snap an image, merely click the Shutter button below the large video screen that serves as a viewfinder, as shown in the picture. A three-two-one countdown ticks off. On zero, the display flashes, and your mug is captured. You can apply funky special effects to your visage either just before or after snapping the picture. For instance, you can make it look as if the picture was taken with a thermal camera or an X-ray, or drawn with a colored pencil. You can turn the image into pop art worthy of Warhol or make it glow radioactively.

The pictures you take end up in an on-screen photo strip. Click the thumbnail you want, and decide what you want to do with the image by choosing an appropriate button: Account Picture, Buddy Picture (to make it your iChat *buddy icon*), E-mail (to the Mac's Mail application), or iPhoto (to your picture library).

Now suppose that instead of Some Limits you selected Simple Finder. Under this setting, Cookie can't alter the dock and will see a sparse, icon-free desktop when he logs on.

You don't have to have kids to implement parental controls. These controls work nicely in setting limits on employees, friends, or visiting relatives.

The Lowdown on Logging On

You can create user accounts for any and all potential family members or visitors who will be using this particular Mac. And you can control how they log in. In this section I describe how.

In System Preferences, again choose Accounts Preferences, and then click Login Options at the bottom of the left pane, under the list of all the account holders on your system. If need be, click the padlock and enter a name and administrative password. Once in, you'll see the window shown in Figure 5-4.

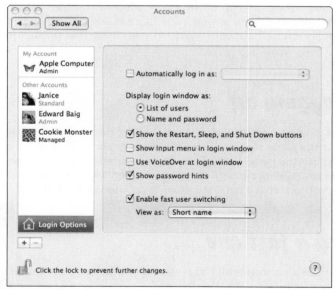

Figure 5-4: Choosing login options.

To automatically log in a particular user (likely yourself), select the Automatically Log In As option and choose the appropriate person from the pop-up menu. You'll have to enter a password.

If the computer is set to automatically log you in, any user who restarts the Mac in your absence will have access to your account.

If automatic log in is not turned on, users who start up the Mac will encounter the computer's Login screen. It will appear differently depending on which radio button you chose under Display Login Window As under Login Options.

Select List of Users to see a Login screen with a roster of people alongside pictures for their respective accounts, plus a check mark if they're already logged in. As if that isn't a clear enough marker, the words *currently logged in* appear under the name.

Select Name and Password, and account holders must type a user name and password in the appropriate boxes on the Login screen.

Either way, press Enter or click after entering the password to actually log in. If you type the wrong password, the entire window wobbles as if having a momentary seizure. Type it wrong a few more times, and any password hints you previously entered appear (provided you chose that option under Login Options).

And logging off

Say you are ready to call it quits for the day but don't want to shut down the machine. At the same time, you don't want to leave your account open for anyone with prying eyes. *Baig's Law: Just because your family, friends, and co-workers are upstanding citizens doesn't mean they won't eavesdrop.* The way to shut down without really shutting down is to choose ➪ Log Out.

Pulling a fast one

Now let's consider another all-too-common scenario. You're in the middle of working when — how to put this delicately — last night's pasta exacts revenge. Nature calls As you get up to leave, your spouse comes running in, *"Honey, can I quickly check my e-mail?"* You could log out to let her do so, but because you are going to be right back, you figure there's got to be a better way. The better way is called *fast user switching.* To take advantage of the feature, you must have previously checked the box next to Enable Fast User Switching, in the Login Options window.

Then, to let your spouse (or any other user) butt in, click your user name in the upper-right corner of the screen. A list of all account holders appears. The person can then click his or her name and type a password. Like a revolving door, your entire desktop spins out of the way while the other user's desktop spins in. When you return moments later, you repeat this procedure by choosing your name and password. Your desktop twirls back into view, right where you left off.

Letting Someone Go

Sometimes being the boss really does mean being the bad guy. The Mac equivalent of terminating somebody is to delete the person's user account from the system. In the Accounts window, click the padlock (it's at the bottom right of the screen) to permit changes. Then select the name of the person getting the pink slip. Click the – button under the list of names.

A dialog box presents two choices: Clicking OK wipes the account from the system but saves the contents of the person's home folder in a file appropriately marked Deleted Users. You may want to retain some of his or her documents and files for your own records. If the user you're booting was particularly naughty (and you don't need their files), you can choose Delete Immediately to completely and instantly wipe out all traces of their existence.

Changing Appearances

Now that you're past the unpleasant act of whacking someone from the system, you can get back in touch with your kinder, gentler side. The part of you solely occupied with making the Mac look pretty.

Altering the desktop

The surreal looking aqua-blue wallpaper Apple put up behind your desktop is attractive enough. It's just not necessarily your taste. You can rip it down and start anew.

Choose ⌘⇨System Preferences. Click Desktop & Screen Saver, and make sure the Desktop tab is highlighted, as shown in Figure 5-5. Click one of the design categories in the list on the left (Apple Images, Nature, Plants, and so on). Various design swatches appear on the right. Best of all, unlike the swatches a salesperson might show you in a home decorating store, you can see what a finished remodeling job here will look like. All you have to do is click.

Figure 5-5:
Becoming
your own
interior
decorator.

The design categories on the left include a listing for the Pictures Folder as well as folders from your iPhoto library (see Chapter 15). Clicking these options lets you choose one of your own images for the desktop background. Apple's designer collection has nothing over masterpieces that include your gorgeous child.

If variety is the spice of life — or you have a short attention span — click to add a check mark to the Change picture every 30 minutes option (or select another timeframe from the drop-down menu). Selecting the Random order option will (you guessed it) change the background in random order. This option cycles through pictures in the folder selected in the left pane.

Choosing a screen saver

"God save the screen. God save the screen? What's that, wrong slogan? "Queen? Oh, royal bummer, never mind."

Screen savers are so-named because they were indeed created to save your screen from a ghostly phenomenon known as burn-in. Whenever the same fixed image was shown on a screen over long periods of time, a dim specter from that image would be permanently etched onto the display. Burn-in ceased to be a problem long ago. But screen savers survived. Today their value is strictly about cosmetics and personalization, in the same way you might choose a vanity license plate or a ring tone for your cell phone.

In the Desktop & Screen Saver window, click the Screen Saver tab. (Not in that window? Choose ➪System Preferences and then click Desktop & Screen Saver.)

Click one of the screen savers in the box on the left side, as shown in Figure 5-6. Some of the pictures are truly stunning. (I recommend Cosmos or Nature Patterns.) You can also select images from your own photo library or install screen savers created by companies other than Apple.

You can preview screen savers in the small screen to the right or click the Test button to get the full-screen impact.

After choosing a screen saver (or again having Apple choose one for you randomly), drag the Start screen saver slider to tell the Mac to choose a time for the screen saver to kick in, ranging from 3 minutes to 2 hours (or never).

Figure 5-6: Beautifying your display with a screen saver.

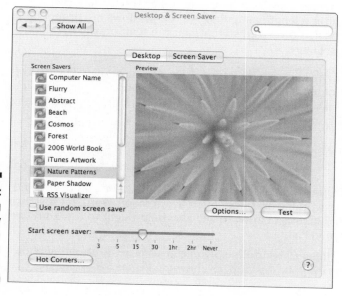

Tidying Up with Exposé

You are so frantically busy that your papers end up strewn every which way, empty coffee cups litter your desk, and boxes pile on top of boxes. Worse, you can't lay your hands on the precise thing you need the very moment when you need it. Sound familiar? Psychiatrists have a technical name for this kind of disorder. It is called being a slob. (Takes one to know one.)

Things can get untidy on the Mac desktop, too, especially as you juggle several projects at once. At any given time, you may have opened System Preferences, the dictionary, iCal, an e-mail program, numerous word processing documents, and then some. Windows lay on top of windows. Chaos abounds. You have fallen into the dark abyss that is multitasking.

Apple has the perfect tonic for MDLS (Messy Desktop Layered Syndrome). The antidote is *Exposé,* and it is as close as your F9 key (or the Fn+F9 combination on some models).

Go ahead and press F9 now (or Fn + F9). Each previously open but obstructed window emerges from its hiding place, like crooks finally willing to give themselves up after a lengthy standoff. All the windows are proportionately and simultaneously downsized so that you can temporarily see them all at once, as shown in Figure 5-7.

Now move the cursor over one of the visible windows. The title of the application or folder is revealed, and the window appears dimmed. Point to the window you want to bring to the front (to work on) and press the spacebar, press Enter, or click inside the window.

Exposé is good for a few other stunts, and these are the default keys to make them happen:

- ✔ **F10:** Opens all the windows in the application you're currently using. If you're working on a document in Microsoft Word, for instance, any other open documents in Word will also be brought to the front lines, as shown in Figure 5-8.

- ✔ **F11:** Hides all windows so you can admire the stunning photograph you chose for your desktop, as shown in Figure 5-9.

Cluttered desktop before putting Exposé to work

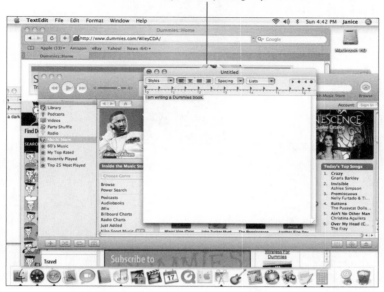

Desktop after pressing F9

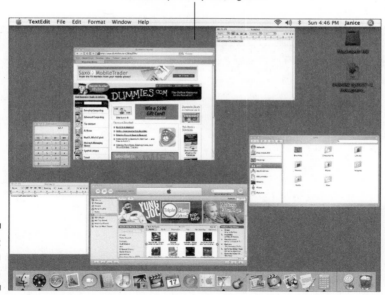

Figure 5-7:
Exposé in
action.

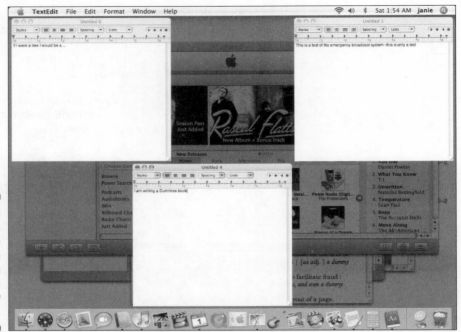

Figure 5-8:
Press F10 to
open all the
windows in
the program
you are
currently
using.

Figure 5-9:
Press F11 to
hide all
windows.

If you have something against F9, F10, and F11 (or are using those keys for other purposes), open System Preferences, choose Dashboard & Exposé, and assign alternative keys. And if you have something against keys in general, you can arrange to have Exposé do its thing by moving the cursor to one of the four corners of the screen.

Incidentally, if you're wondering about the Dashboard part of Dashboard & Exposé, skip ahead to the next chapter. Those who wait will be rewarded with a tour of some of the remaining items in System Preferences.

System Preferences: Choosing Priorities

You may be wondering what's left. We've already dug inside System Preferences to alter the desktop and screensaver, establish parental controls, muck around with Exposé, and then some. But as Figure 5-10 shows, there's still a lot more you can do. Let's explore some of those options now.

Getting in sync with date and time

You established the date, time, and time zone when you set up the Mac initially (Chapter 2). In System Preferences, you can move the location of the clock from the menu bar to a separate window. You can change the appearance of the clock from a digital readout to an analog face with hands. You can display the time with seconds or use a 24-hour clock. You can even have the Mac announce the time on the hour, the half hour, or the quarter hour.

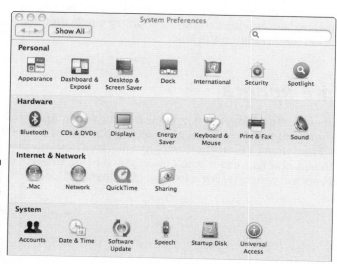

Figure 5-10:
Doing it my way through System Preferences.

Displays

If you are hunky-dory with what your display looks like, feel free to ignore this section. Read on if you are the least bit curious about *resolution* and what changing it will do to your screen. Resolution is a measure of sharpness and expressed by tiny picture elements, or *pixels*. Pixels is such a nice sounding word that I always thought it would make a terrific name for a breakfast cereal, something like new Kellogg's *Sugar-Coated Pixels.* But I digress.

You will see resolution written out as 800 x 600, 1024 x 768, 1680 x 1050, and so on. The first number refers to the number of pixels horizontally, and the second number is the number of pixels vertically. Higher numbers reflect higher resolution, meaning the picture is sharper and you can fit more on the screen. At lower resolutions the images may be larger but fuzzier, though this depends on your monitor. Lower resolutions also *refresh,* or update, more quickly, though you will be hard-pressed to tell with most modern monitors. As it happens, the refresh rate doesn't mean boo on computers such as the iMac with LCD or flat-panel displays.

You can also muck around with the number of colors that a Mac displays (millions, thousands, or down to a puny 256). Best advice: Play around with these settings if you must. More often than not, leave well enough alone.

Sound

Ever wonder what the *Basso* sound is? Or *Sosumi* or *Tink?* I'd play them for you if this was an audio book, but because it isn't, check out these and other sound effects in System Preferences. You'll hear one of them whenever the Mac wants to issue an alert. Sound preferences is also the place to adjust speaker balance, microphone settings, and pretty much anything else having to do with what you'll hear on the Mac.

Software update

Your Mac may be a machine, but it still has organic traits. And Apple hasn't forgotten about you just because you've already purchased one of its prized computers. From time to time, the company will issue new releases of certain programs to add new features it won't make you pay for, to *patch* or fix bugs, or to thwart security threats. For a full log, click Installed Updates.

You can have the Mac check for automatic software updates daily (might be overkill), weekly, or monthly, or on the spot. If you choose, the Mac will fetch important updates in the background, and bother you only when the program update is ready to be installed. Software Update is accessible also directly from the menu.

Universal Access

Some physically challenged users may require special help controlling the Mac. Choose Universal Access under System Preferences, and click the tab you need assistance with: Seeing, Hearing, Keyboard, or Mouse, as shown in Figure 5-11.

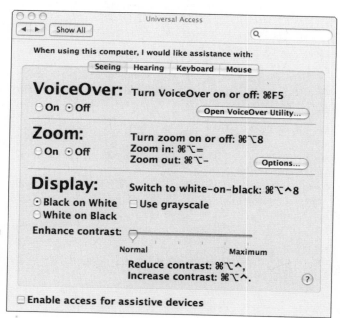

Figure 5-11: Universal Access preferences.

Among the options, you can arrange to

- ✔ Turn VoiceOver on or off, to hear descriptions of what's on your screen.
- ✔ Enhance the contrast, or alter the display from black on white or white on black.

- Flash the screen when an alert sound occurs.

- Zoom in on the screen to make everything appear larger.

- Use a Slow Keys function to put a delay between when a key is pressed and when the result of that keypress is accepted. Or, if you can't easily press several keys at once, use Sticky Keys to press groups of modifier keys (Shift, ⌘, Option, and Control) in a sequence.

The Mac may share a nickname with certain McDonald's hamburgers. But it's actually an old Burger King slogan that is most apt when describing your computer. As this chapter has shown, you can "have it your way."

Chapter 6

Apple's Feline Fetish

- -

- -

Steve Jobs is fond of big cats. Before Apple unleashed Tiger, previous versions of Mac OS X software carried such *purr-fect* monikers as Cheetah, Puma, Jaguar, and Panther. (Apple used the code words Cheetah and Puma internally.) Leopard is coming next, perhaps even by the time this book hits store shelves. Apple is also presumably breeding Lynx and Cougar inside its Cupertino, California, cages.

As strong a release as it is, the name OS X just doesn't have the bite that Tiger or any of the other giant kitty nicknames command. However, X (for ten) is the most celebrated use of Roman numerals this side of the Super Bowl.

Tiger actually represents OS X version 10.4. Every year or so, Apple brings out a new iteration of its operating system software (see the "An operating system primer" sidebar), complete with a boatload of new features, and identified by an extra decimal point. Apple says OS X version 10.4 Tiger piled more than 200 features onto its predecessor OS X version 10.3 Panther. I haven't counted.

During the course of a year, Apple will make interim tweaks to its operating system. You will know because the OS takes on an extra decimal digit. At the time of this writing, Apple was up to OS X version 10.4.7 (pronounced "ten dot four dot seven").

I wonder how many features must be added before Apple changes the designation to OS XI.

To check out the version of Mac software running on your system, choose ⌘⇨About This Mac. Choose Software Update to see whether the OS (and, for that matter, other programs) are up to date.

Bottom line: Tigers are stunning and powerful creatures. They demand respect and awe. Something like Apple's computers.

How Many New Features?
Let Me Count the Ways

As already noted, Apple added more than 200 features to the Mac OS in Tiger (and you can expect lots more features when Leopard prances on stage; Apple was set to preview the new operating system in August 2006). Even if I had the space, I don't claim the expertise to do all the new features justice. As a public service and, um, for your reading pleasure, I thought I'd at least tick off a few of the items on Apple's long laundry list of features. I'm letting Apple do the talking here. I haven't changed any of the company's descriptions (except for the boldface lead-ins).

Disclaimer: I'm not trying to demean any of these enhancements. These obviously provide great value to somebody. I'm just guessing that the items listed here will collectively interest perhaps 1 percent of you. If you want to skip ahead, I'm not going to stop you.

- ✔ **For the international crowd:** Tiger includes the Tamil language script, a new input mode for Korean and extended system fonts to support Greek (modern and classical), Vietnamese, Cyrillic, and Roman script languages of the former USSR.

- ✔ **For UNIX lovers:** Use command line file commands on HFS+ items with proper results. Utilities such as cp, mv, tar, rsync now use the same standard APIs as Spotlight and access control lists to handle resource forks.

- ✔ **For networking types:** Take advantage of the power of distributed computing with Xgrid, Apple's easy-to-use tool that turns a group of Macs into a supercomputer.

- ✔ **For developers:** Take advantage of the latest version of the GCC compiler, featuring support for 64-bit code generation.

An operating system primer

There is software, friends, and there is SOFT-WARE. Make no mistake, a computer's operating system deserves top billing. If this were a movie and the opening credits were rolling, the name of the operating system would appear above the title. All other performers on your computer, no matter how much talent they possess, are supporting players by comparison.

Come to think of it, there would be no movie at all without the operating system, for it is the foundation on which all your other programs run. Minus the OS, that fancy photo editing program you bought recently might as well be chopped liver.

As operating systems go, you are truly fortunate to have Tiger. OS X earns raves not just because it's slick and easy on the eyes. Tiger is robust, reliable, and stable. Its underpinning is something

called *UNIX,* a venerable operating system in its own right. The brilliance of Apple was in figuring how to exploit UNIX without making *you* learn UNIX. Just be thankful it's under the hood and don't give it another moment's thought.

Now I know at least some of you can't leave it there. You want to investigate UNIX. (You're the person I want in the trenches with me.) Okay, here goes. Open the Applications folder, choose Utilities, and delve inside a program called *Terminal.* What you'll find here isn't pretty, as the figure shows. No icons. No easy menus. You have split the town of GUI-ville and are now tooling around with a *command line interface*— meaning you have to type arcane commands to tell the computer what to do. Doing so could wreak havoc on your system, so be careful. You know what they say about curiosity killing the cat.

```
000              Terminal — tcsh — 80x24
Last login: Sat Apr  1 02:19:01 on ttyp1
Welcome to Darwin!
[Edward-Baigs-Computer-3:~] apple% []
```

Searching with Spotlight

Whew! Now that I dispensed with that little piece of trivia, it's time to concentrate on Tiger lilies all Mac users will appreciate. I'll start by putting the spotlight on *Spotlight,* a marvelous desktop search utility I practically guarantee will blow you away. If Spotlight was the only new feature Apple bred into Tiger, those of you who haven't bothered to upgrade a previous version of OS X in the past would have to think long and hard about not doing so this time around.

Here's why. Search is a big deal. A computer isn't much good if you can't easily lay your hands on the documents, pictures, e-mail messages, and other programs you need at any particular moment. When most people think about searching on a computer, they probably have Google, Yahoo!, or some other Internet search engine in mind. Internet search is of course a big deal too, and I spend some time discussing it in Chapter 9.

The searching I have in mind here, however, involves the contents of your own system. Over time, Mac users accumulate thousands of photos, songs, school reports, work projects, contacts, calendar entries, and you name it. Spotlight helps you locate them in a blink. It starts spitting out search results before you finish typing.

What's even better is that Spotlight can uncover material within documents and files. That's incredibly useful if you haven't the foggiest idea what you named a file.

Let's try Spotlight now:

1. **Click the blue magnifying glass icon in the upper-right corner of the menu bar. Or press ⌘ and the spacebar simultaneously.**

   The Spotlight search box appears.

2. **Enter a word or phrase you want to search for.**

   The instant you type the first letter, a window shows up with what Spotlight considers the most likely search matches. The search is immediately refined as you type extra keystrokes, as shown in Figure 6-1. Searching is so fast you'll see results more quickly than it takes you to read this sentence.

Say you're planning a tropical vacation and remember that your cousin Gilligan e-mailed you awhile back raving about the beach at some deserted Pacific island. You can open the Mac Mail program and dig for the missive from the dozens that Gilligan sent you. (Evidently he had a lot of time on his hands.) But it's far simpler and faster to type Gilligan's name in Spotlight.

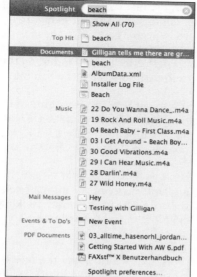

Figure 6-1:
The
Spotlight
search box.

Or maybe you want to give Gilligan a quick buzz. Without Spotlight, you would probably open your Address Book to find your buddy's phone number. The faster way is to type `Gilligan` in Spotlight and then click his name next to Contacts in the results window.

Rummaging through your stuff

Spotlight is built into the very fabric of the operating system. Quietly behind the scenes, Spotlight indexes, or catalogs, all the files on the computer so you can access them in a moment's notice. The index is seamlessly updated each time you add, move, modify, copy, or delete a file.

Moreover, Spotlight automatically rummages through *metadata,* the information about your data. Digital photographs, for example, typically capture the following metadata: the camera model used to snap the image, the date, the aperture and exposure settings, whether a flash was used, and so on. For example, if a friend e-mails you pictures taken with a Kodak camera, you can quickly find those images — as opposed to, say, the pictures you took with your own Canon — by entering the search term `Kodak`.

Spotlight is one confident sucker. It boldly takes a stab at what it thinks is the *Top Hit,* or search result you have in mind. (The Top Hit in Figure 6-1 is a document named *beach.*) Its track record is pretty good. If it guesses right, click the Top Hit entry. That will either launch the application in question, open a particular file, or display the appropriate folder in the Finder. As is often the case, there's a shortcut. Press ⌘ and Return to launch the top hit.

Of course, Spotlight isn't always going to get the Top Hit right, so it also displays what it considers to be the next 20 most likely matches. Results are segregated into categories (Applications, Documents, Folders, PDF Documents, Music, Images, Bookmarks, and so on). Again, just click an item to launch or open it.

Some searches yield more than 20 possible outcomes. Often a heck of a lot more. That's what Show All (refer to Figure 6-1) is all about. Clicking Show All doesn't, in fact, show you everything. Most of the time your screen wouldn't be near big enough anyway.

Instead, Show All opens a separate Spotlight window like the one shown in Figure 6-2. The most probable search results in each category are listed, followed by an indication of how many more results are in each group. Click the *more* line (for example, *20 more*) to scroll through the list of other possible search outcomes.

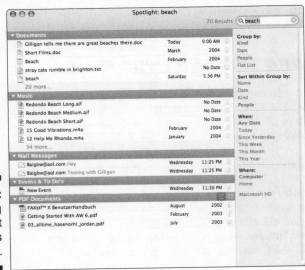

Figure 6-2:
Spotlighting
the Spotlight
results
window.

Intelligent searching

You can customize search results in numerous ways. Take a look at the column on the right side of the Spotlight results window. You can sort outcomes by Kind (Documents, Mail Messages, and so on), Date (Today, Yesterday, Previous 7 Days, Previous 30 Days, Earlier), and People (Gilligan, Ginger, Skipper, and so on). You can also set various sorting preferences *within* a group.

The best way to narrow results is to enter as specific a search term as possible right off the bat. As you plan your vacation, typing beach will probably summon the e-mail message Gilligan sent you. But because Spotlight will find *all* files or programs that match that text, results may also include Power-Point presentations with a beach theme, pictures of your family by the seashore, and songs on your hard drives sung by the Beach Boys. Typing *Gilligan* and *beach* together will help you fine-tune your search.

If you know the type of item you're looking for, such as Gilligan's e-mail as opposed to his picture, you can filter the search in another way. Enter the search term followed by kind and the file type you are looking for, as in

```
Gilligan kind:email
```

If you want to search for a presentation someone sent you on the world's best seaside resorts but can't remember whether the presentation was created in AppleWorks, Keynote, or PowerPoint, try

```
seaside resort kind:presentations
```

And if you want to search only for presentations opened in the past week, type

```
seaside resort kind:presentations date:last week
```

To search for an application such as Microsoft Word, type

```
Word kind:application
```

To search Gilligan's contact information, type

```
Gilligan kind:contacts
```

To search for music, type

```
Beach Boys kind:music
```

To search for pictures at the beach, type

```
Beach kind:images
```

And so on.

Searching your way

Up to now, you've let Spotlight determine how to present search matches. Now let me remind you who's the boss. This being your Mac and all, you can have Spotlight search according to your marching orders.

Spotlight pours through pretty much *everything* on your hard drive — unless you dictate otherwise. To do so, open Spotlight preferences by clicking at the bottom of the Spotlight results window. With the Search Results tab selected, you can check or uncheck the types of items you want Spotlight to search, as shown in Figure 6-3, and drag the categories in the order you want results to appear.

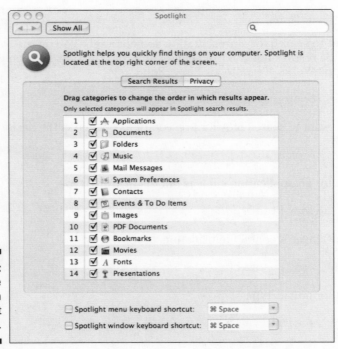

Figure 6-3:
Focusing the limelight on Spotlight Preferences.

If you click the Privacy tab, you can prevent Spotlight from searching particular locations. Drag folders or disks into the Privacy pane to let Spotlight know that these are off-limits. Spotlight will remove any associated files from the index.

Find Me a Find

I've already told you how Spotlight is embedded in the very fabric of the operating system. So it should come as no surprise that Spotlight hangs out as well in Finder windows, the windows you use over and over to browse for files and folders (press ⌘+N to open one).

That there's a search box inside Finder isn't novel to anyone who has spent time with previous versions of OS X. But the similarity ends there. I love baseball analogies, so let me explain it this way. The previous Finder search box was like a solid ballplayer who could hit, say, for a high average. But this newest Finder search box is more like a five-tool player who not only hits for average but can throw, run, field, and hit for power. In other words, he can beat you in a number of ways.

So it goes with the newly powerful Finder search. It lets you tailor searches as never before. To see it in action, open the search box by pressing ⌘+F, or by choosing File⇨Find.

If you click the Privacy tab, you can prevent Spotlight from searching particular locations. Drag folders or disks into the Privacy pane to let Spotlight know that these are off-limits. Spotlight will remove any associated files from the index.

The moment you start typing a few characters in the search box, tabs show up (see Figure 6-4). The top tabs — Servers, Computer, Home, Others — dictate where you want to search. Note the Save button. I return to its purpose in the next section, on Smart Folders.

Just below the tabs are customizable buttons that let you filter a search according to specific parameters. You can add or delete these "criteria" buttons by pressing the + or – at the end of the row (refer to Figure 6-4). Pressing the – button deletes the entire row.

Figure 6-4:
The powerful Finder search box lets you narrow searches by specific criteria.

Among your choices:

- ✓ **Kind:** by Images, Text, PDF, Movies, Music, Documents, Presentations, Folders, Applications, Others. Stick with the default Any if you want to search for all these.

- ✓ **Last Opened, Last Modified, or Created:** Today, Since Yesterday, This week, Last 2 weeks, This month, Exactly, Before, After, and so on.

- ✓ **Keywords or Contents:** Enter the specific word.

- ✓ **Size:** Greater than, less than.

- ✓ **Color Label:** Choose one of the color dots.

Suppose you want to search for all the songs with the word *Lost* in the title that you listened to within the last two weeks. You would tailor a search that would include Kind, Music, and Last Opened, Within The Last 2 weeks.

Fans of the hit TV series *Lost* may feel a chill at the mere mention of the *Others*. (For those who don't watch the show, they're the bad guys.) But you may welcome the Others when it comes to running the most specialized search queries on your Mac. I'll explain. Under Kind, choose Other as your search criteria. A dialog box lists filtered attributes you can use in your search, plus a description of their purpose, as shown in Figure 6-5.

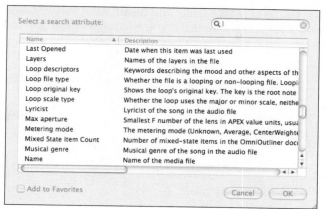

Figure 6-5:
Choosing
other
search
attributes.

For instance, you can choose a search attribute based on the authors of an item, makers of a device, due date, duration in seconds, lyricist of a song, musical key of a song, genre, pixel height of a document, year an item was recorded, and dozens more attributes.

Before closing out of your Finder window, you may want to save your search results. To do that, continue with the next section.

Smart Folders

When you go to all the trouble of selecting specific attributes for your search query, you may want to revisit the search in the future — incorporating the latest information, of course. And that's why the Finder window has a handy Save button.

Traditionally, the files on your computer are organized by their location on your disk. *Smart Folders* change the organizing principle based on the search criteria you've chosen. These folders don't give a hoot where the actual files that match your search criteria reside on the machine. Those stay put in their original location. You are, in effect, working on *aliases,* or shortcuts, of those files. (See the next chapter for more on aliases.)

What's more, behind the scenes, Smart Folders are constantly on the prowl for new items that match your search criteria. In other words, they're updated in real time.

To create a Smart Folder, click that Save button from inside the Finder window. (The Save button is shown in the upper right in Figure 6-4.) A box pops up asking you to specify a name and destination for your newly created Smart Folder, as shown in Figure 6-6. If you want, select the Add to Sidebar option to easily find the Smart Folder you just created.

Figure 6-6:
The Smart
Folder
window
looks like
this.

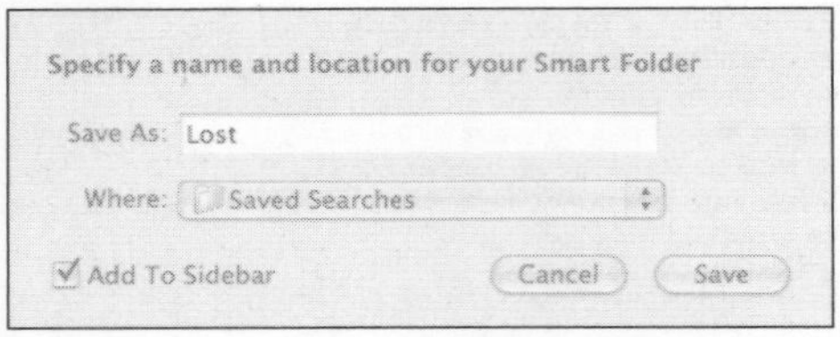

Specify a name and location for your Smart Folder

Save As: Lost

Where: Saved Searches

☑ Add To Sidebar   (Cancel) (Save)

Alternatively, choose New Smart Folder under the Finder File menu to create a new Smart Folder.

You may want to create a simple Smart Folder containing all the documents you've worked on in the past seven days. Give it an original name. Oh, I dunno, something like *What a Hellish Week!* In any case, all your recent stuff is easily at your disposal. Your older documents will pass new arrivals on their way out.

Fiddling with Dashboard Widgets

Apart from prowling the virtual corridors of cyberspace or interacting with Apple's iLife programs, most of your face time on a Mac will find you engaged with some full-blown (and often pricey) software application — even if you take advantage of a relatively narrow set of features.

The wordsmiths among you couldn't subsist without Microsoft Word or some other industrial-strength word processor. You graphics artists live and breathe Adobe Photoshop. But personal computing isn't always about doctoring photos or penning the great American novel (or Dummies book). Sometimes all you want is a quick snippet of information.

Maybe you need to check the temperature or a stock quote. Or you want to look up a phone number or figure out if your plane is on time. Perhaps you want to locate an Italian restaurant for dinner or calculate a mortgage payment.

That's what a gaggle of mini-applications known as *widgets* are all about. Indeed, these lightweight programs generally serve a useful and singular purpose: from letting you track an overnight package to finding out whether your favorite team covered the spread. Frankly, you can perform many of these tasks through the Web or other programs on your desktop. But few do it with the convenience and flair of widgets.

Fronted by large colorful icons, widgets come at you en masse when you summon *Dashboard*. This translucent screen, shown in Figure 6-7, lays on top of your desktop. Nothing underneath is disturbed.

You either click the Dashboard icon in the dock (labeled in Figure 6-7) or press the F12 key to open the Dashboard. Pressing F12 again closes Dashboard. You can exit also by clicking anywhere other than on a widget.

To get you started, Apple supplies a collection of basic widgets (calculator, clock, calendar, weather). The more interesting widgets are available online. (More than 2000 were available as of this writing.) You can embark on a widget hunt at `www.apple.com/downloads/dashboard`.

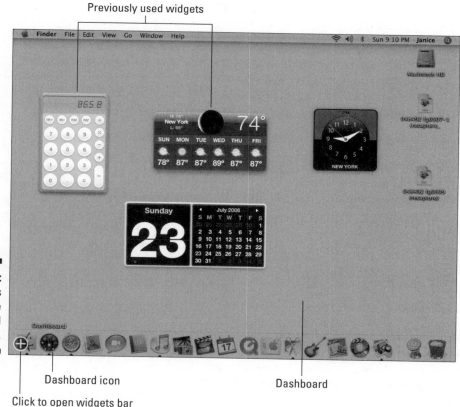

Previously used widgets

Dashboard icon

Click to open widgets bar

Dashboard

Figure 6-7: Widgets star in the Dashboard collection.

You either click the Dashboard icon in the dock (labeled in Figure 6-7) or When you call up Dashboard, only the widgets you previously used appear on the screen, right where you left them. The rest are cozying up to the *widgets bar,* which you can open by clicking the + button (labeled in Figure 6-7). If you want to enlist one of the widgets, just drag it onto the Dashboard area. It will dazzle you with a ripple effect as it makes its grand entrance. Click the X button (labeled in Figure 6-8) to close the widgets bar.

The great majority of downloadable widgets are gratis. A few are available as *shareware,* meaning you can try them out before paying. Whether you actually fork over the loot is up to your conscience, but unless you think the program is worthless, its creator should be rewarded for his or her efforts.

Some widgets are extensions to other programs on your computer, such as the ones that display data from iCal or your Address Book or bring up blank Stickies.

But most widgets grab feeds off the Internet, so you need an online connection (see Chapter 9). Widgets in this category might tell you what's on the tube tonight or deliver a surfing report (on waves, dude, not cyberspace.)

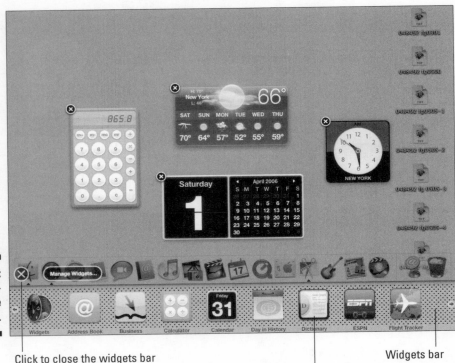

Figure 6-8: Widget-mania at the widgets bar.

Click to close the widgets bar

Widgets bar

Drag icons from the widgets bar to the Dashboard display

Other widgets wizardry:

- ✔ If you hold down the Shift key while you press F12, the widgets will open or close in super-slow-motion.

- ✔ If you hover over an open widget and press ⌘+R, the wizard twists like a tornado and refreshes itself. Any "live" information will be updated.

- ✔ To rearrange widgets on the Dashboard area, just drag them around.

- ✔ You can display more than one of the same widget, which is useful, say, if you want to check out the weather or time in several locations. Just drag the widget out again from its hiding place in the widgets bar.

In Chapter 21, I rattle off ten widget goodies.

Before we skip out on this widgets seminar, let me mention one more in passing, a widget to manage all your other widgets.. The widget shown in Figure 6-9 contains a list of other widgets (People, Researcher, Ski Report, and so on). By unchecking the names of the widgets in the list, you can disable them and in some instances send them to the trash. If you click the More Widgets button, you'll be transported to Apple's main Dashboard Widgets Web page, where you can download other widgets.

Figure 6-9:
The widget
to tame
other
widgets.

Unleashing the Automator

Quick show of hands: How many of you have ever taken a class in computer programming? (You think I can't tell if you have your hand up? Well, I can.) That's what I figured, not many of you.

Tiger includes a feature called *Automator* that lets you program repetitive tasks — renaming a batch of files, say — without having to master programming. This is Apple's way of automating or simplifying a computer practice known as *scripts.*

Automator is built around specific tasks, or *actions* (Open Images in Preview, for example), dragged from an Action list to a workflow area on the right side of the window, as shown in Figure 6-10.

When you've dragged all the actions into the workflow area, click the Run button in the upper-right corner of the Automator window; each action is performed in a natural order with the results of one task flowing into the next one. Thus, various tasks must be performed in sequence and make sense working together.

To open Automator, open Finder, click Applications, and then double-click Automator.

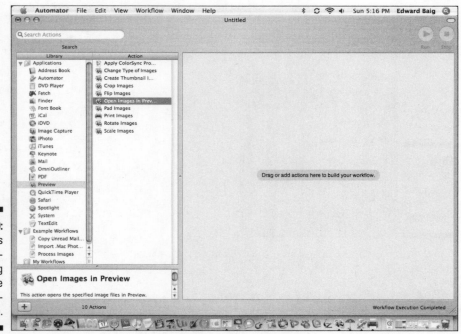

Figure 6-10: Automator is programming without the programming.

A single action can constitute a workflow. To take a rudimentary example, you can automate the process of removing empty playlists in iTunes by dragging that action into the workflow space and clicking Run. A Workflow Execution Completed message at the bottom-right corner of Automator signifies that the job is finished. (For more on playlists and iTunes, read Chapter 14.)

Often multiple tasks make up a workflow. In the simple workflow shown in Figure 6-11, the computer will search the address book for people having a birthday this month, and send an e-mail greeting (with picture) to those folks.

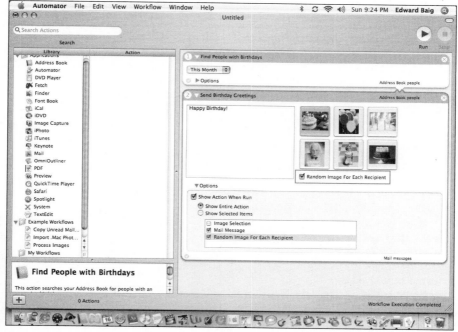

Figure 6-11: Automator removes excuses for missing a birthday.

You can save and reuse workflows by pressing ⌘+Shift+S.

Third-party developers are creating workflow actions for their applications. You can check some of these out at www.apple.com/downloads/macosx/ automator.

Automator is just one more reason to feel good about the Tiger in your tank.

Chapter 7

Handling All That Busy Work

In This Chapter

▶ Preparing your documents

▶ Selecting text

▶ Dragging, dropping, cutting, and pasting

▶ Revealing fonts

▶ Formatting documents

▶ Saving your work

▶ Making revisions

▶ Taking out the trash

▶ Understanding aliens

. . . .

*I*n professional football, the skill position players — quarterback, running backs, and wide receivers — get a disproportionate amount of the glory when a team wins and assume most of the blame when they fall on their collective fannies. But any halfway-competent field general will tell you that those in the trenches typically determine the outcome.

Sure you want to draw up a razzamatazz game plan for your Mac. Probably something involving stupendous graphics and spine-tingling special effects. A high-tech flea-flicker, to keep it in the gridiron vernacular.

There he goes again: using a sports analogy.

After all, you bought the computer with the intention of becoming the next Mozart, Picasso, or at the very least Steve Jobs. (*What, you expected Joe Montana or Lawrence Taylor?*)

I'm not here to dash anybody's dreams. But for this one itty-bitty chapter, I am asking you to keep your expectations in check. You have to make first downs before you make touchdowns. Forget heaving Hail Mary's down the field. You're better off grinding out yardage the tough way.

In coach-speak, the mission of the moment is to master the computing equivalent of blocking and tackling: basic word processing and the other fundamentals required to get you through training camp and ultimately your daily routine.

Practice these now. You can pour the Gatorade on my head later.

Form and Function: The Essentials of Word Processing

I'm old enough to recall life before word processors. (Hey it wasn't *that* long ago.)

I can't possibly begin to fathom how we survived in the days before every last one of us had access to word processors and computers on our respective desks.

Pardon the interruption, but I'm not thrilled with the preceding sentence. Kind of wordy and repetitious. Permit me to get right to the point.

I can't imagine how any of us got along without word processors.

Thanks, much more concise.

The purpose of this mini-editing exercise is to illustrate the splendor of word processing. Had I produced these sentences on a typewriter instead of a computer, changing even a few words would hardly seem worth it. I would have to use correction fluid to erase my previous comments and type over them. If things got really messy, or I wanted to take my writing in a different direction, I'd end up yanking the sheet of paper from the typewriter in disgust and begin pecking away anew on a blank page.

Word processing lets you substitute words at will, move entire blocks of text around with panache, and apply different fonts and typefaces to the characters. You won't even take a productivity hit swapping typewriter ribbons in the middle of a project (though, as the next chapter reveals, you will at some point have to replace the ink in your printer).

Before running out to buy Microsoft Word (or another industrial strength and expensive) word processing program for your Mac — and I'm not suggesting you don't — it's my obligation to point out that Apple includes a respectable word processor with OS X. The program is *TextEdit,* and it calls the Applications folder home. TextEdit will be our classroom for much of this chapter.

Creating a Document

The first order of business using TextEdit (or pretty much any word processor) is to create a new *document*. There's really not much to it. It's about as easy as opening the program itself. The moment you do so, a window with a large blank area on which to type appears, as Figure 7-1 shows.

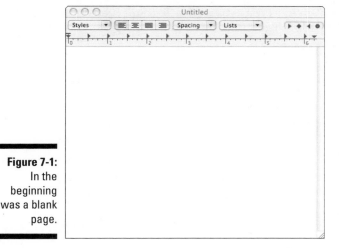

Figure 7-1:
In the beginning was a blank page.

Have a look around the window. At top you see *Untitled* because no one at Apple is presumptuous enough to come up with a name for your yet-to-be-produced manuscript. We'll get around to naming (and saving) your stuff later. In my experience it helps to write first and add a title later, though, um, scholars may disagree.

Notice the blinking vertical line at the upper-left edge of the screen, just below the ruler. That line, called the *insertion point,* might as well be tapping out Morse code for "start typing here."

Indeed, friends, you have come to the most challenging point in the entire word processing experience, and believe me it has nothing to do with technology. The burden is on you to produce clever, witty, and inventive prose, lest all that blank space go to waste.

Okay, got it? At the blinking insertion point, type with abandon. Something original like

It was a dark and stormy night

If you type like I do, you may have accidentally produced

It was a drk and stormy nihgt

Fortunately, your amiable word processor has your best interests at heart. See the dotted red line below *drk* and *nihgt* (see Figure 7-2)? That's TextEdit's not-so-subtle way of flagging a likely typo. (This presumes you've left the default Check Spelling As You Type activated in TextEdit Preferences. Since we're at the beginning of this exercise, that seems a safe presumption.)

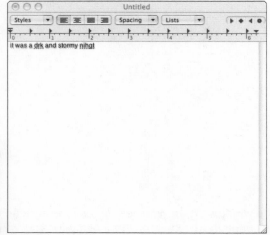

Figure 7-2:
Oops, I
made a
mistake.

You can address these snafus in several ways. You can use the computer's *Delete* key to wipe out all the letters to the left of the insertion point. (Delete functions like the backspace key on the *Smith Corona* you put out to pasture years ago.) After the misspelled word has been quietly sent to Siberia, you can type over the space more carefully. All traces of your sloppiness disappear.

Delete is a wonderfully handy key. I'd recommend using it to eliminate a single word such as *nihgt*. But in our little case study, we have to repair *drk* too. And using Delete to erase *drk* means sacrificing *and* and *stormy* as well. Kind of overkill if you ask me.

Back to football. It's time to call an audible. Two quick options:

✔ Use the left-facing arrow key (found on the lower-right side of the keyboard) to move the insertion point to the spot just to the right of the word you want to deep-six. No characters are eliminated when you move the insertion point that way. Only when the insertion point is where it ought to be do you again hire your reliable keyboard hit-man, Delete.

✔ Eschew the keyboard and click with the mouse to reach this same spot to the right of the misspelled word. Then press Delete.

Now try this helpful remedy. Right-click anywhere on the misspelled word. A list appears with suggestions, as shown in Figure 7-3. Single-click the correct word and, voila, it instantly replaces the mistake. Be careful in this example not to choose *dork*.

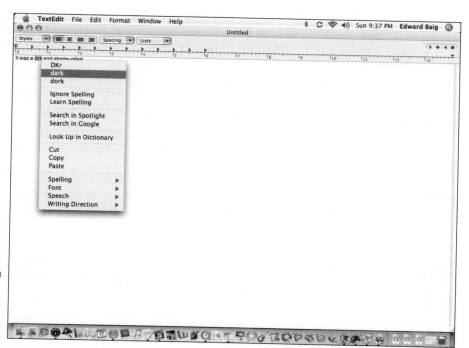

Figure 7-3:
I'm no dork.
I fixed it.

Selecting Text in a Document

Let's try another experiment. Double-click a word. See what happens. It's as if you ran a light-blue marker across the word. You've *highlighted,* or *selected,* this word so that it can be deleted, moved, or changed.

Many times, you'll want to select more than a single word. Perhaps a complete sentence. Or a paragraph. Or several paragraphs. Here's how to highlight a block of text to delete it:

1. **Using the mouse, point to the block in question.**

2. **Press and hold down the left mouse button and drag the cursor (which bears a slight resemblance to the Seattle Space Needle) across the entire section you want to highlight.**

   The direction in which you drag the mouse affects what gets highlighted. If you drag horizontally, a single line is selected. Dragging vertically selects an entire block. You can highlight text also by holding down Shift and using the arrow keys.

3. **Release the mouse button when you reach the end of the passage you want highlighted, as shown with *Once upon a time* in Figure 7-4.**

4. **To immediately wipe out the selected text, press Delete.**

   Alternatively, start typing. Your old material is exorcised upon your very first keystroke and filled in with the new characters you type.

To select several pages of text at once, single-click at the beginning portion of the material you want to select, and then scroll to the very bottom. While holding down the Shift key, click again. Everything in between clicks is highlighted.

Now suppose you were overzealous and selected too much text. Or maybe you released the mouse a bit too soon so that not enough of the passage you have in mind was highlighted. Just click once with your mouse to de-select the selected area and try again.

Another screw-up. This time you annihilated text that upon further review you want to keep. Fortunately, the Mac lets you perform a do-over. Choose Edit⇨Undo Typing. The text is miraculously revived. Variations of this lifesaving Undo command can be found in most of the Mac programs you encounter. So before losing sleep over some silly thing you did on the computer, visit the Edit menu and check out your Undo options.

Figure 7-4:
Highlighting
text.

Dragging and Dropping

In Chapter 3 I discuss *dragging and dropping* to move icons to the dock. In this chapter, we drag an entire block of text to a new location and leave it there.

Select a passage in one of the ways mentioned in the preceding section. Now, anywhere on the highlighted area, click and hold down the mouse button. Roll the mouse across a flat surface to drag the text to its new destination. Release the mouse button to drop off the text.

You are not restricted to dragging and dropping text in the program you're in. You can lift text completely out of TextEdit and into Word, Stickies, or Pages, an Apple program for producing spiffy-looking newsletters and brochures.

Alternatively, if you know you'll want to use a text block in another program at some point in the future — you just don't know when — drop it directly onto the Mac desktop (see Figure 7-5) and call upon it whenever necessary. Text copied to the desktop will be shown as an icon and named from text in the beginning of the selection you copied. Moving text in this manner to an external program or the desktop constitutes a Copy command, not a Move command, so the lifted text remains in the original source.

Figure 7-5:
Dropping
text on the
desktop.

Cutting and Pasting

In the preceding section, we copied material from one location and moved a copy to another location. By contrast, cutting and pasting lifts material from one spot and moves it elsewhere without leaving anything behind. (In the typewriter era, you literally cut out passages of paper with scissors and pasted them onto new documents.)

After selecting your source material, choose Edit⇨Cut (or the keyboard alternative ⌘+X). To paste to a new location, navigate to the spot and choose Edit⇨Paste (or ⌘+V).

The Cut command is easily confused with Copy (⌘+C). As the name suggests, the latter copies selected text that can be pasted somewhere else. Cut clips text out of its original spot.

The very last thing you copied or cut is temporary sheltered on the *clipboard*. It remains there until replaced by newer material you copy or cut.

If you can't remember what was last on the clipboard, choose Edit⇨ Show Clipboard when Finder (the dock icon to the furthest left) is activated.

Changing the Font

When typewriters were in vogue, you were pretty much limited to the typeface of the machine. Computers being computers, you can alter the appearance of individual characters and complete words effortlessly. Let's start with something simple.

In the TextEdit window, click the pop-up menu Styles (see Figure 7-6) and choose Italic. Highlighted text becomes *text*. Now try Bold. Highlighted text becomes **text**.

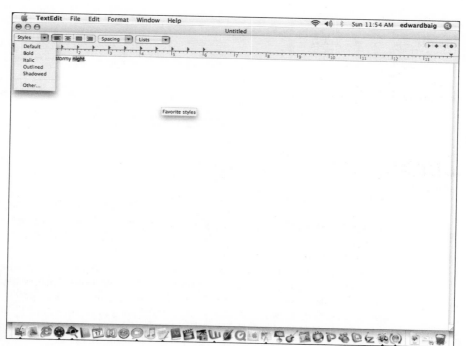

Figure 7-6:
The Styles
menu.

I recommend using keyboard shortcuts in this instance. Just before typing a word, try ⌘+I for *italics* or ⌘+B for *bold*. When you want to revert to normal type, just press those respective keyboard combinations again.

Making words bold or italic is the tip of the proverbial iceberg. You can dress up documents with different *fonts,* or typefaces.

Open the Format menu and choose Font⇨Show Fonts. The window in Figure 7-7 appears. You can change the typeface of any highlighted text by clicking a font listed in the pane labeled Family. Choices carry names like Arial, Baghdad, Chalkboard, Courier, Desdemona, Helvetica, Papyrus, Stencil, and Times New Roman.

Figure 7-7:
A fonts
funhouse.

Unless you wrote your graduate thesis on *Fontomology* (don't bother looking the word up; it's my invention), nobody on the Dummies faculty expects you to have a clue about what any of the aforementioned fonts look like. I sure don't. Cheating is okay. Peek at your document to see how highlighted words in the text change after clicking different font choices.

As usual, another way is available. In the lower-left corner of the Font window, click the icon that looks like the sun. Choose Show Preview from the menu (see Figure 7-8). You'll be able to inspect various font families and type-faces in the preview pane that appears above your selection. Click the sun icon again to choose Hide Preview.

Previewing your font

Figure 7-8:
Previewing your fonts.

Click to hide or show font preview

You can also preview the *type size* of your chosen font, as measured by a standard unit called *points*. In general, one inch has 72 points. You can also type your own words to see how they would look in a given font.

Revealing the Font Book

You likely have well over a hundred fonts on your computer, if not a lot more. Some were supplied with TextEdit. Some arrived with other word processing programs. You may have even gone on a font hunt and added more yourself on the Internet. At the end of the day, you may need help managing and organizing them.

That's the purpose behind an OS X program called *Font Book,* found in the Applications folder. It's shown in Figure 7-9. Think of Font Book as a gallery to show off all your finest fonts. Indeed, fonts here are grouped in collections.

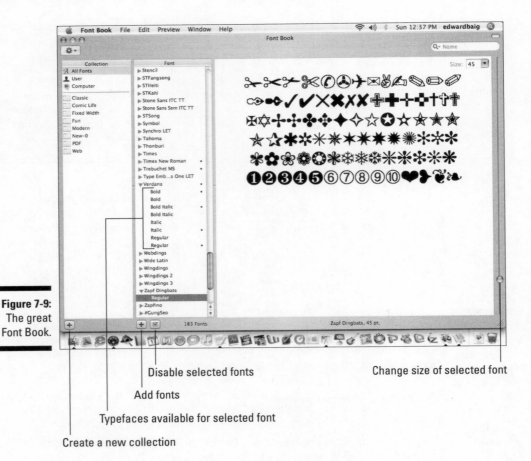

Figure 7-9:
The great
Font Book.

Disable selected fonts

Change size of selected font

Add fonts

Typefaces available for selected font

Create a new collection

The main font groupings are listed as following:

- ✔ **User:** The private fonts unique to your user account (Chapter 5).

- ✔ **Computer:** The public fonts available to anyone who uses this machine.

- ✔ **Classic:** Fonts that work with applications in the ancient pre-OS X Classic mode. Despite their prehistoric pedigree, nothing in the rule book prevents you from employing these with Tiger.

You can create your own font collections by choosing File⇨New Collection and typing a name for the collection. Then just drag fonts from the Fonts column into your new collection.

All in the fonts

Admit it, you're curious about the genealogy behind the font named Zapf Dingbats. Me too. For that matter, you may be wondering about the roots of other fonts on the system. Hey, it's your computer, you have a right to know. Press ⌘+I and the Font Book window reveals all, including the full name of a font, the languages in which it is used, and any copyright and trademark information. Best I can tell, Zapf Dingbats was not created by Archie Bunker.

By clicking a name in the Font column, you can sample what your font of choice looks like in the pane on the right. Drag the slider (labeled in Figure 7-9) to the right of that pane to adjust the type size of the fonts you're sampling.

If you're like most mortals, you'll use a small set of fonts in your lifetime. I'll lay odds you'll never take advantage of such esoteric fonts as Ayuthaya or Zapf Dingbats (see the "All in the fonts" sidebar). Trust me, I am not making these names up.

You can disable the fonts you'll rarely if ever use by clicking the little box with the check mark under the Font list (labeled in Figure 7-9). The word *Off* appears next the font's newly grayed-out name. If you change your mind, choose Edit⇨Enable *font you disabled*.

If, on the other hand, you want to add fonts to the machine, click the + button under the same column and browse to the font's location on your machine. But you can also install new fonts you've downloaded or purchased by simply double-clicking them. The fonts are automatically imported into Font Book.

When a dot appears next to a name in the Font list, duplicates of that font family are installed. Select the font in question and choose Edit⇨Resolve Duplicates.

Formatting Your Document

Fancy fonts aren't the only way to doll up a document. You have important decisions to make about proper margins, paragraph indentations, and text tabs. And you must determine whether lines of text should be single or double-spaced. Hey it's still a lot easier than using a typewriter.

Okay, we're back in our TextEdit classroom. Set your margins and tab stops by dragging the tiny triangles along the ruler.

Now click the drop-down menu that says Spacing, just above the ruler. Clicking Single separates the lines in the way you are reading them in this paragraph.

If I go with Double, the line jumps down to here, and the next line

jumps down to here.

Got it?

The control freaks among you (you know who you are) might want to click Other under the Spacing menu. It displays the dialog box shown in Figure 7-10. Now you can precisely determine the height of your line, the way the paragraphs are spaced (that is, the distance from the bottom of a paragraph to the top of the first line in the paragraph below), and other parameters, according to the points system.

Line height multiple	1.0 ⊕ times
Line height ○ Exactly ⊙ At least ☐ At most	0.0 ⊕ points 0.0 ⊕ points
Inter-line spacing	0.0 ⊕ points
Paragraph spacing before after	0.0 ⊕ points 0.0 ⊕ points
	Cancel OK

Figure 7-10: When it has to look just like this.

Here are other tricks that make TextEdit a capable writing companion:

- ✔ **Aligning paragraphs:** After clicking anywhere in a paragraph, choose Format⇨Text and choose an alignment (left, center, justified, or right). Play around with these choices to determine what looks best.

- ✔ **Writing from right to left:** I suppose this one's useful for writing in Hebrew or Arabic. Choose Format⇨Text⇨Writing Direction and then click Right to Left. Click again to go back the other way, or choose Edit⇨Undo Set Writing Direction.

- ✔ **Locating text:** You can use the Find command under the Edit menu to uncover multiple occurrences of specific words and phrases and replace them individually or collectively.

✔ **Producing lists:** Sometimes the best way to get your message across is in list form. Kind of like what I'm doing here. By clicking the Lists drop-down menu, you can present a list with bullets, numbers, roman numerals, uppercase or lowercase letters, and more, as shown in Figure 7-11. Keep clicking the choices until you find the one that makes the most sense.

✔ **Creating tables:** Then again, you may want to emphasize important points using a table or chart. Choose Format➪Text➪Table. In the window that appears (see Figure 7-12), you can select the number of rows and columns you need for your table. You can select a color background for each cell by clicking the Cell Background drop-down list and choosing Color Fill, and then choosing a hue from the palette that appears when you click the rectangle to the right. You can drag the borders of a row or a column to alter its dimensions. You can also merge or split table cells by selecting the appropriate cells and then clicking the Merge Cells or Split Cells button.

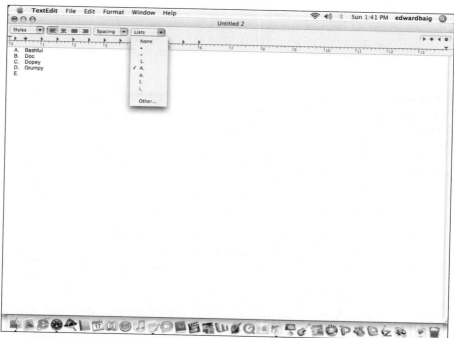

Figure 7-11:
Formatting
a list.

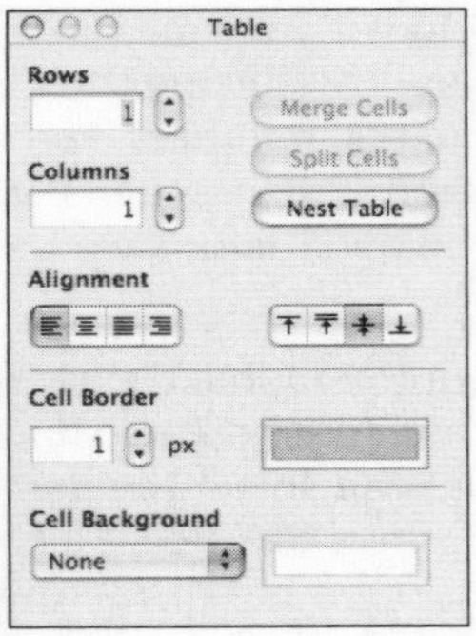

Figure 7-12:
Creating a
table.

Saving Your Work

You've worked so darn hard making your document read well and look nice that I'd hate to see all your efforts go to waste. And yet in the cruel world of computers that's precisely what could happen if you don't take a second to *save* your file. And a second is all it takes to save a file — but you can lose everything just as fast.

Stable as it is, the Mac is a machine for goodness sakes and not immune to power failures or human foibles. Odd as it may seem, even tech authors pound a calamitous combination of keys from time to time.

All the work you've done so far exists in an ethereal kind of way, as part of *temporary* memory (see Chapter 2). Don't let the fact that you can see something on your computer monitor fool you. If you shut down your computer, or it unexpectedly crashes (it's been known to happen even on Macs), any unsaved material will reside nowhere but in another type of memory. Your own.

So where exactly do you save your work? Why on the *Save sheet* of course (see Figure 7-13). It slides into view from the top of your document when you press the keyboard combo ⌘+S, or choose File➪Save.

Remember way back in the beginning of this chapter when I mentioned that Apple wouldn't dare name a file for you (except to give it the temporary moniker *Untitled*). Well this is your big chance to call the file something special by filling in a title where it says Save As. Go ahead and name it, I dunno, *Dark and Stormy*.

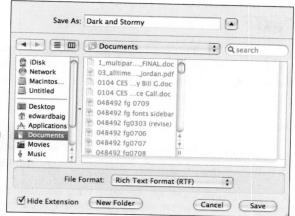

When you click the Save button, the contents of Dark and Stormy are assigned to a permanent home on your Mac's hard drive, at least until you're ready to work on the document again.

But there's more. You get to choose in which folder to stash the file. The Mac suggests the Documents folder, which seems like and often is a logical choice. But you can choose among several other possible destinations, as becomes clear when you click the arrow next to where you just named your document. You will see the sidebar we first became acquainted with in Chapter 3. You can stuff your manuscript in any existing folder or subfolder or create one from scratch by clicking the New Folder button and giving the folder a name.

It's time to confess. I've been holding back. When you christened your opus Dark and Stormy little did you know that you were actually giving it a slightly longer name: *Dark and Stormy.rtf*. The little suffix, or *extension,* stands for *Rich Text Format,* one of the file format types the Mac makes nice with. You could have saved the file in the Microsoft Word format, which would have given the file the .doc extension. Or you could have chosen HTML, the language of the World Wide Web (see Chapter 9). If you want to see what extensions are tagged to your various files, deselect the Hide Extension check box.

So let's review: As you work on documents, you are hereby advised to save and save often.

Making Revisions

Dark and Stormy is safe and sound on your hard drive. But after downing a few chill pills overnight, you have a brand-new outlook on life in the morning. You're past your brooding period. You want to rework your inspiration's central theme and give it a new name too, *Bright and Sunny*.

Back to TextEdit we go.

Choose File➪Open. A dialog box appears. Scroll down in the folder where you last saved your document, and double-click its name or icon when you find it.

You are now ready to apply your changes. Because your document is only as permanent as the last time you saved it, remember to save it early and often, as you make revisions. Along the way, you can rename your bestseller by using Save As and choosing a new name, though you'll still have a version under the old name.

You may be better off renaming a file by selecting it (from a Finder window or the desktop) and pressing Enter. Type the new name and press Enter again.

As always, your Mac tries to assist you in these matters. The computer makes the assumption that if you worked on a document yesterday or the day before, you might want to take another stab at it today. And to prevent you, Oh Prolific One, from having to strain too hard digging for a document you may want to edit, choose File➪Open Recent. Your freshest files will turn up in the list. Just click the name of the document you want to revisit.

Perhaps the fastest way to find a file you want to revise is to use the Spotlight tool, featured in the Chapter 6. Choose Spotlight by single-clicking its icon at the upper-right corner of the screen and type the name of the manuscript that requires your attention.

Taking Out the Trash

Like much else in life, documents, if not entire folders, inevitably outlive their usefulness. The material grows stale. It takes on a virtual stench. It claims hard drive space you could put to good use elsewhere.

Yes it's time to take out the trash.

Use the mouse to drag the document's icon above the trash can in the dock. Release the mouse button when the trash can turns black.

As usual, there's a keyboard alternative, ⌘+Delete. Or you can choose File➪ Move to Trash.

You'll know you have stuff in the trash because the icon shows crumpled paper. And just like your real life trash bin, you'll want to completely empty it from time to time. (Your neighbors might complain otherwise.)

To do so, choose Empty Trash under the Finder menu or press ⌘+Shift+Delete. A warning will pop up (see Figure 7-14), reminding you that once your trash is gone, it's gone, as if it was going through a shredder. (Even then you may be able to get it back, but you'll have to fork over some coin by purchasing data recovery software or hiring an expert.)

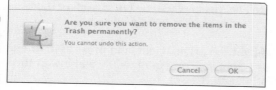

Figure 7-14:
Think before
trashing.

Are you sure you want to remove the items in the Trash permanently?

You cannot undo this action.

Cancel   OK

Never Mind: Retrieving What You've Tossed

It's pretty easy to pull something out of the trash, provided you didn't take that last Draconian measure and select Empty Trash. And it's less smelly or embarrassing than sticking your hands in a real trash bin. Click the Trash icon in the dock to peek at its contents. If you find something worth saving after all, merely drag it back onto the desktop or into the folder where it used to hang out.

If you're absolutely, positively certain that you want to get rid of the contents of your trash — and paranoid about industrial spies recovering the docs, choose Secure Empty Trash from the Finder menu instead of the regular Empty Trash command.

Making an Alias

You can create an *alias* of a file to serve as a shortcut for finding it, no matter where it's buried on your Mac. To understand what an alias is, it helps to understand what it's not. It's not a full duplicate of a file. (If you want to create a full duplicate, press ⌘+D or choose File⇨Duplicate.)

Instead, you are effectively copying the file's icon, not the file itself, meaning you are barely using any disk space. Clicking an alias icon summons the original file no matter where it's hanging out on the computer and even if you've renamed the file.

Why create an alien in the first place? Perhaps you're not sure where to place a file that you could easily justify putting in any number of folders. For instance, if you have a document titled Seven Dwarfs, it might belong in a folder for Snow White, one for Bashful, one for Doc, and so on. Because the Mac lets you create multiple aliases, you can effectively place the file in each of those folders (even though you and I know it really resides in only one place.)

To create an alias, highlight the original icon and press ⌘+L or choose File⇨ Make Alias. You can also drag an icon out of its file window at the same time you hold down the Option and ⌘ keys.

As you can see in Figure 7-15, the alias looks like a clone of the original icon, except the *alias* suffix is added to its name, and a tiny arrow appears on the lower-left corner of the icon. Clicking either brings up the same file.

If you want to find the location of the original file, highlight the alias icon and choose File⇨Show Original.

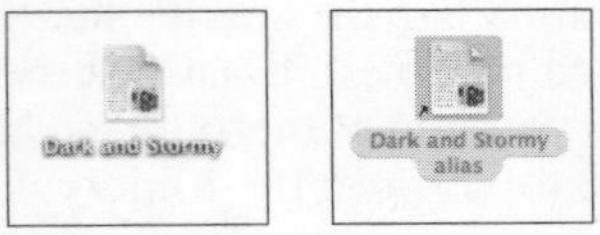

Figure 7-15:
The original
icon and
its alias.

To get rid of an alias, drag it to the trash. Doing so does not delete the original file.

If you had separately deleted the original file, the alias can't bring it back. But you can link the alias to a new file on the machine.

Chapter 8

Printing and Faxing

Computers are supposed to bring relief to packrats. The idea that you can store documents and files in their electronic state on your hard drive — thus reducing physical clutter — has widespread appeal. A few trees might breathe a sigh of relief too.

Yet for all the buzz over the years surrounding the potential for a "paperless" society, I don't reckon pulp industry executives are losing much sleep.

Fact is, you want to pick up something tangible for your own edification and convenience. And you want hard copies to show people. It's better to hand grandma printed pictures of the newborn rather than pull out a computer (or other gizmo) to show off your latest bundle of joy. What's more, even in the age of e-mail and electronic filings, you still usually print documents and reports for employers, teachers, financial institutions, and (sigh) the Internal Revenue Service.

Which reminds me: Despite wonderful advances in state-of-the-art printers, the counterfeiters among you will find no helpful hints in this chapter about printing money.

Choosing a Printer

What are those state-of-the-art printers? So kind of you to ask. Today's print-ers generally fall into two main camps: *inkjet* or *laser,* with the differences coming down to how ink makes its way onto a page. Printers vary by speed, features, resolution (sharpness), quality of the output, and price.

The most popular models are produced by Canon, Epson, and Hewlett-Packard, but you can buy printers of one type or another from a host of competitors.

Believe it or not, you can still find an el-cheapo hand-me-down *daisy-wheel* or *dot-matrix* printer on eBay and elsewhere. But these so-called *impact printers* are most definitely *not* the state-of-the-art I have in mind. Keep them a safe distance removed from your very modern Mac. Purchasing a daisy-wheel for a Mac would be along the lines of adorning the Queen of England with cos-tume jewelry. Not to mention the royal pain you'd have trying to hook up these relics.

In this section, we take a closer look at your most realistic printing options.

Inkjets

Inkjet printers consist of nozzles that squirt droplets of ink onto a blank sheet of paper. Models may be equipped with a single black cartridge and a single color cartridge. Or they may contain several color cartridges.

Where's that magenta cartridge when I need it?

Most of you, I suspect, will end up with an inkjet printer. They are the least expensive to buy, with some rock-bottom models costing as little as $40.

Bargains aren't always what they seem, however. The *cost of ownership* of inkjet printers can be exorbitant. You must replace pricey ($30 or so) ink car-tridges on a routine basis, more often if you spit out lots of photographs of your pet kitten Fluffy. So an inkjet printer's cost-per-page tends to be consid-erably higher than that of its laser cousins.

Having said that, inkjets are generally the most flexible bet for consumers, especially if you demonstrate shutterbug tendencies. Besides standard size 8½-by-11-inch paper, some inkjet models can produce fine looking 4-by-6-inch color snapshots on glossy photographic paper. (Photo paper, I'm obligated to point out, is expensive.)

Granted, black text produced on an inkjet won't look nearly as crisp as the text produced by a laser, though it can be quite decent just the same. Under certain conditions, some inks bleed or smudge. But for the most part, the quality of inkjets is perfectly acceptable for producing, say, family newsletters or brochures for your burgeoning catering business.

Lasers

It's somewhat remarkable that a focused laser beam can produce such excellent quality graphics. Then again, if lasers can correct nearsightedness and perform other medical miracles, perhaps printing isn't such a major deal after all.

Laser printers use a combination of heat, ink, and static electricity to produce superb images on paper. Such printers, especially color models, used to fetch thousands of dollars. To be sure, you'll still find prices for some models in the stratosphere. But entry-level color lasers are now south of $500.

However affordable they have become in recent years, lasers still command a premium over inkjets. But they are far more economical over the long term. Toner cartridges are relatively cheap and don't need to be replaced very often. A highly efficient laser might cost a couple of cents per page to operate, a small fraction of what an inkjet costs to run.

Lasers remain a staple in corporate offices. Businesses appreciate the photocopier-like output and the fact that lasers can handle high-volume printing loads at blistering speeds. The machines typically offer more paper handling options as well.

All-in-ones

Printers print, of course. But if your Mac is the centerpiece of a home office, you probably have other chores in mind. Copying and scanning, for instance. And faxing too. (Although as you discover later in this chapter, Macs with built-in modems can fax without a separate fax machine.) An *all-in-one* model, otherwise known as a *multifunction* printer, can provide some combination of these tasks. Most multifunction workhorses in home offices are inkjet based.

It's cheaper to buy a single multifunction device than several standalone devices. That lone machine takes up less space too. And many current all-in-ones are photo friendly.

If your fax, copier, or scanner goes on the fritz, you may also have to live without a printer while the multifunction unit is under repair.

What else to think about

Other features to consider when shopping for a printer follow:

- ✓ **Large paper trays:** Few things are more annoying than having to load a fresh stack of paper in the middle of an important printing job. With a fat paper tray, you won't be hassled quite as often. And some models have separate trays for photo paper, so you won't have to constantly shuffle different types of paper in and out depending on what you're printing.

- ✓ **Memory slots:** Maybe I shouldn't mention this feature in a Mac book. Because frankly, their purpose is to take the Mac out of the equation. Indeed, you can print images stored on a memory card without getting a computer involved.

- ✓ **LCD display:** You use this for peeking at the pictures you want to print (see preceding item) without the benefit of a computer. You can use the display also for various menu functions on the machine.

- ✓ **Two-sided printing:** This is useful (you guessed it) for printing on both sides of a sheet of paper.

- ✓ **Networking capabilities:** For sharing your printer among multiple Macs or Windows PCs or both. Wireless network printers cost more. I'll speak more of networking in Chapter 18.

Connecting and Activating a Printer

Almost all printers compatible with OS X, and that includes most printers sold today, connect to your Mac through the *Universal Serial Bus (USB)* port we became acquainted with in Chapter 2. So much for un-retiring the printer in the closet that connects through what's called a *parallel* port.

Here's one of my pet peeves. You shell out all this loot for a dandy printer only to have the salesperson tell you it doesn't come with the USB cable you need to connect it. In fact, that's the norm. Manufacturers are notoriously chintzy when it comes to supplying this *necessary* accessory. They'll tell you they don't include such a cable because people already have them. I'm not buying it. My feeling is that it's the company's way of advertising a lower price for a printer, while ultimately making a generous markup.

Indeed, you'll almost certainly leave the store considerably poorer than you would have first imagined. *Gotta* buy stacks of paper. Plus extra ink because the starter cartridges included with your printer may not last very long. And the aforementioned USB cable.

Ready, Set, Print

You have ink. You have paper. You have a USB cable. You are antsy. Time's a wasting. I sense a certain impatience. So let's get around to the task at hand.

Plug the printer into an AC wall jack. Plug the USB cable into the USB port on the Mac and make sure it's connected snugly to the printer itself. Turn on your printer. The thing is warmed and ready for action. Tiger big-heartedly assembled most of the software *drivers* required to communicate with modern printers. Chances are yours is one of them. If not, it probably resides on the software that came with the printer. Or visit the company's Web site.

Configuring wireless or wired (through Ethernet) networked printers is a tad more complicated. For now, we'll assume we've connected a USB printer. Open the Mac's trusted word processor, TextEdit. Then follow these steps:

1. **Open the document you want to print.**

2. **Choose File⇨Print, or use the keyboard shortcut ⌘+P.**

   Even though we're doing this exercise in TextEdit, you'll find the Print command under the File menu across your Mac software library. The ⌘+P shortcut works across the board too. The print window shown in Figure 8-1 appears.

3. **Click the Printer drop-down list and select your printer, if available.**

Figure 8-1:
Fit to print?

4. **If your connected USB printer is not in the print window:**

   a. **Click Add Printer in the drop-down list.**

      The Printer Setup Utility opens. You can access the utility also from the Utilities folder inside the Applications folder.

b. **If your printer appears in the list, click to select it (if it's not already selected) and you're golden. Continue with Step 5.**

c. **If your printer isn't listed, choose Add from the Printer List.**

A Printer Browser sheet appears.

d. **Click the printer connection type at the top and make the appropriate selection, as shown in Figure 8-2.**

In that connection type box, choices likely include USB, AppleTalk (signifying a network), Bluetooth (a type of wireless connection), and so on. When you make your choice, the Mac will search for any available printers and their drivers.

e. **Highlight the printer you want to use and then click Add.**

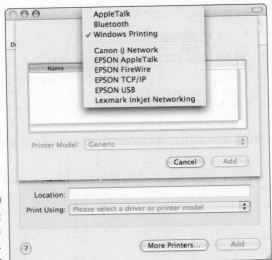

Figure 8-2:
Adding a
printer.

5. **Make your selections in the print window.**

Select which pages to print (All is the default, but you can give any range by tabbing from one From box to the other.) You also get to select the number of copies you need. You can check a box to indicate whether you want pages collated. And you can choose whether to save your document in the Adobe PDF format.

Note that print dialog boxes differ slightly from program to program. In Microsoft Word, for instance, you can get a quick preview of the document you want to print.

6. When you're satisfied with your selections, click Print.

If all goes according to plan, your printer will oblige.

Even if the Mac instantly recognizes your printer, I recommend loading any Mac installation discs that came with the printer. I specify Mac installation disc because printers that work with both Macs and Windows — and again that includes most models — may well supply separate discs for each operating system.

I know what you must be thinking. Why bother? My printer is already printing stuff out. So smart of you to ask. The answer is that the disc might supply you with extra fonts (see Chapter 7), as well as useful software updates.

It wouldn't hurt to also visit the printer manufacturer's Web site to see whether updated printer drivers are available.

Printing it your way

The Mac gives you a lot of control over how your printer will behave and your printouts will look.

You may have noticed another pop-up menu in the print sheet called Copies & Pages. Click, and a gaggle of other choices are revealed. Let's examine most of them:

✔ **Layout:** You can select the number of "pages" that will get printed on a single sheet of paper, and determine the ways those pages will be laid out, as shown in Figure 8-3. You can also choose a page border (Single Thin Line, Double Hairline, and so on).

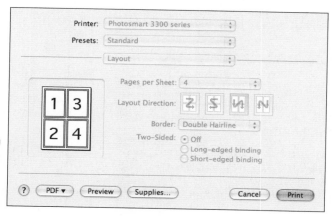

Figure 8-3:
Choosing a print layout.

- ✔ **Scheduler:** Suppose that you have to print dozens of invitations for your spouse's surprise birthday party and want to make sure to do so when your honey is out of the house. Set your Mac to print at a time when the two of you are out together.

- ✔ **Paper Handling:** You can choose to print only odd- or even-numbered pages or to print pages in reverse order. You can also scale a page so that it fits a legal- or letter-sized sheet, an envelope, or a variety of other paper sizes.

- ✔ **ColorSync:** Choose this setting if you want to add black and white, blue tone, sepia, or other filters.

- ✔ **Cover Page:** Pretend you work for the CIA. Then print a cover sheet stating that everything else you're printing is classified, confidential, or top secret? (Yea, like they're not going to look.)

- ✔ **Two-Sided Printing:** For printers that can handle such a requirement.

- ✔ **Paper Type/Quality:** Clues the printer in on the type of paper you loaded (such as inkjet, transparency film, brochure.) You also get to choose the print quality. A fast draft uses less ink than printing in the spiffiest, or best, quality. If your printer has more than one tray (for example, a main tray and a photo tray), you can also choose the source of the paper to use.

- ✔ **Borderless Printing:** Tell your printer to print without borders. Or not.

This seems as good a time as any to drop in on System Preferences, which is under the menu. Under the Hardware section, click the Print & Fax icon. As you can see in Figure 8-4, three tabs appear: Printing, Faxing, and Sharing. I'll touch on Faxing later in this chapter.

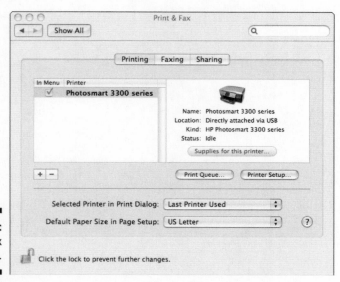

Figure 8-4:
Print & Fax
preferences.

If you click the Printing tab, you can choose a default paper size, click the Print Queue button to check the status of any current printing jobs, and more. If you click the Sharing tab, you can designate which of your other computers can share a particular printer.

Previewing your print

Before you waste ink and paper on an ill-advised print job, you probably want to be sure your documents meet your lofty standards. That means the margins and spacing look jiffy and you have a clean layout with no *widows*. That's publishing-speak for a lonely word or two on a line of text all to itself.

The Mac lets you take a sneak peek. Click the Preview button in the sheet that appears when you click Print in TextEdit. In Microsoft Word or other programs, you can choose File⇨Print Preview to see a version of what you are about to print. Word also gives you a preview in a small window that appears in the Word print sheet.

If you're satisfied, press ⌘+P. If not, go back and apply the necessary changes to your documents.

One more nice thing about printing on your Mac: The various programs you work in give you lots more custom printing options. For example, you can print a CD jewel case insert in iTunes (Chapter 14) or a pocket address book in Address Book.

When Printers Stop Printing

As sure a thing as you'll get in computing is that sooner or later (but probably sooner) your printer will let you down. I've already hinted at why.

Running out of ink or toner

Ink is perishable. Especially with an inkjet printer. The symptoms will be obvious. The characters on a page get lighter and lighter each time you print, to the point where they become barely legible. The software that came with your printer may give you an estimate on how much ink you have left each time you print. You can also check supply levels in the Print Queue, found again by clicking the Printing tab under the Print & Fax section of System Preferences.

Digital longevity?

Does the paper you buy make a difference? Some experts believe it does. Scientists maintain that the ink and paper combination you use to print digital photographs has a major effect on how the images will endure through the decades. Wilhelm Imaging Research has conducted accelerated aging tests that have indicated that, even on the same printer, prints made on high-quality paper could last more than 70 years when exposed to light, as compared to just two or three years using inferior paper. Regardless of the paper you use, you can bolster the lifespan of printed photographs by keeping them from light, humidity, and cigarette smoke and other pollutants.

Running out of paper

Unless you make a habit of peeking at your printer's paper tray, you won't get a fair warning when your paper supply is exhausted. Of course, the rule of thumb is that you will run out of paper the hour before an important term paper is due (or legal brief or journalism deadline; feel free to insert your own catastrophe).

Click the Supplies button in the TextEdit print sheet (and other print sheets). It whisks you off to the Apple store on the Internet, where you can buy replacement ink cartridges and paper. Because Tiger knows the kind of printer you have, you won't have to waste your time locating the requisite supplies. Tiger serves as your personal shopper, ushering you to the correct aisle in the store. If you have, say, an HP printer, Tiger will find the cartridges compatible with your particular printer model.

Alternatively, click Supplies for This Printer in the Print & Fax section of System Preferences.

Wherever you buy your ink and paper, I recommend having a spare set around.

Sometimes a printer stops working for no apparent good reason. In the Print Queue, try clicking Resume or Start Jobs. If all else fails, turn off and restart your printer.

Hooking Up a Scanner

As with printers, connecting a *scanner* is no big deal. It usually hooks up through USB, though FireWire models are in the marketplace as well. Or you may gain a scanner as part of a multifunction, or all-in-one, device.

Scanners are kind of anti-printers because you already have a printed image that you want to reproduce on your computer screen, such as receipts, newspaper clippings, or photo slides and negatives. Standalone scanners may cost less than $50, though you pay a lot more as you add features.

If you click Scanner in the Print Queue, you can tinker with the software provided by your scanner manufacturer. The software may let you remove dust or scratches from an image and restore faded colors.

Turning the Mac into a Fax Machine

If you bought a Mac with a built-in, dial-up fax modem (see Chapter 9), you don't need a dedicated fax machine. Just connect a telephone cord to the Mac's modem jack and you're all set. Unfortunately, the dial-up modem is no longer standard on the latest Macs. Instead, it's a $49 USB add-on.

Sending a fax

If you have the Apple modem, you'll appreciate the convenience of computer faxing. You don't have to print a document and go to the trouble of feeding a dedicated fax machine. Instead, you dispatch faxes directly from any program with printing capabilities.

1. **Open the document you want to fax.**
2. **Chose File➪Print.**
3. **Click the PDF button and choose Fax PDF from the pop-up menu.**

    A sheet such as the one shown in Figure 8-5 appears.

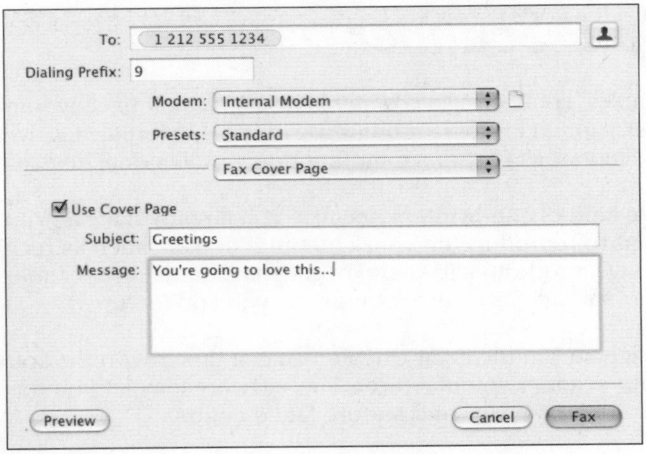

Figure 8-5:
Fill in the
necessary
fields to
send a fax.

4. **In the To field, type the fax number of the person to whom you want to send the fax, including 1 and the area code.**

   If necessary to access an outside line, add a dialing prefix such as 9 in the box marked as such.

   Alternatively, chose an entry from your Address Book by clicking the shadowy silhouette icon to the right of the To field and then double-clicking the card of the contact to whom you want to fax.

5. **In the Modem box, select Internet Modem (or whatever) as the means for dispatching your fax.**

6. **If you want a cover page, select the Use Cover Page option and type a subject line and brief message.**

7. **If you click the pop-up menu that says Fax Cover Page, you can choose other options to schedule the delivery of your fax or alter the layout.**

8. **To review the fax before sending it, click the Preview button.**

9. **Click the Fax button.**

   You should hear that awful, grinding faxing sound. It's the best evidence that your fax is on its merry way.

Receiving a fax

It makes sense that if a Mac can send a fax, it can receive one too. Make sure you have an available phone line and your computer is awake. A Mac in sleep mode cannot receive a fax. Then follow these steps:

1. **From System Preferences, choose Print & Fax and then click the Faxing tab.**

2. **Select the Receive Faxes on This Computer option.**

3. **Type your fax number in the box, as shown in Figure 8-6.**

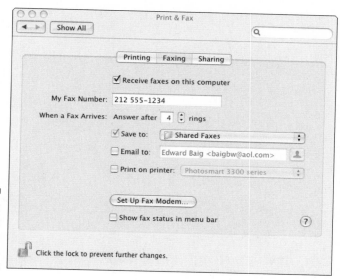

Figure 8-6:
Hold on. I'm getting a fax.

3. **Designate the number of rings before the fax is answered.**

   Make sure the computer gets to pick up before an answering machine connected to the same phone line.

4. **Choose how you want the incoming fax to be treated:**

   • Save the fax as a PDF in the Shared Faxes folder that Apple suggests, or save it to another folder

   • Send the fax to a specific e-mail address

   • Automatically print the fax

You can accept an incoming fax even if you haven't bothered to set up the system to receive faxes automatically. Go to System Preference, choose Print & Fax, and click Faxing. Select the box Show Fax Status in Menu Bar option. When the phone rings, choose Answer Now from the Fax Status icon in the menu bar.

Part III
Rocketing into Cyberspace

The 5th Wave   By Rich Tennant

"Wow, I didn't know OS X could redirect an e-mail message like that."

In this part . . .

Do you sometimes feel like the last person on Earth to figure out the Internet? The chapters here will direct you online, and help you survive after you get there. You also find out why e-mail is so wonderful — and so horrific at times — and give some deep thoughts to the merits of .Mac membership.

Chapter 9

Stairway to the Internet

*R*emember what life was like prior to the middle half of the 1990s? Before this nebulous thing called the Internet changed only *everything*.

Way back in the Dark Ages people routinely set foot in record stores to buy music. Students went to the library to do research. Folks paid bills with checks and read newspapers on, gosh, paper. They even picked up the telephone to gab with friends.

How passé.

Nowadays, such transactions and exchanges occur gazillions of times a second on the Internet. Cyberspace has become the place to shop, meet your soul mate, and conduct business. It is also a virtual playground for the kids.

You can fetch, or *download,* computer software, movies, and all kinds of other goodies. You may even get the stuff for free. Let your guard down, however, and you can also lose your shirt. (You really have to question how you won the Sri Lankan lottery when you never bought a ticket.)

Nobody in the early days of the Internet could have envisioned such a future. What eventually morphed into the Net was invented by the nerds of their day, 1960s Defense Department scientists. They constructed — in the interest of national security — the mother of all computer networks.

Hundreds of thousands of computers would be interconnected with hundreds of thousands more. The friendly face of cyberspace — what became the *World Wide Web,* or *Web* for short — was still decades away.

Has this somehow passed you by? Forget about fretting if you haven't boarded the cybershuttle just yet. Getting up to speed on the Internet isn't as daunting as you might think. You can enjoy a perfectly rewarding online experience through your Mac without ever deciphering the Net's most puzzling terms, everything from *domain names* to *file transfer protocols.* And you certainly don't have to stay up late cramming for any final exams.

But the Internet is not for people who cherish siestas either. It's as addictive as nicotine. Expect a warning from the surgeon general any day now: Spending time online is hazardous to your sleep cycle.

Feeling brave? Want to take the online plunge anyhow? The rest of this chapter will clue you in on how best to proceed.

Dialing In

Let the games begin. You can find your way online in two main ways, and both involve getting chummy with an important piece of computer circuitry, the *modem.* I address *dialup* modems here and *broadband* modems in the next section.

Dialup is the simplest and cheapest scheme. It's nearly as brainless as making a phone call. Wait a second, it *is* making a phone call. When the modem works its magic, it dials the Internet over a regular phone line as if you were calling your mother. The difference is that no one at the other end will make you feel guilty for not visiting often enough. With any luck, you won't get a busy signal, either.

In many cases you won't actually see the modem because it resides inside the Mac. That's okay. You only need to locate the phone jack on the back or side of the computer (depending on the model). A little phone icon lets you know you've arrived at the right place. On recent Macs, a built-in dialup modem is no longer standard, probably because Apple reckons that most users are embracing broadband; you can buy an optional dialup modem that connects to a USB port on the machine. Either way, connect one end of a standard phone cord into the modem jack and the other end into the wall jack where your telephone was connected.

Speed kills

When geeks speak of modem speeds, they typically talk in terms of *kilobits per second,* or *kbps,* which is the equivalent of one thousand bits per second. The itty *bit* or *binary digit* is the tiniest unit of measurement for data. Dialup modems are typically rated at 56 Kbps (often expressed as 56K). Reality check: Rarely are the maximum speeds achieved, so a 56K modem is probably transmitting data at 48K or so. If you don't have a clean connection, you might creep along at much slower speeds than that. You'll be counting "one Mississippi, two Mississippi, three Mississippi" and so on before the Web page you clicked on even *starts* to show up.

Now consider *broadband* modems. The ones that truly rock might blaze along at 5000kbps or faster (sometimes expressed as 5 *megabits per second,* or 5 M*bps.*) The broadband to dialup difference is like comparing an Olympic sprinter to a weekend jogger. Web pages can turn up *thisfast,* downloaded files also show up in a jiffy, and videos appear much more fluid, as if you were watching TV rather than viewing the equivalent of a herky-jerky slide show.

This all sounds fine and dandy, save one knotty problem. You still want to be able to make and receive regular calls using the phone whose cord you removed. The answer is a small, inexpensive, plastic doodad called a *splitter* (or Y-jack), which as its name suggests splits a single phone jack into two. So now you can plug your computer and phone into the same wall jack, though you still can't handle regular calls and use the Internet at the same time.

If doing both simultaneously is an essential requirement, you can always have the phone company come out to install a second phone line in your house. You can then dedicate one line to the modem and another to the phone. This peachy little arrangement will cost you a pretty penny each month, however, and is not necessarily the ideal solution, as I expand on in the next section. It's time to consider broadband.

Taking the Broadband Express

If the traditional dialup modem is the local, broadband is the express. Who can blame you for wanting to take the fast train? You'll pay more for a ticket — monthly charges can amount to $35 to $50 on up, often more than double the dialup fees. The positive spin is that you won't need a second phone line. Besides, the broadband express is almost always worth it. After you've experienced a fast hookup, you'll have a difficult time giving it up.

DSL or cable?

Broadband service comes in three flavors. Depending on where you live, you may have a choice of all, some, or none of the various alternatives. All three broadband types have dedicated modems that reside outside the computer. In many but not all cases, a technician will come to your house (generally for a fee) and connect a broadband modem to the service you have selected. The options are

- **Cable modem:** Typically the fastest of the broadband choices and the one that probably makes the most sense if you already subscribe to cable TV. The reason is your cable company is likely to cut you a small break on the monthly fee. The connection involves hooking up the cable TV cord to the modem.

- **DSL:** As with dialup, DSL, which stands for Digital Subscriber Line, works over existing telephone lines. But a big difference compared to dialup is that you can prowl the Internet and make or receive phone calls at the same time. And DSL, like a cable modem, is leagues faster than a dialup modem. As with cable, deals can be had if you take on service from the same company supplying your regular phone service.

- **Satellite:** Possibly the only alternative if you live in the boondocks. You get the Internet signal the same way you receive satellite TV, through a dish or antenna mounted on your house. If you go the satellite route, make sure your modem can send, or *upload,* information as well as receive, or *download,* it. Upload speeds are typically much pokier than download speeds, and satellite service in general is sluggish compared to other broadband choices. (Of course, uploading and downloading are components of all modem types.) Satellite also commands higher upfront costs than cable or DSL because you have to shell out for the dish and other components.

Always on, always connected

In the dialup world, you make your call, wait for a connection to be established, grab what you are looking for on the Net, and say adios. Heaven forbid you forget something. Each time you want to go back online, you have to repeat this drill. Amounts to too many phone calls, too many hassles.

Broadband generally has fewer hang-ups. The experience is far more liberating because you have a persistent, always-on connection, at least as long as the Mac itself is turned on. You won't have to compete with your teenagers for access to the only phone in the house. Web pages get updated. E-mails and instant messages usually arrive in a blink. What's more, you can share your Internet connection with other computers in the house (see Chapter 19).

Let Me In

This whole Internet business has one more essential piece: deciding on the outfit that will let you past the Net's front gate. That company is called an *Internet Service Provider, ISP* for short. You'll invariably have to slip this gate-keeper a few bucks each month, though sometimes paying annually lowers the price of admission. Many ISPs, such as AOL, Comcast, EarthLink, and MSN, are large, well-known enterprises. But tiny unfamiliar companies may also serve the bill.

As always, there are exceptions: You may not have to shop for an ISP if your employer provides the Internet gratis. Students often get complimentary access on college campuses, though the costs are likely buried in tuition.

If you signed up for broadband, chances are you've already met your ISP because it's the cable or phone company that set you up. But if you're playing one company off against another, here are key points to consider:

- ✔ **Service:** An ISP's reputation is the whole enchilada. Seek companies that do a lot of handholding, from Getting Started pamphlets to toll-free technical-support phone numbers. If they do provide toll-free support, give the number a try before you sign up. Look elsewhere if it takes forever for a live person to answer your call.

- ✔ **Fees:** Membership fees vary, and companies often run promotions. Compare rate options if you live in a town with lots of dialup and broadband choices. Choose a plan in which you are given unlimited access for a generous chunk of hours. Metered pricing in which you are billed hourly isn't smart for anyone but the most disciplined user who rarely expects to go online.

- ✔ **Local number:** This is an important consideration for dialup customers. If possible, choose a plan where you can dial the Net without incurring long-distance charges. If you travel a lot, it's also helpful to have a choice of local numbers in the city or cities you most often frequent.

- ✔ **E-mail:** Just for being a customer, some ISPs give you one or more e-mail accounts. More is obviously better if you intend on sharing the computer with family members. Ask also whether the ISP provides tools for cutting down on spam. I'll have more to say on this topic in Chapter 10.

- ✔ **Family protection:** If you have kids, find out whether the ISP offers parental controls or takes other steps to help protect the little ones in cyberspace.

Whither online services

America Online remains the colossus of ISPs, but it also is the prime representative of a crumbling institution: the online service as we once knew it. (An *online service* is essentially a private club where you can pontificate in chat rooms and on bulletin boards, download files, get news, seek help with technical problems, and access e-mail.) In the days when only nerds had heard of the Internet, AOL competed against and ultimately clobbered consumer rivals such as Prodigy and more technically oriented online services such as CompuServe and GEnie. In fact, AOL eventually acquired CompuServe.

As with any ISP, subscribers today rely on AOL as the gateway to the unfettered Internet. But you also must fork over a premium for the privilege. At $25.90 a month for an unlimited plan, you'd be hard-pressed to find a more expensive dialup alternative.

Throngs of members, including lots of Net beginners, or *newbies,* made AOL the online champ because of the way the company cleverly prepackaged and organized material inside its "walled garden." Sure, you could eventually venture out to the Internet at large, but more than likely you'd remain inside AOL's friendly confines. The environment was pretty safe — AOL offered excellent parental controls and tried to rid the joint of its relatively few bad apples. The company also made it a breeze to get started. AOL's free software disks turned up in shops, in your mailbox, and as magazine inserts.

In recent years, though, AOL members started ditching the service in droves. Folks discovered broadband and figured that much of what they were getting inside AOL for hefty fees, they could find on their own in cyberspace for less. It hardly mattered to these people that AOL peddled broadband connect services like its rivals. They couldn't care less that AOL reduced the tab for its proprietary content when they arrived online through another ISP. Bottom line: AOL became less relevant.

AOL got the hint. It quietly transitioned from a company that has traditionally trumpeted the flagship online service into one that aggressively competes in the free Web *portal,* or entryway space, against the likes of Yahoo!, MSN, and Google. This means that much of the material previously available only to subscribers can be accessed for free by visitors to its Web pages. What's more, as of this writing, AOL parent Time Warner was reportedly considering a plan that would drop subscription fees for high-speed broadband customers. (Dial-up members would still have to pay.) Such an altered landscape begs an obvious question: Is AOL membership worthwhile? A slew of AOL critics sneer that AOL wasn't worth the price of admission even in its heyday. The reasons for staying put are dwindling even for AOL loyalists. Although AOL still provides fine parental controls, most of the other PC protection and security features it offers with a subscription mean little to the Mac community. Viruses and spyware are mostly somebody else's problem (see Chapter 14).

Still, Mac users will appreciate some of the content that remains solely available to AOL subscribers, notably all XM satellite radio's music channels. Perhaps the most compelling reason to stick with AOL: Veteran members may not want to go through the hassle of telling friends and cohorts that the AOL e-mail address they've used for years is now out of service.

Going on a Safari

It is virtually impossible to ignore the World Wide Web. Practically everyone you come across is caught up in the Web in one way or another. On a typical day, you might hear how "little Johnny built this amazing Web page at school." How your best friend researched symptoms on the Web before heading to the doctor. And how you can save a bundle booking your vacation online. Web addresses are plastered on billboards, business cards, and the cover of books like this one.

Just browsing

Technologists have an uncanny knack for making simple things hard. They could ask you to make a phone call over the Internet. But if they told you instead to make a *VoIP* or *Voice over Internet Protocol* call, they'd pretend to be really smart. So it is unbelievably refreshing to discover that to browse or surf the World Wide Web, you need a piece of software that is called, um, a *Web browser.* Okay, so they might have called it a Web surfer.

Because you had the good sense to purchase a Mac, you are blessed with one of the best browsers in the business. It's aptly named *Safari* because much of what you do in cyberspace is an expedition into the wild. See Figure 9-1.

Learning to tame Safari means getting fluent with the concept of a Web address, or what those aforementioned technologists dub a *URL* (*Uniform Resource Locator*). Scary stuff. I told you, these guys can't seem to help themselves.

Just because of the way things are, all Web addresses begin with *http://* or *www.* and end with a suffix, typically *.com* (pronounced "dotcom"), *.edu, .gov, .net,* or *.org.* What you type in between is often (but not always) an excellent indicator of where you will end up on the Web. So typing www.usatoday.com takes you to the nation's largest newspaper. Typing www.espn.com leads to a popular sports destination. And so on. You enter the URL into an *address box* at the top of the browser window (labeled in Figure 9-1).

Back

Forward

Home page

Enter Web address here

Figure 9-1:
The Safari
Web
browser.

Clicking links

Web surfing would be awfully tedious if you had to type an address each time you wanted to go from one site to another. Fortunately, the bright minds who invented Safari and other browsers agree.

On the Safari *address bar* you'll typically see a series of buttons or icons to the left of the box where you entered the URL. The buttons you see and the order in which they appear vary, depending on how you customize the browser. To make the address bar disappear entirely, choose View⇨Hide Address Bar. To make it reappear, choose View⇨Show Address bar.

The left- and right-facing arrow buttons on the address bar function as the back and forward buttons, respectively. So clicking the left arrow transports you back to the last page you were looking at before the page that is currently displayed. Click the right, or forward, button to advance to a page you have already looked at.

TIP

Click the address bar icon that looks like a house, and you go to your starting base, or *home page*. That's the site that greets you each time you fire up the browser for the first time. It's no coincidence that Apple chose one of its own Web pages as the default Safari starting point. That way, it can promote the company and try to sell you stuff. As you might imagine, home pages are valuable pieces of screen real estate to marketers. Everyone from AOL to Google to Yahoo! would love for you to choose their *portal* as your start page. Fortunately, changing Safari's home page is simple. Select Preferences from the Safari menu, click the General tab, and then type the Web address of your page of choice in the box labeled Home page, shown in Figure 9-2.

You'll notice that some text on various Web pages is underlined in blue. That means it's a *link*. Clicking a link takes you to another page without having to type any other instructions.

Some links are genuinely useful. If you are reading about the Indianapolis Colts game, you may want to click a link that would lead to, say, quarterback Peyton Manning's career statistics. But be wary of other links that are merely come-ons for advertisements.

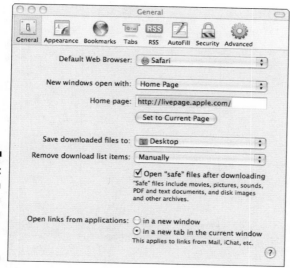

Figure 9-2:
You can change a Home page in Safari preferences.

Using bookmarks

Odds are you'll rapidly get hooked on a bevy of juicy Web pages that become so irresistible you'll keep coming back for more. We won't ask, you need not tell. Of course it's downright silly to have to remember and type the destination's Web address each time you return. Create a *bookmark* instead.

Choose the Add Bookmark item under Safari's Bookmarks menu or press the keyboard shortcut ⌘+D. A dialog box appears (see Figure 9-3), asking you to type a name for the bookmark you have in mind and to choose a place to keep it for handy reference later. You can group bookmarks in menu folders called Collections. If you decide to bookmark the Internet Movie Database home page, for example, you might decide to place it in a Collections folder called Entertainment. Whenever you want to pay a return visit to the site, you open the Entertainment folder and click the bookmark.

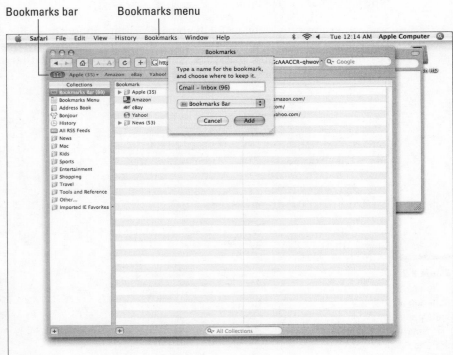

Figure 9-3:
Where to book your bookmarks.

Despite your best organizational skills, your list of bookmarks and Collections may become so, well, overbooked, that it becomes far less functional. I practically guarantee that you will tire of at least some of the sites now cluttering up your bookmarks closet. To delete a bookmark, highlight its name, click the Edit menu at the top of the screen, and then choose Cut. If you change your mind, choose Edit⇨Undo Delete Bookmark.

If all that seems like too much work, highlight an unwanted bookmark and press the Delete button on your keyboard.

You'll want to return to some sites so often they deserve VIP status. Reserve a spot for them in Safari's Bookmarks marquee, otherwise known as the *bookmarks bar,* situated below the browser's address bar. Choose Bookmarks Bar when the dialog box pops up, asking where to place the bookmark you've just created.

Employing the tools of the trade on your Safari

Safari is capable of other neat tricks. I describe some of them in this section.

Pop-up blocker

Tolerating Web advertising is the price to pay for all the rich Web resources at your disposal. Problem is, some ads induce agita. The most offensive are *pop-ups,* those hiccuping nightmarish little windows that make you think you woke up in the middle of the Las Vegas strip. Pop-ups have the audacity to get between you and the Web page you are attempting to read. Turning on the pop-up blocker can shield you from such pollutants. Click Block Pop-Up Windows under the Safari menu or employ the keyboard shortcut ⌘+K. If a check appears, you have successfully completed your mission. Once in a great while, a pop-up is worth viewing; to turn off the pop-up blocker simply repeat this exercise.

Google search bar

You can conduct a Google search by visiting www.google.com. But Safari saves you the time and trouble. You can enter search terms directly into a box right in the address bar. I'll have more to say about Google and other search engines later in this chapter.

Filling out forms

Safari can remember your name, address, passwords, and other information. So when you start typing a few characters into a Web form or other field, the browser can finish entering the text for you, provided it finds a match in its database. From the Safari menu, choose Preferences⇨AutoFill, and select the items you want Safari to use (such as info from your Address Book card). If several choices match the first several letters you type in a form, a menu appears. Press the arrow keys to select the item you have in mind and then press Enter.

Tabbed browsing

Say you want to peek at several Web pages in a single browser window instead of having to open separate windows for each "open" page. Welcome to the high art of *tabbed browsing*. To turn on the feature, choose Preferences in the Safari menu and then click Tabs. The window shown in Figure 9-4 appears. Select the Enabled Tabbed Browsing option and the Select New Tabs As They Are Created option. Then close the Preferences window.

Now each time you ⌘-click, you open a link in a new tab instead of a window. To toggle from one open Web page to another, just click its tab. The tabs appear just under the bookmarks bar. You can also press ⌘+T to open a new tabbed window.

Benefiting from History

Say you failed to bookmark a site and now days later decide to return. Only you can't remember what the darn place was called or the convoluted path that brought you there. Become a history major. Safari logs every Web page you open and keeps the record for a week or so. So you can consult the History menu to view a list of all the sites you visited on a particular day during the week. If you're wigged out by this Internet trail, you can always click Clear History to wipe the slate clean.

Figure 9-4:
Keeping
tabs. The
tabbed
browsing
window.

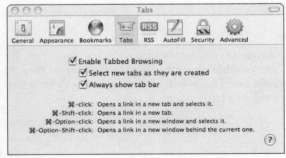

Private browsing

Hey maybe you do have something to hide. Perhaps you're surfing in an Internet cafe. Or just possibly you're being paranoid. Whatever. Turn on a hush-hush Safari feature called *private browsing* by choosing that option on the Safari menu. Now Safari won't add the Web pages you've visited to the History menu (though you can still use the Back and Forward buttons to return to sites you've been to). When private browsing is turned on, AutoFill is turned off, and Web *cookie* preferences (see Chapter 14) are also deep-sixed.

Using an Alternative Browser

Safari is swell, but it's not the only game in town. Eventually, you'll stumble upon a Web site that doesn't make nice with the Apple browser. That's likely because the site was programmed to work solely with the Grand Poobah among browsers, Microsoft's Internet Explorer. Hey, no one ever said life was fair (see the "Putting up with Internet Explorer" sidebar).

Other fine browsers abound and choosing one is like deciding between Coke and Pepsi. Check out Mozilla Firefox, iCab, and Opera at their respective Web sites.

Putting up with Internet Explorer

For years Microsoft adopted a kind of *laissez-faire* approach when it came to revving up its famed Web browser. It generally left tabbed browsing and other innovations to others. Such is the complacency that sets in when you've bagged a monopolistic share of the market. Still the venerable browser comes in handy at times, especially if Safari has difficulty communicating with a particular Web page you're trying to view. On older Macs, you'll find Internet Explorer in the Applications folder. On newer systems, you have to fetch the program yourself from the Internet.

Just don't expect any niceties from the folks at Microsoft headquarters in Redmond, Washington. In the middle of 2003, Microsoft announced that IE for the Mac would undergo no further development. A couple of years later, Microsoft said it would no longer offer tech support for the Mac version of IE and indicated it wouldn't provide security or performance updates either. The message was practically deafening: Go book a Safari.

The Skinny on Search Engines

So all these plum pickings are on the Internet, along with quite a lot of garbage. This leads to the obvious question: Where in goodness sakes do you uncover the gems amidst all the junk? A search engine is the best place to begin. These useful tools scan Web pages to find links based on instances of the search terms you enter.

Google this

Anyone who is anyone — and that might as well include you — uses Google. Google has become so popular that it's often treated as a verb, as in, I googled something. It is also why Google's founders have become richer than Croesus.

Haven't the foggiest idea who Croesus was? Just Google the name, and you'll soon discover how this sixth-century Lydian monarch managed to amass a fortune without launching an IPO.

The slowpoke way to Google something is to visit www.google.com. Type your search query, Croesus in this example, and click the Google Search button. Safari, however, provides a faster alternative. Just enter your query in the Google text box inside the Safari address bar, as shown in Figure 9-5.

Google text box

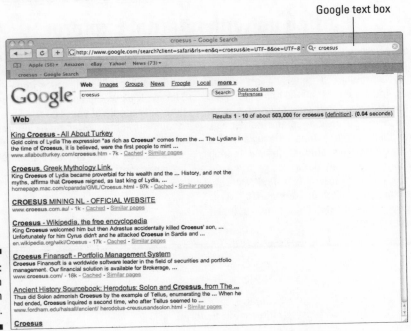

Figure 9-5:
A rich
search in
Google.

Either way, Google will rapidly spit back a list of findings, or hits, containing links to Web pages. That would be all there is to it, except you'll probably have to help Google narrow things down a tad. The Croesus example yields about 503,000 hits, which is more than you probably bargained for.

Enter an even broader search term such as *rockets,* and Google responds with something in the order of 45 million hits. I don't know about you, but I have time to pore through only half of them. What's more, smart as Google is, it has no way of knowing whether you mean the flying machine that soars into outer space, the basketball franchise that plays in Houston, or even the hamburger chain Johnny Rockets.

The obvious takeaway: the more descriptive you are the better. Two or three search terms almost always work better than one.

You can assist Google in several ways. Putting quotation marks around your search term narrows the returns because the browser thinks you're searching for that exact phrase. This works wonders with song or book titles.

Conversely, you can exclude topic areas by putting a minus sign next to the word. For example, if you enter

```
rockets -houston
```

you shouldn't receive references to the basketball team. If you want to find pages that include either of two search queries, use an OR between the words. For example

```
Rockets OR Jets
```

displays results for two professional sports franchises. But proving again how tricky the search biz can be, you would have to be more explicit if the rockets and jets you have in mind are the kind that require astronauts and pilots.

Here's a sampling of other nifty Google tricks that would make a professional researcher proud:

- **Solve arithmetic:** Enter a math problem, such as *63/7.8 =* and Google supplies the answer (8.07692308).

- **Provide the forecast:** By adding *weather* next to a city name or postal zip code, you can peek at the current temperature, wind, and humidity and get a quick weather snapshot of the days ahead.

- **Do a reverse phone lookup:** Type an area code and a phone number, and Google will reveal whose number it is (if listed).

- **Track airline delays:** Google can tell you whether a plane is on time. Just type in the flight number.

  ✔ **Take over for Webster:** Place *define* before a word and Google offers a definition.

  ✔ **Convert currency:** Want to determine how many dollars there are to the euro? Type, for example, *250 us dollars in euros.*

MSN and Yahoo!

Google is the search engine of choice for your humble author, but other alternatives are available. Yahoo! and MSN (from Microsoft) are probably the best-known rivals, and both do a decent job. In fact, Yahoo! is kind of the granddaddy of the search business. Moreover, when you go to the Yahoo! or MSN site, at www.yahoo.com or www.msn.com, respectively, you'll be taken to their respective Web portals, where you can do a lot more than search. *Portals* are launching pads for a gaggle of goodies, including news and entertainment links, stock quotes, games, and e-mail.

The Davids to the search Goliaths

You may want to do a Google search on search engines because so many smaller, specialized ones pop up all the time. (I suppose the creators of these sites want entrée into the same country clubs as the Google guys.) Search companies may narrowly focus on news, health, travel, local goings-on, politics, or shopping. And some, such as Dogpile (www.dogpile.com), merely aggregate or compile results from other leading search engines into one.

A particularly interesting approach is taken by Clusty, found at www.clusty.com. It groups similar items together into folders, or clusters. If you type *Giants,* for example, Clusty generates groupings such as New York Giants, San Francisco Giants, Barry Bonds, Corporate Giants, Dinosaurs, and Land of the Giants. Click the appropriate cluster, and the displayed search results pertain only to that grouping.

Chapter 10

Going Postal over E-Mail

*E*lectronic mail is a blessing and a curse.

Why you can't live without e-mail: Messages typically reach the person to whom they're addressed in a few seconds as compared with a few days for *snail mail*. (That's the pejorative label geeks have tattooed on regular postal mail.) You won't waste time licking envelopes either.

Why e-mail drives you batty: It won't take long before you're likely buried under an avalanche of messages, much of it junk mail, or *spam*.

Not that any mail system is perfect. You can only imagine the snide comments heard in the day of the Pony Express: *Love that I got my tax refund and Sharper Image catalogue, but the stench on that steed. . . .*

If you're an e-mail tyro, you discover the basics in this chapter. But even those who have been sending electronic missives for years might be able to collect a useful nugget or two.

Understanding E-Mail

In broad terms, *e-mail* is the exchange of messages over a communications network, typically the Internet but also a network within an organization.

To use e-mail, you need an e-mail account, such as the ones traditionally offered by employers, schools, or Internet Service Providers (ISPs) such as AOL, EarthLink, or MSN. You also need e-mail software to send, receive, and organize these messages. Fortunately, Apple includes such an application with OS X, and there can't be any doubt about what the program does. It's aptly named Mail.

To access Mail, single-click the icon that looks like a stamp on the dock. If for some reason the icon isn't there, double-click the Mail icon inside the Applications folder.

By the way, don't let the stamp representing the Mail icon fool you. E-mail doesn't require postage; for that matter, many e-mail accounts are free. Well, like most things in life, e-mail is not really free. You pay for it

- ✔ As part of your ISP fees
- ✔ As part of your college tuition
- ✔ By having to read irritating online advertisements
- ✔ By the aggravation accompanying your boss's e-mails

The Worldwide E-Mail Exchange

Before telling you how to set up e-mail accounts to work with the Mac's Mail program, know that you can continue to send and read mail inside such applications as Microsoft Entourage (like Outlook for the Mac crowd). What's more, if you've been sending and receiving e-mail on other computers through Web accounts such as Google's Gmail, Microsoft's MSN Hotmail, or Yahoo! Mail, you can continue right along on the Mac. AOL, the outfit that popularized the phrase "You've Got Mail," works too.

Having one or more Web-based e-mail accounts is nice. You get the tremendous advantage of being able to access mail from any Internet browser (on a Mac or PC). Plus, popular Web e-mail accounts are free and loaded with gobs of storage.

Setting Up a New E-Mail Account

Sending and reading e-mail through the Mac's Mail program is a breeze, after you set the thing up. Indeed, the process for first-timers can be a slightly harrowing experience:

1. **Open Mail by clicking the Mail icon (it looks like a stamp) on the dock or by double-clicking Mail in the Applications folder.**

   You are greeted with a Welcome to Mail window, shown in Figure 10-1.

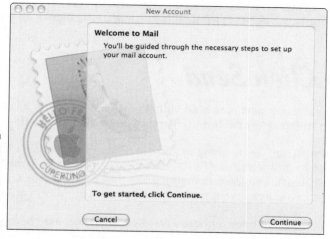

Figure 10-1:
Setting up a
new Mail
account
begins here.

2. **Click Continue.**

3. **Fill in the General Information required in the next screen.**

   You must fill in an Account Type (from a drop-down menu), Account Description, Full Name, User Name, and Password.

4. **In the next few screens, you have to supply other dreadful sounding particulars, such as the name of the incoming mail server (something like pop.*yourprovider*.com).**

   This is where your e-mail congregates before it is retrieved. There's also the outgoing mail server (typically SMTP.*yourprovider*.com). Okay, I won't keep you in the dark any longer: SMTP stands for *Simple Mail Transfer Protocol*, POP is short for *Post Office Protocol*, and IMAP for *Internet Mail Access Protocol* or *Internet Message Access Protocol*.

Setting up additional mail accounts involves repeating these steps. Begin by choosing File⇨Add Account in Mail.

Piece of advice: Unless you're looking for an excuse to get away from the chatterbox you've been kibitzing with at a cocktail reception, avoid dropping these unfriendly terms into your conversation. It's like having a big *N* (as in *Nerd*) stamped to your forehead.

If the IMAPs and SMTPs and the rest are not exactly at your fingertips (and why should they be?), call your ISP or poke around the company's Web site for assistance.

Incidentally, setting up e-mail through a .Mac account (see Chapter 12) is a far simpler endeavor because Apple fills in some of the blanks on your behalf.

Before You Click Send

I promise the difficult part is behind you. And if you're already an e-mail whiz, you can skip the next few sections. I'll greet you on the other side.

If you're still with me, you're going to find out how to send e-mail, with minimal attention paid to protocol. E-mail addresses always have the @ symbol somewhere in their midst. They look something like this: paula@americanidol.com, deputyfife@mayberrysheriff.gov, or costanza@nyyankees.com.

With the Mail program open, choose File⇨New Message, use the keyboard alternative ⌘+N, or click New in the Mail toolbar. (Once again, if Mail isn't open, click the stamp icon on the dock.) A window like the one shown in Figure 10-2 appears.

Addressing your missive

With the New Message window on your screen, you're ready to begin the process of communicating through e-mail with another human being.

In the *To* box, *carefully* type the recipient's e-mail address. If you type even a single letter, number, or symbol incorrectly, your message will not be sent (you should get a bounce-back notification) or worse, will be dispatched to the wrong person.

Click to save a message you're not ready to send

The main recipient of your message

These folks are copied but can't see who else received the message

Click to send the message

These folks are copied

Message subject

Click to attach a file

The main body of the message

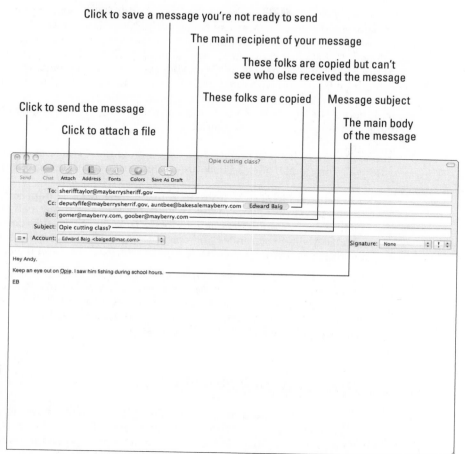

Figure 10-2:
How to send an e-mail message.

As you start banging out an e-mail address, the Mac tries to be helpful. It fills in the name and address of the person it thinks you are trying to reach (culled from your Address Book). Don't worry if the wrong name shows up at first. Keep typing until either Apple guesses correctly or you have manually entered the full address.

If you are sending mail to more than one recipient, separate the addresses with a comma.

If you want to send mail to folks who are not the primary addressees of your letter, type the addresses for these people (again separated by commas if you have more than one) in the *Cc:,* or *carbon copy,* box.

There's an even easier way to add an e-mail address, provided your recipient already resides in your Address Book. In the New Message window, click the Address button. Then just double-click the name of the person from your Address Book who you want to send mail to, and the Mail program takes care of the rest. The real names of these Address Book people appear in the To box (or cc box); you won't see their actual e-mail address. For example, you'd see the name `Tony Soprano` rather than `boss@sopranos.com`. Have no fear, under the hood, Apple is making all the proper arrangements to send your message to the rightful recipient.

You may want to keep the recipients' list confidential. (The Feds need not know where all Tony's mail goes.) There are a couple of ways to accomplish this:

✔ You can send mail to a Group in your Address Book (Chapter 3) just by typing the Group name in the To field. Mail then automatically routes mail to each member's e-mail address. To keep those addresses private, choose Mail➪Preferences and select Composing. Make sure the "When Sending to a Group, Show All Member Addresses" option is *not* checked.

✔ To keep the addresses of recipients who are not members of the same group private, click the little drop-down arrow to left of the Account box in the New Message window. Choose Bcc Address Field. Bcc stands for *blind carbon copy*. Everyone included in the list will get the message, but they won't have a clue who else you sent it to.

Composing messages

Keep a few things in mind before pounding out a message. Although optional, it's good e-mail etiquette to type a title, or Subject, for your e-mail. (See the "E-mail etiquette" sidebar.) In fact, some people get right to the point and blurt out everything they have to say in the Subject line (for example, *Lunch is on at noon*).

To write your message, just start typing in the large area provided below the address, subject, and account lines. You can also paste passages (or pictures) cut or copied from another program.

The standard formatting tools found with your word processor are on hand. You can make words **bold** or *italic* and add spice to the letters through fancy fonts. Click the Fonts button to display different typefaces. Click the Colors button to alter the hues of your individual characters. Both the Font window and the color wheel are shown in Figure 10-3.

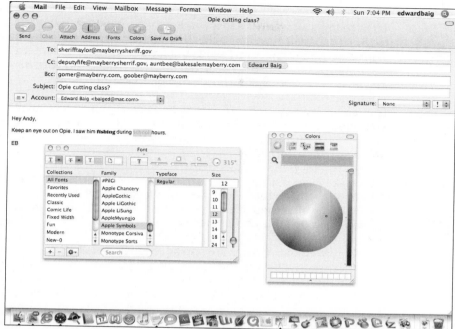

Figure 10-3:
Changing
fonts and
colors in
your
e-mails.

You're almost there. But what if you're waiting to insert an updated sales figure? Or decide it wouldn't be a bad idea to let off a bit of steam before submitting your resignation (via the cold harsh world of e-mail)? Click the Save as Draft button and do whatever it is you do to calm down. When you're ready to resume working on the message, demanding a raise instead, choose Mailbox⇨Go To, and click Drafts. Or press ⌘+3.

Attaching files

You can attach a payload to your e-mail. *Attachments* are typically word processing documents, but they can be any type of file: pictures, music, spreadsheets, videos, and more.

To send a file with your e-mail, click the Attach button. In the window that appears, select the file you have in mind from the appropriate folder on your hard drive.

Given the market dominance of that *other* operating system, it's a fair bet you're sending attachments to a Windows user. Windows is particular about the files it can read. It wants to see the *file extension,* such as .doc (see Chapter 7). Because Apple apparently wants to play nice with the rest of the computing public, all you need to do is check the box that reads Send Windows Friendly Attachments before sending an attachment to a Windows pal.

Windows users may receive two attachments when you send mail from a Mac. (And you *coulda* sworn you sent a single file.) One reads "*TheNameofthe FileISent*" and the other "*._TheNameoftheFileISent.*" Your recipients can safely can ignore the latter.

You'll make everyone happy if you clue recipients in ahead of time if you're planning on sending them large files, particularly high-resolution images and video. And by all means refer to the attachment in the message you send. You should do for a couple of reasons.

✔ Many Windows viruses are spread through e-mail attachments. Although you know the files are harmless, your Windows pals may be understandably skittish about opening a file without a clear explanation of what you're sending. Mac users have managed to avoid such headaches.

✔ Sending oversized attachments can slow down or even clog your recipient's e-mail inbox. It can take him or her forever to download these files. Moreover, ISPs may impose restrictions on the amount of e-mail storage users can have in their inboxes or in the size of a file that can transported. The company you work for may enforce its own limits. In fact some employers prevent staffers from sending messages (or replying to yours) until they've freed up space by wiping out older messages and attachments.

To get past an ISP's size restrictions, Mail gives you the option to resize images. Click the tiny pop-up menu at the bottom-right corner of the New Message window, which shows up along with the image you are sending. The menu appears in Figure 10-4.

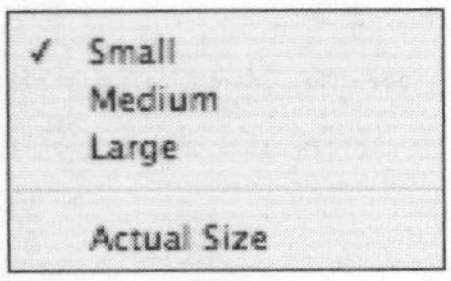

Figure 10-4:
Changing
the size of a
picture
before
sending the
photo by
e-mail.

✓ Small
  Medium
  Large

  Actual Size

Spell checking

There's a certain informality to e-mail. Rather than type a sentence that says, "How are you?" you might instead type "How r u?" But not always.

Spelling counts (or ought to) when you are corresponding with potential employers or, for that matter, the person currently responsible for your paycheck. I know you won't want to be reprimanded if you send e-mail with misspellings to your seventh-grade English teacher.

Fortunately, Apple provides assistance to the spelling-challenged among us. A spell checker is a basic feature.

To access the e-mail spell checker, choose Mail⇨Preferences, and then click Composing. Under the Check Spelling pop-up (see Figure 10-5), choose As I Type, When I Click Send, or Never.

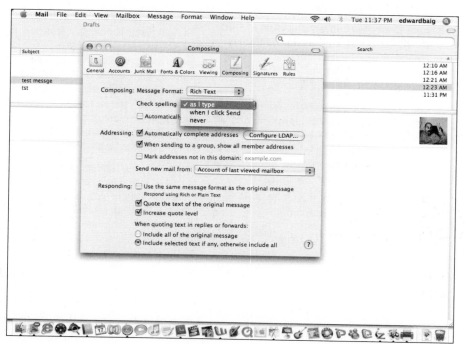

Figure 10-5:
Spelling
counts.

Assuming you ignored that last option, the Mail program will underline in red what it thinks are misspelled words, just as TextEdit and other word processors do, provided you selected As I Type in the Composing section of Mail Preferences (which you can access from the Mail menu). Right-click the suspect word and click the properly spelled word from the list of suggested replacements.

E-Mail etiquette

If Emily Post were alive today, she would surely draw up a list of acceptable practices for handling e-mails. In her absence, permit me to school you on e-mail decorum. I've already mentioned a few proper conventions: It helps to add a title or subject line to your e-mail and warn people if you're going to send large attachments. In some instances, you'll also want to use Bcc to protect the anonymity of the other people receiving your messages.

Here are some other conventions. DON'T SHOUT BY USING ALL CAPITAL LETTERS. Typing in lowercase letters like these is much more civilized. And you will avoid someone SHOUTING BACK and deliberately insulting, or *flaming,* you.

Do not forward e-mail chain letters. They will not bring you or your comrades vast riches. Or good luck. On the contrary, chain letters have been proven to cause people to stick needles in voodoo dolls representing the person who passed on the chain letter.

If replying to an e-mail, include the original *thread* by clicking *reply* rather than composing a new message from scratch. If the original thread does not automatically show up (as is the case with AOL mail), try this trick. Highlight the pertinent passages (or all of) the incoming message you want to respond to. When you click Reply, the original text will be there. Tailor your reply so the responses are right next to the original queries.

Keep *emoticons,* such as :) — a smiley face — and text shortcuts, such as LOL (laugh out loud) and IMHO (in my humble opinion), to a minimum. You can use these more often when sending instant messages, as I elaborate in the next chapter.

In general, keep messages short and sweet. Some people get hundreds of e-mails a day. If you want your message to be among those that are read, don't compose an e-mail that is the text equivalent of a filibuster.

Take care to ensure that the message is going to the right place. Nothing's worse than mistakenly sending a message that says "Jack is a jerk" to Jack. For that matter, think long and hard before sending the "Jack is a jerk" memo to Jill. E-mails have a life of their own. They can be intentionally or accidentally forwarded to others. Maybe Jill is on Jack's side. (They've been spotted together fetching a pale of water, you know.) Maybe she thinks *you* are the jerk.

Along this line, remember that e-mails lack the verbal or visual cues of other forms of communication. Maybe you were kidding all along about Jack being a jerk. But will Jack know you are merely pulling his chain? To make sure he does know, this is one instance where it is perfectly acceptable to use a smiley.

In general, ask yourself how you'd feel receiving the same message. And don't assume your message will remain private. Think before sending anything in an e-mail that you'd be reluctant to say in public.

Ignore these suggestions at your own peril. Somewhere Emily Post is watching.

If your spell checker keeps tripping over a word that is in fact typed correctly (your company name, for instance), you can add it to the spell checker dictionary. Control-click the word and select Learn Spelling from the pop-up list. Your Mac should never make the same mistake again.

Signing off with a signature

You can personalize Mail with a *signature* plastered at the bottom of every outgoing message. Along with your name, a signature might include your snail mail address, phone number, iChat account name, and a pithy slogan.

To add your e-mail "John Hancock," choose Mail⇨Preferences. Click the Signatures tab, and then click the Add (+) button. You can accept or type over the default signature Apple suggests and choose whether to match the font already used in the message.

Managing the Flood of Incoming Mail

The flip side of sending e-mail, of course, is having to sift through the mess of messages that may come your way. You can spend hours trying get through an e-mail inbox, depending on your line of work.

The little red balloon on the Mail icon on the dock indicates the number of unread messages demanding your attention.

New e-mails arrive as a matter of course through the Internet. You can click the Get Mail button on the Mail toolbar to hasten the process, as shown in our little tour of the Mail program in Figure 10-6. Tiny status circles next to each of your e-mail accounts spin until the number of messages in that account pop up.

If you click the Get Mail button and nothing happens, make sure your account isn't offline (the account name appears dimmed). To remedy the situation, choose Mailbox and then choose Go Online.

If that too fails to alleviate the problem, choose Window⇨Connection Doctor. It verifies that you're connected to the Internet and examines each e-mail account to make sure it's properly configured.

The number of unread
e-mails in the account

Mesages with a blue
dot haven't been read

Drag bar to adjust window size

Drag slider to scroll through
messages in your inbox

Drag divider to adjust
column width

Click column header to
sort by that criteria

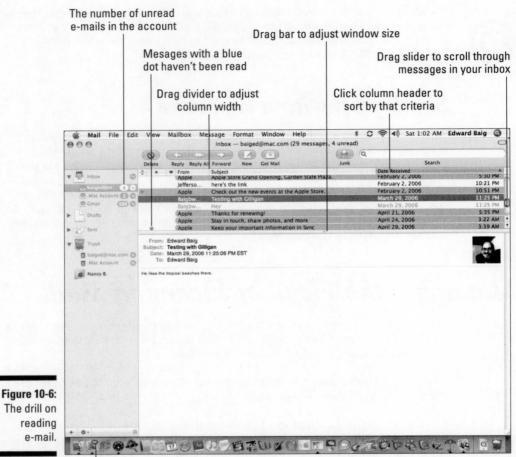

Figure 10-6:
The drill on
reading
e-mail.

The red balloon on the Mail icon tells you how
many unread messages demand your attention

Single-click an incoming message to read it in the lower pane of the Mail
window. Or double-click the message to read it in a window like you see in
Figure 10-7.

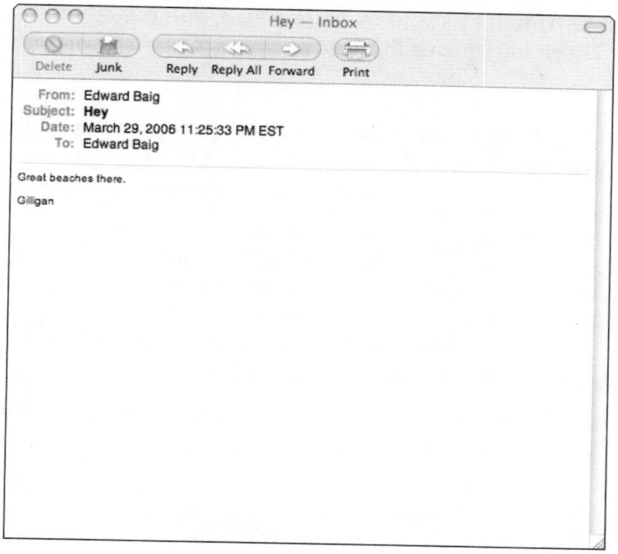

Figure 10-7:
Opening
mail in its
own
window.

Choosing what to read

I'm no censor. I'd never tell you what you should or should not read — online or off. So know that I have only your best interests at heart when I urge you to maintain a healthy dose of skepticism when it comes to tackling your inbox.

As you pore through said inbox, you'll probably notice mail from companies, online clubs, or Web sites you might have expressed an interest in at one time or another. You might have subscribed to e-mail newsletters on subjects ranging from ornithology to orthodontics. Most of the mail you get from these outfits is presumably A-OK with you.

I'll also take it as a given that you're going to read all the e-mails you get from colleagues, friends, and family. Well, maybe over time you'll come to ignore mail from Uncle Harry and Aunt Martha, especially if they insist on sending you the lamest of joke lists. If your mother is now using e-mail to hassle you about how you still aren't married, you have permission to ignore those too.

That leaves e-mail from just about everyone else, and it likely falls into one of three buckets. These categories fit most people's definition of junk mail, or *spam:*

- **They're trying to sell you something.** If might be Viagra or Xanax. It might be a (supposedly) cheap mortgage. It might be a small-cap growth stock. It might be a Rolex. It probably means trouble.

- **They're trying to scam you.** You have to ask yourself, why me? Of all the deserving people on the planet, how is that you have been chosen by a private international banking firm to collect a small fortune left by a rich eccentric? Or the secret funds hidden by a deposed Third World diplomat? This too will probably get you in a pickle. (In Chapter 13, I discuss a special type of scam known as *phishing.*)

- **They're sending you pornography.** It's out there. In a major way.

Opening mail from strangers

What was it your parents taught you about not talking to strangers? That's generally sound advice with e-mail too. As I hinted at in the preceding section, cyberspace has a lot of misfits, creeps, and (I knew I'd have to throw this phrase somewhere in the book) bad apples. They're up to no good. Because I don't want to cast aspersions on every unknown person who sends you e-mail, go with your gut. Common sense applies.

You can learn a lot from the subject line. If it refers to someone you know or what you do, I don't see the harm in opening the message.

If the greeting is generic — *Dear Wells Fargo Customer; Get Out of Debt Now* — I'd be a lot more cautious. Ditto if there's no subject line or there are gross misspellings.

If a sender turns out to be a decent business prospect or your new best friend, you can always add him or her to your Address Book by choosing one of the following alternatives.

- Choose Message⇨Add Sender to Address Book.

- Right-click a sender's name or address in the From line of a message and select Add to Address Book. (If you have a one-button mouse, the alternative is Ctrl-click.)

A few other handy shortcuts appear when you right-click a sender's name. You can Copy the person's Address, reply to the person, send him or her a new message, create a *smart mailbox* (more on this later in this chapter) or run an instant Spotlight search on the person.

Junking the junk

If senders turn out to be bad news, you can sully their reputation. At least on your own computer. Throw their mail into the junk pile. It's easy: Just click Junk on the message toolbar.

Marking messages happens to be your way of training the Mail program in what you consider spam. Apple updates its databases accordingly. The company flags potentially objectionable mail by highlighting messages with a brown tinge. Click Not Junk in the message if Apple applies the junk label to the innocent.

You can direct Apple on how to handle the junk. Choose Mail⇨Preferences, and then click the Junk Mail tab. The screen shown in Figure 10-8 appears.

By default, the Mail program leaves junk mail in your inbox so that you get to be the final arbiter. If you want Tiger to segregate suspect mail in its own mailbox, click the Move It to the Junk Mailbox option.

As a matter of course, Apple exempts certain messages from spam filtering. This includes mail from senders who are in your Address Book, as well as senders who already received mail from you. Messages that use your full name are also exempt. In the Junk Mail section of Mail Preferences, remove the check mark next to any Mail preferences you want to change.

Most reputable ISPs attempt to fight spam on their own. If you're satisfied with the job they're doing, leave the box "Trust junk mail headers set by my Internet Service Provider" checked. Apple's Mail program will leverage your ISP's best efforts.

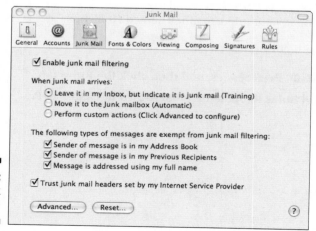

Figure 10-8:
The junk
yard.

Tips for avoiding spam

You can do your part to eliminate spam too. Spammers are resourceful and can get your e-mail address through various methods:

- ✔ They employ automated software robots to guess at nearly every possible combination of addresses.

- ✔ They watch what you're doing. Do you fill out online sweepstakes forms? There's a winner, all right, the spammer.

- ✔ Do you hang out in chat rooms and Internet newsgroups? Bingo.

- ✔ Do you post messages in a public forum? Gotcha again.

You can stop engaging in these online activities, of course, but then the Internet won't be nearly as much fun. I have a better idea. Set up a separate e-mail account to use in these out-in-the-open kinds of scenarios. (ISPs such as AOL let you set up myriad accounts or screen names.) You'll still get spam there. Just don't bother using those accounts to send or receive e-mail. Instead, treat your other account or accounts as the sacred ones you share with family, friends, and colleagues.

Setting the rules

Potent as Apple is at filtering spam, you can set up your own filters, or *rules*, for combating junk. But you can set rules also to automatically reorganize the messages on hand that are perfectly acceptable. When incoming mail meets certain conditions such as who sent the mail or the subject matter, the Mail program automatically forwards, highlights, or files them accordingly. For instance, you might want to redirect all the messages you've received from your investment advisor into a mailbox named stock tips.

To set up a rule, follow these steps:

1. **Choose Mail⇨Preferences, and then click the Rules tab.**

2. **Select Add Rules to open the pane shown in Figure 10-9.**

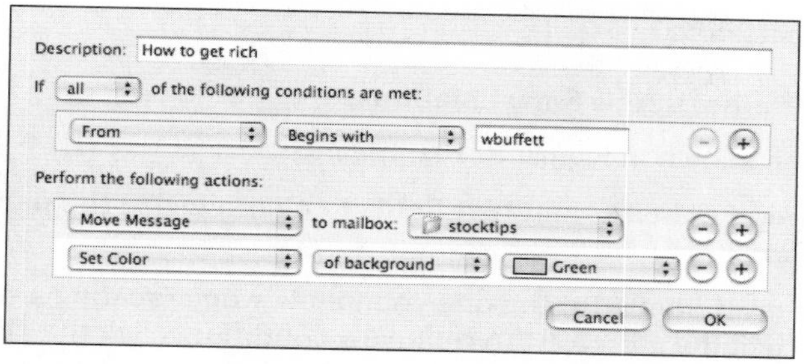

Description: How to get rich

If [all ‡] of the following conditions are met:

[From ‡] [Begins with ‡] [wbuffett] ⊖ ⊕

Perform the following actions:

[Move Message ‡] to mailbox: [📁 stocktips ‡] ⊖ ⊕

[Set Color ‡] [of background ‡] [☐ Green ‡] ⊖ ⊕

(Cancel) (OK)

Figure 10-9:
You have to
establish
rules.

3. **Choose parameters identifying which messages are affected by the rule.**

   To redirect e-mail from your financial guru, for example, choose From in the first box, Begins With in the second box and the name in the third.

4. **Now choose parameters for what happens to those messages.**

   In this instance, those messages will be highlighted in green and moved to the stocktips mailbox.

5. **When you've finished entering parameters, click OK.**

Smart mailboxes

In Chapter 6, you discover dynamic smart folders. Welcome to the e-mail variation, *smart mailboxes*. Just as smart folders are constantly on the prowl for new items that match specific search criteria, smart mailboxes do the same. They are tightly integrated with Tiger's Spotlight search technology.

You can set up smart mailboxes as a way to organize all mail pertaining to a specific project or all mail from a specific person. For instance, you might want to create a smart mailbox containing all correspondence with your boss for the most current fortnight. Mail older than two weeks is replaced by the latest exchanges.

Incidentally, the messages you see in a smart mailbox are virtual; they still reside in their original locations. In that sense, they are similar to aliases, described in Chapter 7.

To create a smart box:

1. **Choose Mailbox⇨New Smart Mailbox.**

   The screen shown in Figure 10-10 appears.

2. **Use the pop-up menus and text fields to characterize the parameters of the mailbox.**

   The process is similar to the one you follow when creating a rule. To add criteria, click the + button. To remove a condition, click the - button.

3. **When you're finished, click OK.**

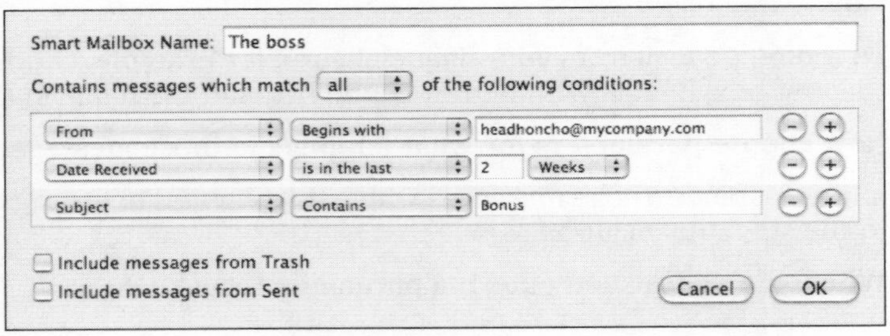

Figure 10-10: The smartest mailbox around.

Smart Mailbox Name:	The boss	

Contains messages which match [all ⬍] of the following conditions:

From ⬍	Begins with ⬍	headhoncho@mycompany.com	⊖ ⊕
Date Received ⬍	is in the last ⬍	2	Weeks ⬍	⊖ ⊕
Subject ⬍	Contains ⬍	Bonus	⊖ ⊕

☐ Include messages from Trash
☐ Include messages from Sent   (Cancel)   (OK)

Searching mail

With an assist from Spotlight, the Mac's fast and comprehensive search system, you can find a specific e-mail messages, or the content of those messages, in a jiffy.

✔ To search an open message, choose Edit⇨Find and type the text you're looking for.

✔ You can also enter a search term in the search box at the upper-right portion of the Mail program screen. Use the All Mailboxes, Entire Messages, From, To, or Subject headers (which appear only when you've entered a search) to determine how to display the results.

Opening attachments

You already discovered how to send attachments. But now the tide has shifted, and someone sends you one (or more). Attachments appear with an icon in the body of the message, as shown in Figure 10-11.

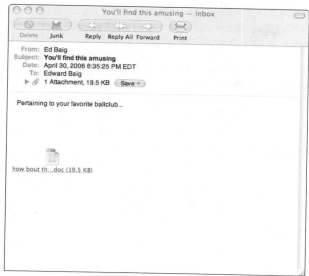

Figure 10-11:
Attachments
show up
with an icon
in the
message
body.

You have a few choices:

- ✔ Drag the icon onto the desktop or a Finder window.

- ✔ Double-click the icon, and the attachment should open in the program designed to handle it (for example, Word for a Word file or Preview for an image).

- ✔ Click Save to save the file to a particular destination on your computer.

Normally, I tell people not to open attachments they weren't expecting, even if they know the sender. Mac users can be a little more relaxed about this than their Windows cousins. While the times they are *a-changin'*, the odds that the attachment will damage the Mac, even if it did carry some type of Windows virus, are low.

If you want to remove an attachment from an incoming message, choose Message➪Remove Attachments. As a reminder, the body of the message will include a line telling you that the attachment in question has been "manually removed."

Making the Most of Your Mail

Before leaving this chapter, I want to introduce other ways to get the most out of your e-mail:

✔ **View a photo slideshow:** Picture attachments are afforded special treat-ment. Click the Slideshow button that appears when someone sends you pictures and you can view the attached images in a lovely full-screen slideshow. From an on-screen control panel, you can go back to the pre-vious image, pause the slideshow, or advance to the next slide. You can also click to add pictures to your iPhoto library (see Chapter 15). When you're finished with the slide show, press the Escape key on the key-board to go back to the original e-mail.

✔ **Pass it on:** Sometimes you get stuff that is so rip-roaringly hysterical (or at the other extreme, tragic and poignant) you want to share it with everyone you know. To forward a message, click the Forward button inside the e-mail and enter the recipient's address in the New Message window that pops up. The entire previous e-mail will go out intact, save for a couple of subtle additions: the *Fwd:* prefix in the Subject line, and the phrase "Begin forwarded message" above the body of the message. You can add an introductory comment along the lines of "This made me laugh out loud" or "I'm sorry to have to call this to your attention."

✔ **Synchronize e-mail:** If you have a .Mac account (Chapter 12), you can synchronize all your rules, signatures, and other settings across all your Tiger computers.

✔ **Use parental controls:** You can restrict who junior can correspond with through e-mail to only those addresses you've explicitly okayed. Visit System Preferences under the menu and choose Accounts. You'll be notified when your kid gets (or tries to send) messages to addresses not on your authorized list.

✔ **Get rid of mail:** You can dispose of mail in a number of ways. Highlight a message and press Delete on the keyboard. Drag the message to the Trash folder. Or click the Delete button on the toolbar. The messages aren't permanently banished until you choose Mailbox⇨Erase Deleted Messages. Apple can automatically extinguish mail for good after one day, one week, or one month, or when you quit the Mail program. To set this up, go to Mail Preferences, click Accounts, choose an account, and select Mailbox Behaviors.

Chapter 11

Caught Up in the Web

*F*olks routinely surf the Web seeking specific types of information. Headlines, stock quotes, vacation deals, weather, homework help, sports scores, and technical support. But as much as anything, the Internet is about meeting and connecting with people. These people could be job prospects or would-be employers. Or people who share your zeal for the Chicago Cubs, sushi, and Macintosh computers. Persuasion takes on a major role in cyberspace too. You'll get on your virtual high horse and attempt to coax others around to your way of thinking.

And, yes, finding companionship, romance, and (under the best of circumstances), long-lasting relationships is part of the cyber-experience too.

Critics have often sneered, "these people need to get a life." But many *Netizens* (citizens of the Internet) have rewarding lives online and offline, thank you very much. And on the Net, they're congregating in vibrant *communities* with individuals of similar interests and passions.

We'll explore many of these avenues in this chapter.

Chat Rooms

A lot of congregating on the Net happens in *chat rooms,* areas where you can converse in real time on pretty much any topic: knitting and quilting, cricket, fad diets, parenting, biotechnology, model airplanes, extraterrestrial sightings, and on and on. The conversing has typically been left up to your fingertips. Indeed, typos be damned; expect to bang away at the keyboard with reckless abandon because text exchanges in chat rooms come fast and furious. There may be a few dozen people or more in a room. Good luck determining who's talking to whom.

As broadband hookups becoming increasingly common, audio and video chats (through the use of a small cameras called webcams) are likewise becoming more widespread.

Chat is also a staple in the online gaming environment. In an immersive three-dimensional virtual fantasy world, your persona may be represented by an animated *avatar.* One such setting (available to Mac users with a recent version of OS X) is called *Second Life* (www.secondlife.com). Be aware that the environment sometimes exceeds PG-13 sensibilities.

Some chat rooms are monitored by people who make sure that the discourse is civil and courteous. In rare instances, monitors may dictate who can and cannot speak, or they may boot somebody out.

The first exposure many people had to chat rooms was inside the virtual confines of America Online. AOL established a set of community guidelines, mostly having to do with banning hateful speech as well as threatening or abusive behavior. As you can see in Figure 11-1, the subject categories in chat rooms are quite varied. AOL's primary rivals, Yahoo! and MSN, run their own chat areas.

I tell people visiting a chat group for the first time to say hi to everyone and then take a backseat. Observe. Get a feel for the place. Figure out whether participants are around the same age (or maturity level) as you. Determine whether they're addressing topics you care about — and speak the same language. Participants in these joints come from all over the planet (and sometimes it seems from outer space).

Along those lines, don't be surprised if it appears as though members of the chat community are typing in tongues. You'll notice strange uses of punctuation and abbreviations. Check out the "And you thought mastering Latin was difficult?" sidebar for a crash course in *emoticon* linguistics.

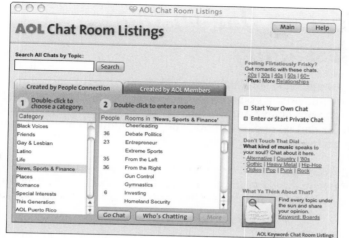

Figure 11-1:
Spending
time in AOL
chat rooms.

And you thought mastering Latin was difficult?

Becoming fluent in the lingo of chat rooms and instant messaging is crucial if you want to fit in or merely understand what's taking place. However, remember to resist the overuse of emoticons in your e-mails and real-world correspondence.

Common Emoticons

:) = smile

;) = wink

:D = laughing

:(= frown

:'(= crying

>:-} = a devil

0:-) = an angel

{ } = hug

:* = kiss

:P = sticking out tongue

Common Acronyms

BTW = By The Way

ROTF = Rolling On The Floor (Laughing)

LOL = Laugh Out Loud

IMHO = In My Humble Opinion

BRB = Be Right Back

TTFN = Ta-Ta For Now

GMTA = Great Minds Think Alike

F2F = Face to Face

FOAF = Friend Of a Friend

WB = Welcome Back

Communicating One-on-One: Instant Messaging

You may be speaking (broadcasting really) to dozens of people at a time in a chat room. But what if you strike a bond with the mysterious stranger whose quips catch your fancy? And want to whisper sweet nothings behind this person's ear and no one else's? Such intimacy requires a private conversation. It requires an *instant message,* or *IM.*

Instant messages need not originate in chat rooms, and for most people they do not. Participants instead rely on dedicated instant messaging *client* software that can be downloaded for free from AOL, Yahoo!, Microsoft, and Skype.

Just as the company did with e-mail, AOL gets the lion's share of the credit for spreading IMing — yes, you can treat it as verb — among the masses in the United States. AOL owns the popular *AOL Instant Messenger,* or *AIM,* software, as well as the exceedingly popular global IM program, *ICQ.* You can fetch these free without joining AOL at www.aim.com and www.icq.com, respectively. In fact, as we'll see shortly, you need not even download AIM, because Apple's own iChat program lets you kibitz with the AIM community.

Instant messaging has become a mainstay in business as well as in social circles. It's a complement to e-mail and in many ways more appealing. Here's why: Just as in a chat room, instant messaging conversations occur in real time, without the delays associated with e-mail. In addition, IM permits the kind of spontaneity that's not possible through e-mail or even an old-fashioned phone call. Through a concept known as *presence,* you can tell not only whether the people you want to IM are currently online but also whether they're willing to chat. Status indicators next to their names on a *buddy list* clue you in on their availability.

Instant messaging has at least one major downside compared to e-mail and the plain old telephone: the lack of *interoperability* among the major IM purveyors. For competitive reasons, market leader AOL carefully guards its buddy list, so an AIM member can't send a direct instant message to a Yahoo! or MSN user, at least not without techie workarounds. Think about what would happen if a Verizon cell phone customer, say, couldn't call a friend who was a Cingular subscriber, and vice versa.

Just as regular chat has evolved well beyond a text-only communications channel, so has instant messaging. Today's IM programs let you engage in audio exchanges and make free computer-to-computer Internet phone calls.

Moreover, if you have a webcam — and owners of certain new Macs are blessed with built-in iSight cameras — you can also hold face-to-face conversations. And that leads us to Apple's own ever-evolving instant messaging application, iChat AV.

iChat AV

In truth, calling iChat AV an instant messaging program is selling it way short, kind of like telling somebody that Michael Jordan knows how to make free throws. The *AV* part stands for *audio visual* or *audio video,* depending on who you ask.

So yes, iChat is a competent instant messenger for handling traditional text chatter. But consider some of iChat's other tricks:

- You can exchange files while talking with someone.
- You can have a *free* audio conference with up to nine other people.
- You can engage in a video conference from your Mac desktop with up to three other people.

You'll need at least one of the following to get going with iChat:

- **An existing AIM or AOL screen name and password.** As noted, iChat is tied in with AOL's popular instant messaging program.
- **A Jabber ID.** You can use a Jabber ID to exchange messages with cohorts who share the same Jabber servers. Jabber is an open standard chat system employed in many organizations. Through Jabber, you can exchange instant messages with a Google Talk member. Although iChat is still not directly compatible with screen names from the MSN or Yahoo! instant messaging systems, you may be able to do a technological workaround through Jabber.
- **By using or signing up for a fee-based .Mac account.** You can get a free .Mac account just for the purposes of using iChat by sampling all the other .Mac features on a trial basis. (You have to pay to keep using these other features, which I elaborate on in Chapter 12; you can hold onto your iChat account for as long as you want.)
- **On a local network or in a classroom using Apple technology called Bonjour, formerly known as Rendezvous.** Through this built-in technology, iChat lets you see who on your local network is available to chat. Bonjour, however, is used for configuration-free networking throughout OS X.

If you want to exploit video, you'll need a fast broadband Internet connection, plus a compatible camera. Apple's own iSight camera (standard on recent iMac and MacBook Pro models) works well, but any FireWire-based camera should do. You'll also need a Mac with OS X version 10.2.5 or later.

Hey buddy

Naturally, iChat AV is useless without one more essential component: At least one other person with whom to schmooze. If you signed up with an AIM account and have been using AOL's instant messenger for awhile, your buddy list may already be populated with a bunch of names.

To add new people to the list, click the + button at the bottom of the Buddy List window, choose Buddies⇨Add Buddy, or press Shift+⌘+A. You're given the option to choose an entry from your Address Book. (Data you put there is made available to iChat.) Otherwise, click New Person to add, well, a new person. You type the person's chat name (under Account Name) and fill in the other blanks shown in Figure 11-2. The person's name turns up instantly on your buddy list. A buddy list is as long as you are popular.

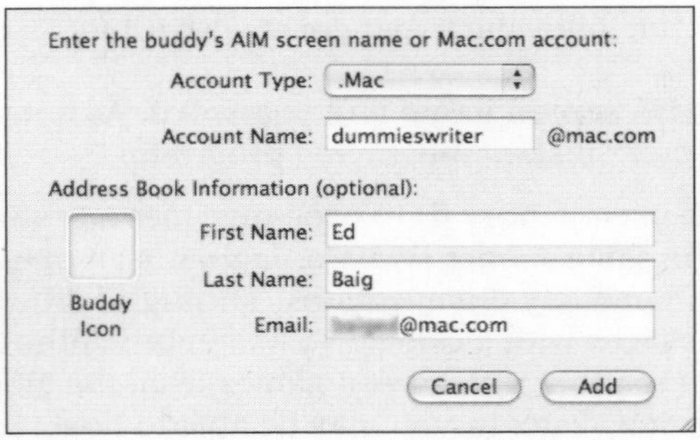

Figure 11-2:
Adding new
buddies to
the list.

Enter the buddy's AIM screen name or Mac.com account:

Account Type: .Mac

Account Name: dummieswriter @mac.com

Address Book Information (optional):

First Name: Ed

Last Name: Baig

Buddy
Icon

Email: @mac.com

Cancel   Add

You can also lump your buddies into groups (such as co-workers and soccer team). To do so, Choose View⇨Use Groups and click + to add or edit a group.

The buddy list has a bunch of visual status cues. Your buddy may have included a mug shot, perhaps through the Mac's Photo Booth feature (see Chapter 5). Or your buddies may express themselves through small images called *buddy icons*. What's more, a telephone symbol tells you whether you can connect through voice, and a movie camera icon indicates that you can connect through video, as shown in Figure 11-3.

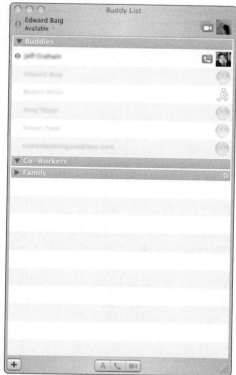

Figure 11-3:
Visual cues
let you know
how to
instantly
contact your
buddies.

Mostly you'll be able to tell whether your buddies are online at the moment and willing to give you the time of day. Here's how:

- A green circle to the left of a person's name means he or she is ready and (presumably) willing to talk.

- A red circle means the person is online but otherwise engaged. The person is considered Away.

- A yellow circle means the person on your list is idle and has not used the machine for awhile (the window tells you how long the person has been in this state). Your buddy just hasn't bothered to change his or her status from Available to Away.

- If a name is dimmed, your buddy isn't logged on to iChat or AIM.

You can set your own status for everyone else to see. And you are not limited to Available or Away. Click under your own name and choose Custom from the drop-down list. You can choose a custom message to appear next to a green or red circle, depending on your circumstance. Type any message you want, such as, *can chat in a pinch but busy* or *back after lunch.*

Incidentally, if you've been absent from the computer for awhile, the Mac will kindly welcome you back to the machine and ask whether you want to change your iChat online status from Away back to Available.

Chatting

To initiate an instant message, double-click a name in the buddy list, which pops up whenever you open iChat. Type something in the bottom box. *Hey stranger* will suffice for now.

Alternately, you can chose File➪New Chat and enter the name of the person with whom you would like to chat. This can be done even if the individual is not in your buddy list or Address Book.

What you type instantly appears in a comic-strip bubble in the upper portion of the window. If the person responds, what he or she has to say appears in its own comic-strip bubble. And so on.

To illustrate this point, check out Figure 11-4. It shows yours truly having a silly conversation with yours truly. (Honestly, I don't normally talk to myself. This little exercise is strictly for the benefit of the reader.)

Figure 11-4:
I don't normally talk back to myself. Right Ed?

Now say you're having an important IM exchange with your lawyer or accountant. Or swapping tuna casserole recipes with your best friend. You may want a record of your conversation that you can easily refer to later. To create a transcript of your chitchatting, open iChat Preferences, shown in Figure 11-5. To do so, click the iChat menu and then click Preferences. Choose the Messages icon and then select the Automatically Save Chat Transcripts option.

Sharing a tune

You can tell your IM chums what music you are listening to in iTunes. From the iChat drop-down list indicating your availability status, choose Current iTunes Track. This serves a few purposes, best I can tell. For one thing, your pals will discover how hip you are (assuming they don't know it already). What's more, you become an *influencer:* If your friends click your musical selection, they can preview the song in the iTunes Music Store (Chapter 14). If your buddies purchase ten or more of the songs you're listening to over a two-week period, Apple sends you a computer. Okay, so I made the last part up. But know this: Steve Jobs will really like you.

You can use iChat also to send files to your IM buddy (or get a file in return). Not only is it convenient, but unlike with e-mail there's no size restriction on the file you're sharing. (You can send only one file at a time, however.) Select a name on your buddy list and then choose Buddies➪Send File. Select the file you want to send. Alternatively, drag a file to a buddy's name or into the area of an open chat window. Either way, your buddy has the option to accept or reject the incoming file.

While we're on the painful subject of rejection, if one of your buddies (or anyone else) initiates an IM and you don't feel like talking, click Decline in the window that pops up.

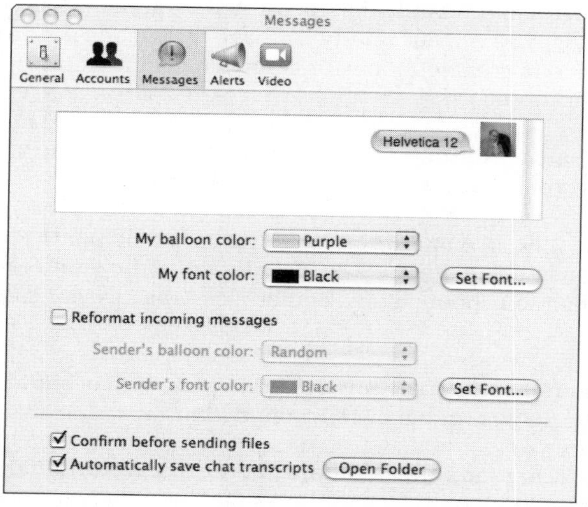

Figure 11-5:
Chatting the way you like it through iChat Preferences.

If the person gets on your nerves, click Block to prevent the person from ever sending you IMs again. (Just know that your would-be buddies can do the same to you.)

You can proactively determine who can see that you're online and send you messages. Under iChat Preferences, click the Accounts icon and then click the Security tab. Choose a Privacy Level that you're comfortable with. The options are

- Allow anyone.
- Allow people in my buddy list.
- Allow specific people. If you make this choice, you have to type each person's AIM or .Mac address.
- Block everyone.
- Block specific people. Again, type the appropriate addresses.

Seeing is believing; hearing too

As I already alluded to, IMing and text chatting in general are kind of yesterday's news (though still darn useful). The twenty-first-century way of communicating is through a video phone call. (Never mind that a primitive version of this technology was exhibited at the 1964 New York World's Fair.)

Assuming your camera and microphone are configured to your liking, click the video camera icon in the buddy list or, for just an audio session, click the telephone icon. Members of your buddy list have little icons next to their names too; these icons are telephones or video icons depending on their respective configurations.

As usual your IM partner has the option to accept or decline the invitation. If he or she accepts, you can gaze at each other full screen.

This stuff is super slick. In a multiroom conference, participants appear in a virtual three-dimensional conference room with authentic video effects that make people's reflections bounce off a conference table, as you can see in Figure 11-6.

The quality is generally pretty good, though the picture may show some distortion, depending on your cable or DSL connection.

The video used in iChat (and QuickTime) adheres to a video standard known as H.264 or Advanced Video Codec (AVC). It's meant to deliver crisp video in smaller file sizes, saving you bandwidth and storage.

Courtesy of Apple

Figure 11-6:
Videocon-
ferencing
through
iChat AV.

If you have a webcam but your IM buddies do not, they still get the benefit of seeing your smiling face at least. And provided they have a mike, you still get to hear them.

Having an Online Voice

There are lots of places on the Internet for you to be heard and seen. In this section we explore some of these places.

Newsgroups

The term *newsgroups* may make you think of journalists retreating to the nearest watering hole after deadline. (Been there, done that.) Or a posse of friends sitting around together watching, I dunno, Katie Couric. Newsgroups are defined differently in the chapter you are so kindly reading.

Newsgroups go by numerous descriptors: electronic (or online) bulletin boards, discussion groups, forums, and Usenet (a techie name that dates back to Duke University in the late 1970s). Google acquired the Usenet archives in 2001; through Google Groups, you can read more than one billion Usenet postings dating back to 1981.

In a nutshell, people post and respond to messages on everything and anything: pipe smoking, low-carb diets, monster movies, world-class tenors, nanotechnology, canine incontinence, alternative sources of energy, snake charmers . . . Thousands of these discussions are taking place online.

Newsgroups generally adhere to a hierarchical structure. At the top level, you'll see *comp* for computers, *rec* for recreation, *sci* for sciences, *soc* for socializing, *talk* for politics, *news* for Usenet, *misc* for miscellaneous. *alt* for alternative and so on. As you move down the food chain, the categories become more specific. So you might start at *alt*, then drill down to *alt.animals*, then *alt.animals.cats*, then *alt.animals.cats.siamese*.

You'll need a newsgroup reader program to read these posts. If you bought Microsoft Office for the Mac, it includes a newsreader in the Entourage e-mail program.

You can also download free or low-cost shareware newsreaders for the Mac. They go by names such as Hogwash, MacSoup, MT-NewsWatcher, NewsHunter, Thoth, and Unison.

Blogs

Blogs, or weblogs, have become an Internet phenomenon. The blogging search engine Technorati is tracking more than 47 million blog sites and counting. Some 70,000 new blogs pop up every day, and there are about 700,000 posts daily.

Although still in its relative infancy, the *blogosphere* has already been exploited by politicians, educational institutions, marketers, publicists, and traditional media outlets. And as you might imagine, you can also find Mac-related blogs, such as `blog.wired.com/cultofmac`, `www.tuaw.com` (The Unofficial Apple Weblog), and `www.theappleblog.com`.

Some bloggers may dream of becoming journalistic superstars overnight, though few achieve such status. And many in the mainstream media fret that bloggers lack editorial scrutiny and journalistic standards. But most blogs are nothing more than personal journals meant to be read by a tight circle of friends and family. Bloggers share their musings, provide links to other content, and invite comments from others.

Destinations for creating and hosting a blog include Google's free Blogger.com service, WordPress, also free, and SixApart's TypePad (starting at $5 a month). You can subscribe to or read other blogs through technology known as *RSS*. See the "What the heck is RSS?" sidebar? for more information. You can use the Mac's new iWeb program to publish a blog through the .Mac service ($100 a year).

What the heck is RSS?

Blogs and other news feeds are distributed through a technology known as RSS, shorthand for *Really Simple Syndication*. You can view RSS feeds in a Safari browser (they're sometimes called *XML* feeds). When you subscribe to an RSS feed, you'll get a barebones summary (and title) for articles listed, such as the feed shown here from my *USA TODAY* tech column. You can click the <u>Read more</u> link to check out the full article. If Safari finds a feed, *RSS* appears in the address bar, as shown in the figure.

If you want to be notified when new feeds arrive, go to Safari preferences (found in the Safari menu), click RSS, and select how often to check for RSS updates (every 30 minutes, every hour, every day, or never). To peek at all RSS feeds (from multiple sites) at one time — a great way to customize your own newspaper, in effect — place all your feeds in a single bookmark folder. Then click the folder's name and choose View All RSS Articles.

You can even turn your RSS feeds into a cool screensaver with flying news headlines that charge at you like the credits in a Tinseltown blockbuster. Choose System Preferences under the menu, click Desktop & Screen Saver, and then click the Screen Saver tab. Next, in the Screen Savers list, click RSS Visualizer. Then click the Options button and select a specific RSS feed. If you want to read the underlying news story, you'll be instructed to press the 1 key to read one feed, 2 key to read another, and so on.

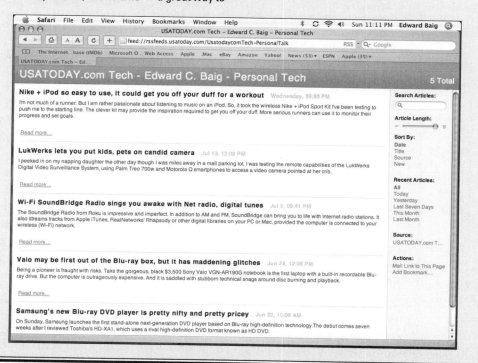

Social Networking

Who do you know? Who do your friends know? Who do the friends of your friends know? Oh, and how can *I* benefit from six (or many fewer) degrees of separation?

That's pretty much what online social networks are all about. By leveraging your direct and indirect contacts, you might find a place to live, broker the deal of the century, or land a recording contract. That's the hope anyway. Hate to be a glass-is-half-empty kind of guy, but none of these outcomes is guaranteed.

Still, social networking sites can help you network and help you be social. They may combine blogs, instant messaging, photo sharing, and other tools. Some are difficult to pigeonhole, so don't take offense if the dozen sites listed next don't fit the classic definition of social networking, assuming there is such a thing:

- ✔ www.classmates.com: Looking for an old high-school flame? An Army buddy? Classmates is a good place to wax nostalgic and find reunions.

- ✔ www.craigslist.com: A network of global community sites in dozens of international cities with forums and free classifieds advertising jobs, gigs, housing, personals, and more.

- ✔ www.facebook.com: Social networking on the college campus and in select corporations.

- ✔ www.flickr.com: Image sharing site (owned by Yahoo!). Members tag their uploaded pictures so they can be discovered by others.

- ✔ www.friendster.com: An early pioneer in online social networking, with more than 27 million member profiles.

- ✔ www.imeem.com: Instant messaging meets social networking.

- ✔ www.jokebox.com: Billed as MySpace.com meets Comedy Central.

- ✔ www.linkedin.com: Geared toward helping you with business and professional connections.

- ✔ www.MySpace.com: A popular hang-out (more than 70 million members) for young people, including burgeoning musicians. Now owned by Rupert Murdoch's News Corp.

- ✔ www.orkut.com: An invitation-only community owned by Google that seems to attract an intelligent crowd.

✔ 360.yahoo.com: A place to share blogs, pictures, recommended books, music, movies, and more.

✔ www.youtube.com: A place to upload and share amateur videos, including bootleg footage from concerts.

The Virtual Meet Market

As you might have surmised by now, Cupid spends a lot of time on the Internet. You may even run into him in one of the aforementioned social networking sites. But if you're determined to find a mate in cyberspace at all costs, the direct approach is probably best. Dating sites often let you peruse online personals and fill out detailed online profiles for free. With some variation in subscriptions and fees, they typically start charging only when you're ready to get in touch with Mr. or Ms. Right.

Rest assured, there's a dating site to fit your lifestyle. Online matchmakers focus on particular communities, political beliefs, sexual preferences, religions, hobbies, and even love of four-legged creatures (check out datemypet.com).

The following sites are among the major mass-market online matchmaking destinations:

✔ www.americansingles.com: Lets you send "flirts," or one-liners, to members you're interested in. The object of your affection can flirt back if he or she so desires.

✔ www.eharmony.com: For the marriage-minded. eHarmony eschews the term *dating site* and is instead an online matchmaker that attempts to find people it thinks are right for you. Founder Dr. Neil Clark Warren says he has identified the 29 "dimensions" of compatibility that make for a successful, long-term relationship. (I don't think it's among the blessed 29, but it helps if you and your potential mate both have Macs.)

✔ www.match.com: Features relationship insights from Dr. Phil.

✔ personals.yahoo.com: Offers two pay services — basic membership for casual daters and premium membership for those seeking serious, long-term relationships.

✔ www.true.com: Says it will prosecute married men and criminals who try to use the service.

A few important disclaimers: I take no responsibility for who you meet online through these or other Web sites (unless it works and then you can invite me to the wedding). And I can't predict what kind of sparks will fly if a Windows user pairs up with Mac loyalist.

Buying Stuff Online

Grandpa, what was it like when people shopped in stores?

I doubt you'll hear such a conversation anytime soon. But more and more people are purchasing products online, and those products are not just books, music, and software. Increasingly, folks go to the Net to shop for big-ticket items: backyard swing sets for the kiddies, high-definition televisions, and even automobiles. Electronic commerce, or *e-commerce,* is alive and kicking.

Shopping over the Internet has many plusses. For example:

- ✔ You avoid crowds and traffic.
- ✔ You save on gas or commuting costs.
- ✔ You avoid pushy salespeople.
- ✔ You can easily compare products and prices across numerous Web sites, increasing the likelihood that you'll end up with an excellent deal. Visit such comparison shopping sites as www.mysimon.com, www.price-grabber.com, and www.shopzilla.com.
- ✔ You can choose from a large inventory of products (which is not to suggest that stuff won't be out of stock).
- ✔ You can get buying recommendations from your cyber-peers.

Shopping online has a few negatives too:

- ✔ You can't "kick the tires" or otherwise inspect the items under consideration.
- ✔ You won't get personal attention from a reliable salesperson.
- ✔ You might get spammed.
- ✔ Without proper safeguards, your privacy could be at risk.

✔ Instant gratification becomes an oxymoron, except on such items as downloadable software and music.

✔ You can't make goo-goo eyes with attractive strangers you might meet cruising the aisles.

Amazon.com

As an e-commerce pioneer, Amazon.com is probably still best known for selling millions of discounted books online. But you can shop for items across more than 30 product categories, from video games and computers (including Macs) to gourmet foods and pet supplies.

Before spending any loot on a book or other merchandise, you can read online reviews from fellow customers. You might also want to consult the "Customers who bought this item, also bought this" list. Amazon has been at the forefront of many online shopping initiatives, including 1-Click Shopping (rapid way to process an order as long as your credit card and shipping info are on file) and Wish List (letting folks know what you want for your birthday).

Indulging the eBay addiction

I don't know who first uttered the cliché "one person's junk is another person's treasure," but he or she could have been describing eBay. The famed Internet auction site has listings for more than 10 million items in thousands of product categories, and more than 100 million registered users. Many buyers are insanely obsessed — and believe me I say that with affection.

eBay is the ultimate garage sale. It's only a slight exaggeration to suggest that if you can't find the thing you're looking for on eBay, you probably can't find it anywhere. Many of the products peddled on eBay have long since gone out of circulation. It's a hodgepodge that includes obscure products, interesting inventions, memorabilia, and collectibles. Maybe you're looking for vintage comic books, an original Cabbage Patch Kid doll, replacements for broken china dishes, or even a 1970s, 8-track cartridge player (heaven knows why?). Sellers on eBay peddle new stuff too, from digital camcorders to acoustic guitars. (Some folks make a decent living selling wares through the service.)

Indeed, eBay may be a godsend if you finally get around to cleaning the attic. Keep it quiet, but you can also get rid of that homely "what-were-they-thinking" serving plate you received as a wedding gift.

Managing travel

It used to be that people bought airline tickets and booked hotels over the Internet strictly for convenience. After all, booking online beats languishing on hold waiting to talk to an airline customer service rep. And you can choose seats from the comfort of your own keyboard and even print boarding passes. (Okay, when things get complicated with connections or flying with pets, you might still want to go through an airline staffer or a travel agent.). Nowadays, carriers want you to go through the Web and take advantage of e-tickets. In fact, you're typically penalized for requesting a paper ticket.

Although you can find deals elsewhere, the big three online travel sites — www.expedia.com, www.orbitz.com, and www.travelocity.com — are worth a visit. Also check out the carrier's own Web site and ask to get on an e-mail list in which the airline notifies you of last-minute bargains.

Putting Sherlock on the Trail

Sherlock, Apple's Internet sleuth, is meant to help you get to the bottom of specific kinds of Web searches on the quick, from tracking stocks and eBay auctions, to finding out whether your flight is on time and when flicks you want to see are playing. Searches are assigned to specific Sherlock channels, known as Dictionary, Translation, and so on (see Figure 11-7).

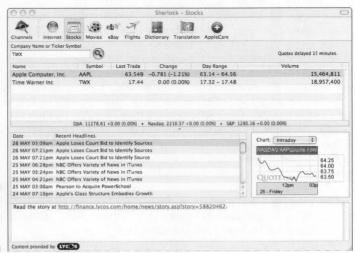

Figure 11-7:
Sherlock is
on the case.

A researcher's toolbox

Imagine if you could take the *Britannica* or *World Book Encyclopedia* and alter or update it at will. You now have some idea of what Wikipedia, found at www.wikipedia.org, is all about. It's billed as a free encyclopedia that *anyone can edit*. At the very least, entries are more timely. The collaborative global perspective may provide insights lacking in other reference material.

I know what you're thinking. There's a flip side to all this. What if I'm mischievous? What if I'm biased? What if I'm a misinformed know-it-all? Why couldn't I change the text to read that the South won the Civil War, or Dewey beat Truman? Yes, it can and does happen, because the very essence of a *wiki* allows for anyone

with an Internet connection to mess with any of the references. In most instances, blatant vandalism and dubious submissions are corrected by the collective efforts of honest writers and editors from around the world.

But open-sourced wiki entries are organic and never quite finished, and mistakes are introduced, overtly or subtly, consciously or otherwise. One side of an argument might be presented more eloquently than another. There is almost always room for interpretation and debate. So, Wikipedia is a remarkably useful online resource, provided you recognize its limitations and don't treat everything you come across as gospel.

Sherlock gets on the case when you single-click the dock icon with the detective hat and magnifying glass (if it's there) or call upon its services from the Applications folder. Following are a few of the channels worth noting:

✔ **Translation:** Type the phrase you want to translate in the original text box, and then select the original language and the language you want to translate the words into from the drop-down menu that appears. See Figure 11-8.

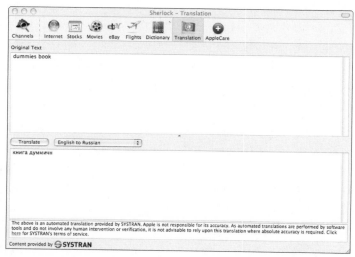

Figure 11-8: How do you say it in Russian?

✔ **AppleCare:** This is a fast way to read troubleshooting tips and other articles in the AppleCare knowledge base.

✔ **Internet:** Lets you quickly search the Web, but it's no Google.

✔ **Stocks:** Enter the company name or the ticker symbol of stocks you're interested in, and Sherlock reports back the price of the last trade (delayed 15 minutes), the change over the previous quote, and the day's range, volume, and relevant headlines. You can even display a mini stock chart showing prices for the year, week, or intraday.

Whenever Apple adds channels, they automatically show up in Sherlock. But has Scotland Yard (or Steve Jobs) put the famed detective on notice? Sherlock already appears to be past his prime. Many of his duties are now handled by newer and slicker Dashboard widgets (see Chapters 6 and 21).

Sayonara Sherlock?

Chapter 12

Joining .Mac, the Club That Will Have You for a Member

*O*ne hundred bucks a year. That's the price to join Apple's .Mac (pronounced "dot Mac") service. The suite of Internet goodies you get for that sum includes an e-mail account, tools to keep multiple Macs in sync, plus online storage. Most .Mac services are cleverly woven into Tiger and iLife.

Okay, so my inner fact-checker compels me to point out that .Mac actually costs $99.95 per annum. What's a nickel among friends? While we're at it, a Family Pack .Mac subscription, (including a single master account and five subaccounts) fetches $180, um, $179.95 per year.

If you really must know, .Mac used to be called iTools and used to be free. Television was once free too, but no one argues when you get a lot more viewing choices for the money. So it goes with .Mac. The folks at Apple have piled on the features these last few years, even as they now make you fork over extra coin.

Which raises the overall question: Is .Mac worth the price of admission? This is where I'd love to pause, run a couple of commercials, keep you hanging for a few minutes. They do it all the time on TV. Oh, well, wrong medium.

At the risk of copping out, the answer is, it depends.

Why Belong?

In general, .Mac is a worthwhile investment for many but not all Mac owners. The service gets a lot more interesting for you creative types looking to share your inspirations — photos, blogs, Web pages, music — in cyberspace.

I suspect that most of you can take advantage of the extra online storage that comes with .Mac membership.

Apple lets you use limited versions of certain .Mac features risk free for 60 days, so give it a shot. If it doesn't work out, well, as they say in basketball, no harm, no foul.

You'll have the opportunity to sign up to a .Mac account (or trial) when you first turn on your Mac. No worries if you're already well past that point: Go to System Preferences and click the .Mac icon (found under Internet & Network). Or visit www.apple.com/dotmac.

Here's a bird's-eye view of .Mac features, some of which I'll delve into in greater detail in this chapter, some in other chapters:

- **iLife Media Publishing:** When you create Web sites or blogs through iWeb or podcasts through GarageBand (see Chapter 17), .Mac gives you a place to host, or publish, your work.

- **Photocasting:** Family and friends can "subscribe" to so-called photocasts consisting of dynamic photo albums you create in iPhoto 6 (Chapter 15). As you update those albums in iPhoto, they're dynamically updated on subscribers' computers.

- **iDisk:** A centralized online storage facility you can use to exchange files with others.

- **Backup 3:** A method of scheduling automatic backups for your Mac.

- **Mail:** An ad-free e-mail account with built-in virus protections.

- **Groups:** Lets you communicate, coordinate, and collaborate with other friends, family, and colleagues who congregate in groups. Groups might consist of classmates who arrange study sessions and field trips online. You might create a group for the Little League team you're managing, to post photos and alert everyone to scheduling changes.

- **Sync:** Keeps contacts, calendars, bookmarks and other info in sync on multiple Macs. .Mac Sync lets you access your Address Book from any computer connected to the Net, including a Windows machine.

✔ **Learning Center:** Provides step-by-step tutorials and other training resources for Tiger, iLife, and other applications.

✔ **Member Central:** A repository for free Mac software downloads and special discounts.

With that, let's examine some of .Mac's most prominent features up close, starting with the online storage lockers called iDisk.

iDisk Backups in the Sky

iDisk is arguably the most useful .Mac feature of all. Who wouldn't want personal storage in the clouds, or in reality on Apple's secure servers (that is, big powerful computers)? For one thing, data copied to your iDisk is safe and preserved if anyone ever drops a bowling ball on your computer (I don't ask). This won't be the only reference in this book to the importance of backing up your digital treasures.

What's more, as long as you have an online connection, you can access the files in your iDisk locker wherever you happen to be, even from a Windows machine. Plus you can easily collaborate or exchange documents with others or access files remotely yourself, especially those too large to e-mail.

Basic .Mac membership comes with 1GB (gigabyte) of storage space (as of this writing), which you can allocate as you want between iDisk and your .Mac e-mail account. You can boost the storage amount to 2GB or 4GB, for an extra $49.95 or $99.95, respectively. Upgrade prices are prorated daily; your .Mac expiration date is unchanged.

Subscribers to .Mac can access iDisk via the Finder by choosing Go⇨iDisk⇨ My iDisk (or by pressing Shift+⌘+I).

The icon for iDisk also shows up in all Finder windows.

You can connect to another user's iDisk or Public folder in the same manner.

Click that icon now. If you didn't know better, you'd think iDisk was like any other hard drive inside or connected to your computer.

An iDisk actually consists of ten folders (or eleven for a Family Pack account) for storing your digital valuables. Storing files inside these folders is as simple as dragging stuff to them, just as with any Mac folder. Most of the folders shown in Figure 12-1, including Documents, Movies, Music, and Pictures, are self-explanatory.

Figure 12-1:
iDisk is
organized
into folders.

I'll highlight the others:

- **Public:** You can share the contents of this folder with anybody in cyber-space who knows your .Mac name and (if you created one) password.

- **Sites:** Holds the Web pages you spawned through a .Mac feature called HomePage.

- **Groups:** Here's where to put files for the Little League team, book club, or the clandestine committee planning to overthrow your company's management. .Mac Groups members can share calendars, photos, files, and so on, and post to group message boards. They also get ad-free e-mail. The iDisk Groups folder has subfolders accessible only to group members.

- **Shared:** This folder appears only if you have a Family Pack .Mac membership. Included are files that can be accessed by the master account holder and subaccounts.

- **Backup:** Houses the files you've backed up using a .Mac software feature called Backup, which I cover later in the chapter.

- **Software:** Includes programs and files available only to .Mac members, plus other software you can download from Apple. You can't drag your own files to this folder.

- **Library:** Another read-only folder. It includes files for .Mac Sync, which lets you keep personal data (such as bookmarks, addresses, mailboxes, and calendars) synchronized among all the Macs you own, provided they're connected to the Net.

If you ever decide not to renew a .Mac account, drag your data back onto your Mac's own hard drive before the account expires.

Other Backup Methods

Backing up your digital keepsakes (pictures, videos, financial documents, and so on) is vital. I hope I've impressed that upon you by now. (If I haven't, what will it take? A drum roll? Sworn affidavit?) If you take nothing else from this book, know that you must back up your important data and do so regularly.

Lecture over.

iDisk is a terrific vehicle for backing up bits and bytes, but it doesn't afford you enough storage if you have, say, a sizable multimedia collection. So today's backup arsenal typically consists of recordable CDs and DVDs, external hard drives, and networks.

As a .Mac subscriber, you can approach this backup business strategically, whether you plan to copy stuff onto iDisk or some other destination. That's thanks to the Backup programs included with a .Mac membership. If you have OS X version 10.3.9 or later, download a program called Backup 3. If you have an earlier version of OS X, download Backup 2.

It's up to you, of course, not only to determine which files and data to back up but when exactly to schedule the backups.

Backup 3 can help. To open the program, click the umbrella icon in your Applications folder. The first time you open the program, you're greeted with the window shown in Figure 12-2.

You're presented with several ready-to-use backup plans, or templates: Personal Data & Settings (to back up your Address Book contacts, for instance), a plan to back up the music and videos you've purchased from the iTunes Music Store (see the next chapter), a plan to backup iLife data, and a plan to back up your Home folder. But you can also back up individual files and folders as *you* see fit.

Apple recommends backing up onto iDisk daily any relatively small files that change often. For larger files that don't change as much, you might choose weekly or monthly backups onto DVDs or external harder drives that can accommodate sizable data storage requirements.

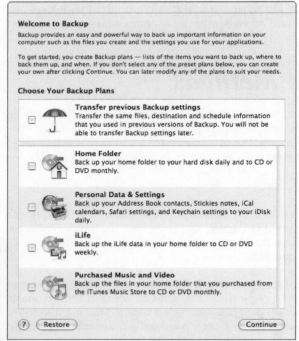

Welcome to Backup

Backup provides an easy and powerful way to back up important information on your computer such as the files you create and the settings you use for your applications.

To get started, you create Backup plans — lists of the items you want to back up, where to back them up, and when. If you don't select any of the preset plans below, you can create your own after clicking Continue. You can later modify any of the plans to suit your needs.

Choose Your Backup Plans

☐ **Transfer previous Backup settings**
Transfer the same files, destination and schedule information that you used in previous versions of Backup. You will not be able to transfer Backup settings later.

☐ **Home Folder**
Back up your home folder to your hard disk daily and to CD or DVD monthly.

☐ **Personal Data & Settings**
Back up your Address Book contacts, Stickies notes, iCal calendars, Safari settings, and Keychain settings to your iDisk daily.

☐ **iLife**
Back up the iLife data in your home folder to CD or DVD weekly.

☐ **Purchased Music and Video**
Back up the files in your home folder that you purchased from the iTunes Music Store to CD or DVD monthly.

⑦　(Restore)　　　　　　　　　(Continue)

Figure 12-2:
You always need a backup plan.

If you already created settings in previous versions of Backup, you are given the option to transfer those settings to Backup 3.

Say you click Personal Data & Settings. The window that appears, shown in Figure 12-3, is divided into two panes. The top shows the backup items you've chosen and the size requirements for those backups. The bottom pane lists the destination and schedule for those backups.

After double-clicking one of these plans in the upper window, choose the Add (+) or Remove (-) buttons to add or delete plans.

If you click the + button, you can choose items to back up in one of three ways:

🗸 **QuickPicks:** These are shortcuts to backup plans involving certain types of files: all your mail messages, your iPhoto library, or Microsoft Excel documents, for example, as shown in Figure 12-4.

🗸 **Files & Folders:** Lets you specify what you want to back up.

🗸 **Spotlight:** Runs a quick search to figure out the files to copy.

Click Done to return to the main Backup window.

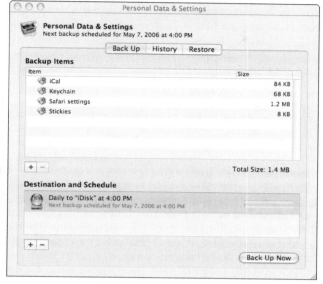

Figure 12-3:
What
exactly are
you backing
up? And
when?

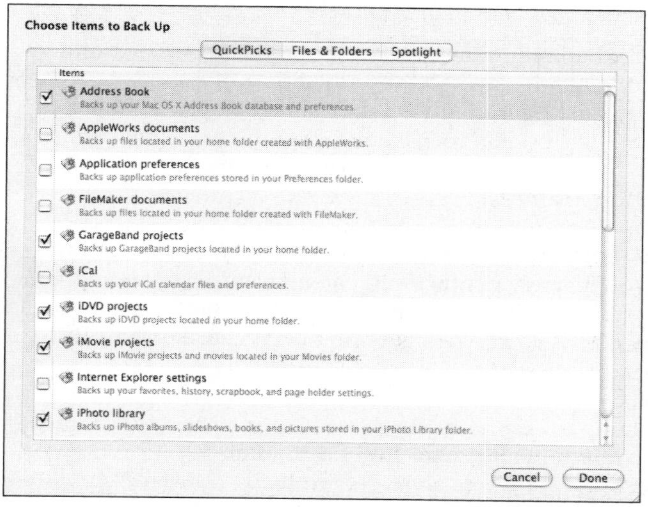

Figure 12-4:
QuickPicks
lets you
back up all
files of a
specific
type.

After you've determined all your backup items, click Back Up Now to begin backing up right away or close the window to begin the backup according to the schedule you've set.

If possible, keep backup discs in a different location than your Mac; that way you may be able to keep your data safe from a fire or other calamity.

The first time you copy a designated set of files, you're doing a full backup. Subsequent files are incremental; only the files altered since your last backup are copied.

.Mac Mail

I'd like to tell you there's something extra special about having a .Mac e-mail account. But it's like any other Web-based e-mail account. You can check .Mac mail from any browser, and it integrates with the Mac's Mail application. The amount of storage you have is directly tied to the amount of storage you use in iDisk. The basic .Mac membership lets you divvy up 1GB between iDisk and .Mac Mail. .Mac storage isn't as generous as other Web-based e-mail accounts such as Google's Gmail, which is free.

.Mac Sync

If you're lucky enough to own two or more Macs, perhaps one for home and another for the office, you can take advantage of .Mac Sync to keep all your computers at least figuratively on the same page. With .Mac Sync, you can synchronize Safari bookmarks, calendars, Address Book contacts, keychains (passwords), and mail preferences. You need OS X version 10.4 or later to exploit all these features.

.Mac Sync is different than iSync, Tiger's own synchronization application that helps you manage contact and calendar info on connected devices such as a wireless Bluetooth cell phone, a Palm handheld, or an iPod. Use iSync to synchronize files if you have a version of OS X earlier than 10.4.

To use .Mac Sync:

1. **Open System Preferences and click .Mac.**

2. **Click the Sync tab.**

3. **Select the Synchronize with .Mac option, and make a selection from the pop-up menu.**

   Your choices are Automatically, Every Hour, Every Day, Every Week, or Manually.

4. **Select the items you want to synchronize, as shown in Figure 12-5.**

Figure 12-5:
It helps to
be in sync.

5. **Enter the same synchronization settings on all the Macs you want synchronized.**

6. **If you want, select the Show Status in Menu Bar option.**

   A little spinning circle will appear in the menu bar while the Macs are synchronizing.

7. **Click the Sync Now button.**

8. **Visit www.mac.com.**

9. **On the .Mac tab, click Address Book and then click Preferences.**

10. **Select the Turn on .Mac Address Book Synchronization option.**

    This keeps your desktop Address Book in sync with your .Mac Address Book. If you have a lot of entries in your Address Book, your first synchronization may take awhile.

Sharing Your Digital Masterpieces

The iWeb software introduced with iLife '06 lets you build striking Web pages and create online journals, or blogs, by laying your own content on top of placeholder text and images found on predesigned Apple templates. After you're satisfied with your new creation, you can foist it on a waiting public by publishing through your .Mac account.

Click the iWeb icon in the dock or open the program in the Applications folder. Then, in iWeb, choose File⇨Publish to .Mac to make your page visible to others.

Incidentally, iWeb, which is part of the iLife suite, differs from HomePage, which consists of sites included with .Mac membership stored on Apple's servers. You can't edit HomePage sites in iWeb, though you can link between HomePage and iWeb sites.

Consider adding a password to lock out strangers from viewing your site. Do you really want to share your thoughts with *everyone?* In iWeb's site organizer, select the site (or a specific page), click Inspector, and select the Make My Published Site Private option. Then enter a user name and password that visitors must enter to access your site.

Oh, and don't use your .Mac password for this purpose.

Chapter 13

Mounting a Defense Strategy

This figured to be a short chapter. After all, OS X has been immune from the swarm of viruses that have plagued Windows computers through the years. Folks traditionally have needed to call a security specialist for their Macs about as often as you summon the Maytag repair man.

But times change. Heck, Whirlpool bought Maytag. So when it comes to computers nowadays, you can't take anything for granted — even if you own a Mac.

The Truth about Internet Security

There are suggestions that OS X isn't as bulletproof as was once believed. In May 2006, the McAfee Avert Labs security threat research firm issued a report claiming that the Mac is just as vulnerable to targeted *malware,* or *malicious software* attacks, as other operating systems. According to McAfee, between 2003 and 2005, the "annual rate of vulnerability" on Apple's platform increased by 228 percent, compared to 73 percent on the Microsoft side of the ledger. Although the volume of threats is low, no invisible cloak is protecting Apple's products.

Moreover, the security firm expects malicious hackers to increasingly place the Mac OS (as well as the iPod) in the crosshairs, given Apple's recent transition to Intel chips and especially as Apple's products gain popularity.

The implication is that the bad guys haven't spent much time targeting Apple because the Mac has had such a miniscule market share. Although that argument may have some merit, Tiger and Macs in general have been engineered with your protection in mind. Your operating system is as secure as they come. Of course, now that a Mac can double as a Windows computer (see Chapter 19), all bets are off.

What then are we to make of the McAfee report? Should Mac owners never turn their computers on? Methinks not. But Mac loyalists shouldn't get complacent either. For starters, you should install the security updates that show up on your Mac when you click System Preferences under Software Updates. And you should only load software on your computer from companies and Web sites you trust.

Most of all, security requires a little common sense.

Spies in our mist

Viruses are menacing programs created for the sole purpose of wreaking havoc on a computer or network. They spread when you download suspect software, visit shady Web sites, or pass around infected discs.

Computer viruses take many forms. Windows users are all too familiar with *spyware,* the type of code that surreptitiously shows up on your computer to track your behavior and secretly report it to third parties.

Spyware typically differs from traditional computer viruses, which may try to shut down your computer (or at least one or two programs on the machine). Authors of spyware aren't necessarily out to shut you down. Rather, they quietly attempt to monitor your behavior so that they can benefit at your expense.

At the lesser extremes, your computer is served pop-up ads that companies hope will eventually lead to a purchase. This type of spyware is known as *adware.*

At its most severe, spyware can place your personal information in the hands of a not-so-nice person. Under those circumstances, you could get totally ripped off. Indeed, the most malicious of spyware programs, called *keyloggers* or *snoopware,* can capture every keystroke you enter, whether you're holding court in a public chat room or typing a password.

The good new is that as of this writing, no major reports of OS X–related spyware have surfaced.

But there's always a first time.

Gone phishing

Dear Citibank Member,

As part of our security measures, we regularly screen activity in the Citibank system. We recently contacted you after noticing an issue on your account. We requested information from you for the following reasons:

We have reason to believe that your account was accessed by a third party. Because protecting the security of your account is our primary concern, we have limited access to sensitive Citibank account features. We understand that this may be an inconvenience but please understand that this temporary limitation is for your protection.

This is a third and final reminder to log in to Citibank as soon as possible.

Once you log in, you will be provided with steps to restore your account access. We appreciate your understanding as we work to ensure account safety.

Sincerely,

Citibank Account Review Department

The text from the preceding e-mailed letter sounds legitimate enough. But the only thing real about it is that this is an actual excerpt lifted from a common Internet fraud known as a *phishing* attack.

Identity thieves, masquerading as Citibank, eBay, PayPal or other financial or Internet companies, try to dupe you into clicking phony links to verify personal or account information. You're asked to surrender home addresses, passwords, social security numbers, credit cards numbers, banking account information, and so on.

To lend authenticity to these appeals, the spoof e-mails often are dressed up with real company logos and addresses, plus a forged company name in the From line (for example, From: support@ebay.com).

Phishing may take the form of falsified company newsletters, as Figure 13-1 shows. Or there may be bogus requests for you to reconfirm personal data.

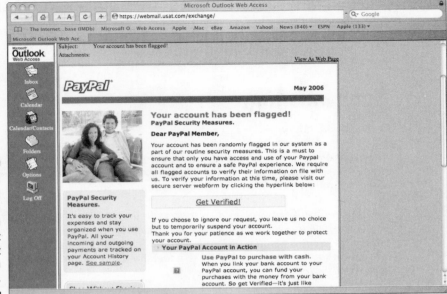

Figure 13-1: Phishing through PayPal. This request to get verification is bogus.

So how do you know when you're being hoodwinked? Obvious giveaways included in some fake e-mails are misspellings, rotten grammar, and repeated words or sentences.

No company on the level is going to ask you to reconfirm data that has been lost. And reputable companies usually refer to you by your real first and last name and business affiliations rather than the more generic Dear Member or Dear PayPal Customer.

If you have doubts that a communication is legit, you can always open a new browser window and type the real company name yourself (for example, www.ebay.com or www.paypal.com.) Your gut instincts concerning phony mail are probably on the mark.

Bottom line: *Never* click links embedded in suspicious e-mails. When you hover the cursor over a link such as www.paypal.com, it actually leads elsewhere.

Firewalls

More than likely, if you're connecting to the Internet through a network router (see Chapter 18), you're protected by a shield known as a *firewall*. But Tiger also has a software firewall, and you can use it to block unwanted Web traffic.

Here's how to access it:

1. **Choose ⬆️System Preferences.**

2. **In the Internet & Network section, click Sharing.**

3. **Click the Firewall tab.**

   This is where you turn on settings to stop incoming Internet traffic to services and ports, except those you specify, as shown in Figure 13-2.

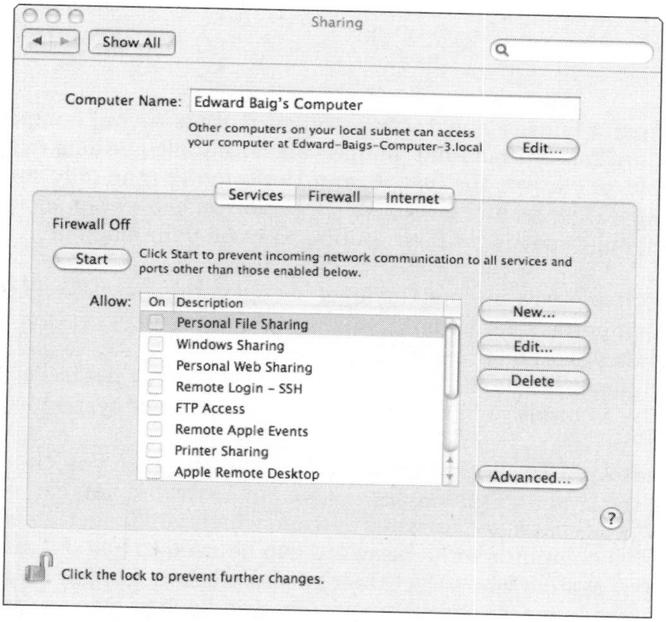

Figure 13-2:
Selecting
the
communica-
tions your
firewall will
let in.

By clicking the New button, you can specify a port on which you'd like to receive inbound networking traffic. Out of the box, Apple keeps all communication ports closed by default.

If you click the Advanced button, you'll be able to log information about unauthorized attempts and destinations blocked by the Mac's firewall.

You can also operate the computer in Stealth mode (by selecting that option in the Advanced section) so that any uninvited traffic receives no acknowledgment or response from the Mac. Malicious hackers won't even know there's a machine to attack.

Still another Advanced option is to block UDP (User Datagram Protocol) traffic. UDP is another Internet communications method. While blocking UDP may help secure your Mac, it may also restrict your Internet connections.

FileVault

If your computer houses truly hush-hush information — your company's financial books, say, rather than Aunt Minnie's secret noodle-pudding recipe — you can scramble, or *encrypt,* the data in your Home folder (and only your Home folder) using a Tiger feature known as *FileVault.* You know your secrets are protected should thieves get their grubby paws on your machine.

FileVault automatically applies the level of encryption employed by Uncle Sam. It's what nerds refer to as AES-128 (for Advanced Encryption Standard with 128-bit keys). And let me tell you, it's *really* secure. Apple claims it would take a machine approximately 149 trillion years to crack the code. Even if they're off by a couple of billion years, I'm thinking your system is pretty safe.

The FileVault window shown in Figure 13-3 turns up when you choose Security under System Preferences. As an administrator, you can set up a safety net *master password* for your system, which you'll need to unlock FileVault. This computer-wide password can be used to bail out authorized users on your system who forget their password. And it might be a lifesaver if you run a small business through your Mac and have to let a wayward employee go. You'll be able to recover any data left behind in that person's account.

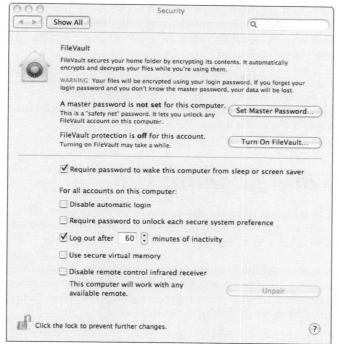

Figure 13-3:
Keeping
your
computer
secure in
System
Preferences.

Heed Apple's warning. If you forget your login password and master password, your scrambled data may as well be toast.

If FileVault is turned on and you're not logged in to the machine, other people you normally share folders with on the computer will not be able to access those folders.

Password Management: The Key to Keychains

Have you stopped to think how many passwords are in your computing life? You probably have so many that you use the same ones over and over, though security experts think that's not such a keen practice.

The pun police will get on me for saying this, but Apple has the key to managing your passwords, account numbers, and other confidential info: a feature known as keychain. A *keychain* can store passwords for programs, e-mail accounts, Web sites, and more.

You can create different keychains for different purposes (one for online shopping, say) by opening keychain access in the Utilities folder under Applications. Your keychain password is initially the same as your login password, and for many users that's the way it'll stay.

Logging In and Logging Out

If you work in an office or other environment where anyone can peek at the monitor to see what you've been up to, log out of your account when you're finished doing what you're doing.

But if you'd rather not bother logging out or you don't think you'll remember, go to the Security pane of System Preferences, and select the Require Password to Wake This Computer from Sleep or Screen Saver option and the Log Out after *x* Minutes of Inactivity option (refer to Figure 13-3).

You also may want to select the options to Disable Automatic Login and Use Secure Virtual Memory. The latter setting ensures that data stored in virtual memory is encrypted. You'll have to restart the computer for the change to take effect.

If you're really distrustful, select the Require Password to Unlock Each Secure System Preference option.

There. I told you this would be a short chapter.

Part IV
Getting an iLife

The 5th Wave   By Rich Tennant

RICHTENNANT

"I could tell you more about myself, but I think
the playlist on my iPod says more about me
than mere words can."

In this part . . .

Come meet and greet the Murderers' Row of multimedia software: iTunes, iPhoto, iMovie HD, GarageBand, and iWeb. Music junkies, photography buffs, auteurs, videographers, aspiring rock stars, podcasters, and bloggers are all invited. So are you and your family. Special bonus: a peek at Apple's remarkably successful iPod. iLife '06 is included on all new Macs and is a $79 upgrade if you have an older system.

Chapter 14

Living in an iTunes Nation

The demographers may have missed it. But we're in the midst of a major population explosion. Everywhere you look, vast colonies of tiny white earbuds are proliferating. They're spotted on subways and on the street. On airplanes, buses, and college and corporate campuses.

Those signature white earbuds, of course, are connected to iPods. And there's every chance you're reading a Macintosh book because of them. Although iPods are meant to work with iTunes software in Windows machines as well as on OS X, your first infatuation with the Mac may well have occurred in an Apple store where you ostensibly went to check out the darling of all portable music players.

You also may be thinking that if Apple hit such a home run with the iPod, perhaps Steve Jobs and crew know something about making darn impressive computers too. (Naturally, you'd be right.)

For its part, the iPod has morphed into such a phenomenon that the *accessories* business for the devices — cases, speaker systems, car radio adapters, armbands, even a distance and pace sensor that fits into Nike shoes — supposedly amount to a billion-dollar-plus business. That's billion with a *B*.

So although this is first and foremost a computer book (and I promise we'll venture back to the Mac before long), please forgive a minor detour into iPod territory. I won't dwell on everything the iPod can do except to quickly mention here that in addition to music and (with some models) video and pictures, iPods can synchronize contacts and calendar information and store text files.

I hope you'll keep reading this chapter even if you don't have an iPod. You can still take advantage of iTunes.

Choosing Your iPod

Sprinkled throughout this book is the disclaimer *as of this writing* because Apple is known for surprises. In late summer 2005, Apple replaced what had been the best-selling iPod model to date, iPod Minis, because it came up with something even more extraordinary, the Lilliputian Nano.

So all bets are off: Notwithstanding a special edition model tied to the rock band U2, as of this writing, there are essentially three iPod classes, each sold with different storage capacities.

By the time you read this, Apple may have finally unveiled a long rumored iPod cell phone combination. (I'm not counting the phones that incorporate iTunes software but otherwise bear no resemblance to genuine iPods.)

The "white" iPod

The so-called white iPod ($299 on up) represents the fifth generation of the original iPod. Roughly the size of a deck of cards, the classic iPod, shown in Figure 14-1, is white on the front with a scratch-prone mirrored finish on the back. The devices are famous for their touch-sensitive *scroll wheel,* which you use to control the gizmo's operations (menus, skipping tracks, play/pause, and more).

Courtesy of Apple

At the time this book was published, the highest capacity iPod could hold up to 15,000 songs, 25,000 photos, and 150 hours of video, from ancient reruns of *Alfred Hitchcock Presents* to highlights from the last Rose Bowl.

The Nano

I can tick off the Nano's weight (1.5 ounces) and dimensions (just 3.5-by-1.6 by-0.27 inches). But you don't truly appreciate how tantalizingly small that is until you place a Nano (see Figure 14-2) next to a grown-up iPod. Of course, giving in on size means giving up some song capacity. The largest capacity Nano can hold around 1,000 songs.

Now Playing

9 of 12

The Journey
Fatboy Slim
Palookaville

3:37   -0:59

MENU

Figure 14-2:
The smaller
Nano.

Courtesy of Apple

Still, if you're looking for an iPod so small you're not even sure whether it's still in your pocket, Nano is the choice. Like it's full-size cousin, Nano sports a version of the scroll wheel. It can show off pictures too (but not videos). Nano, which starts at $149, comes in two flavors, black or customary iPod white.

The iPod Shuffle

Starting at just $69 and smaller than a pack of Trident, Shuffle (see Figure 14-3) gets its name from the shuffle setting found on larger iPods, compact disc players, and other musical devices. Songs on the device play in random order. Moreover, because the Shuffle has no display, the only way to tell what's playing, assuming you don't know just by listening, is to connect Shuffle to your Mac (or Windows machine) through its built-in USB connector. That connector is revealed when you lift off Shuffle's white cap. Incidentally, unlike the hard-drive-based video iPod, Shuffle employs what's called flash memory; so the least expensive model is limited to around 120 songs.

Figure 14-3:
Even
smaller, the
Shuffle.

iTunes: The Great Mac Jukebox

As stand-alone devices, iPods are wonderful examples of exemplary design and superb engineering. But though the iPod name signifies star power, it must share (and truth be told probably relinquish) top billing to the maestro behind Apple's musical ensemble, *iTunes* software.

If the iPod is Lennon, Apple's multimedia jukebox program is McCartney. Or it is Mick to Keith? Or Rodgers to Hammerstein? Well you get the drift; the little player and Apple's software make terrific music together.

Best of all, as part of the iLife suite, iTunes is one of those melodious programs that musical enthusiasts (and everyone else) get just for owning a Mac.

Here's a quick rundown on what iTunes permits you to do, with further commentary to come later in this chapter:

- ✔ Listen to CDs

- ✔ *Rip,* or encode, the songs on a CD into music files that are compressed (see the "Compassionate compression" sidebar) and stored in your digital library

- ✔ Add music to the library from the Internet

- ✔ Create, or *burn,* your own CDs or DVDs, with the proper CD or DVD burner, such as Apple's own Super Drive, which is included in some Macs

- ✔ Listen to Internet radio by clicking the Radio icon in the source list to display a list of *streams* by category, such as Alt/Modern Rock, Blues, and Electronica

- ✔ Watch videos

- ✔ Organize your music by name, artist, time, album, genre, rating, and play-count

- ✔ Segregate your music into customized playlists

- ✔ Stream or share the music in your library across a network — within certain limitations

- ✔ Transfer music onto an iPod

To open iTunes, click the Dock icon, which looks like a musical note resting on top of a CD.

Let's explore some of the iTunes controls referenced in Figure 14-4:

- ✔ **Back/Forward:** The double-arrow pointing to the left and right respectively are your back and forward buttons. Place the cursor above these buttons and hold down the mouse to rewind or fast-forward through a song. If you instead single-click on these arrows, you'll advance or retreat to the next or previous track.

- ✔ **Play/Pause:** Click the single arrow pointing to the right to play a song. When a song is playing, the button changes to two vertical bars. Click again to stop the music. Alternatively, press the spacebar to play or pause.

Click here to enter the Music Store

Click here for Internet radio

Source list

Previous track/back

Play/pause

Forward/next track

Volume

Track list

Click to change to a digital readout

Now playing

Track status

Click column heads to sort

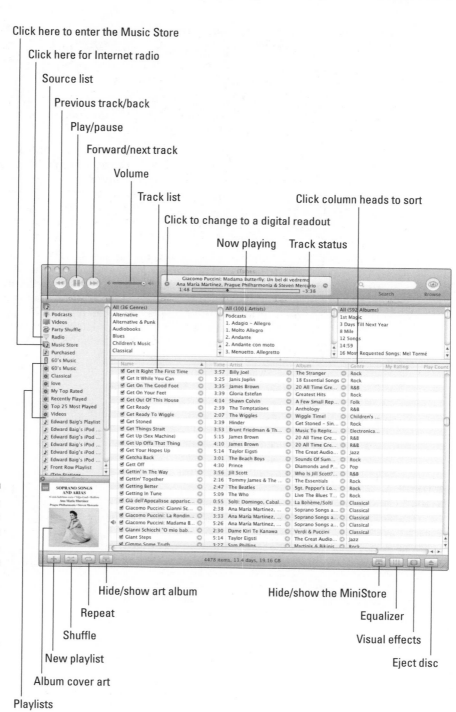

Figure 14-4:
Ode to
iTunes
software.

Hide/show art album

Repeat

Shuffle

New playlist

Album cover art

Playlists

Hide/show the MiniStore

Equalizer

Visual effects

Eject disc

✔ **Volume:** Dragging this slider increases or decreases the volume.

✔ **Shuffle:** When the symbol in this little button is highlighted (it turns blue), tracks play in random order. Be prepared for anything. There's no telling when Eminem will follow The Wiggles.

✔ **Repeat:** Click once to repeat all the songs in the library or playlist you're currently listening to. Click twice so that the number 1 appears on the button. Only the current track will repeat.

✔ **Equalizer:** If you've ever tweaked the treble and bass controls on a stereo, you'll appreciate the equalizer. It allows you to adjust sound frequencies to match the genre of a song, the speakers on your system, or the ambiance of the room in which you are listening. Clicking the equalizer button brings up the list shown in Figure 14-5. You can manually adjust the equalizer by dragging the sliders or choose among more than 20 presets (such as Bass reducer, Flat, Hip-Hop, or Lounge).

✔ **Visual Effects:** If you were conscious during the '60s, you'll welcome these funky psychedelic light animations that dance to the beat of whatever's playing, as shown in Figure 14-6. And if you're the offspring of a Baby Boomer, you'll arrive at this amazing realization: Maybe mom and dad were pretty groovy in their heyday. You can also drum up your visual serenade by pressing ⌘+T. For a full-screen effect when the visualizer is active, press ⌘+F; press Esc, or click the mouse button to return to reality.

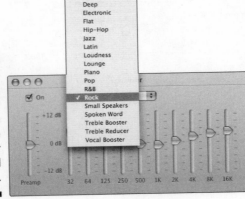

Figure 14-5:
The Equalizer lets you fine-tune your musical mood.

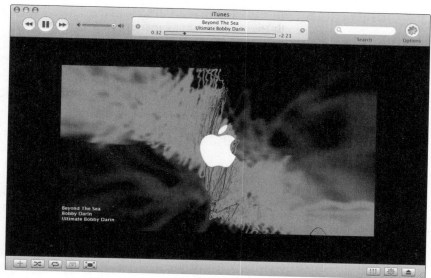

Figure 14-6: Psychedelic light animations.

Managing Your Music

So how exactly does music make its way into iTunes? And what exactly comes of the songs after you have 'em? I thought you'd never ask.

Ripping audio CDs

A remarkable thing happens moments after you insert the vast majority of music CDs into your Mac. The contents of the disc — song titles, artist name, length, album name, and genre — are automatically recognized and copied into iTunes. The software actually fetches this licensed information from a massive online database run by a company called Gracenote.

Now here's another remarkable feat: Next time, you won't have to keep inserting said CD into the computer to hear its music. That's because you can rip, or copy, the contents onto the Mac's hard drive, and then stash the disc somewhere else.

To rip a CD, click the Import CD button in the upper-right corner of the window. Because all songs with a check mark next to their name will be copied, be sure to click to uncheck any songs you have no interest in before proceeding.

As iTunes goes about its business, a tiny orange circle spins next to the song being ripped; the circle turns green and gains a check mark after it's been copied. You can monitor the progress of your imports also by peeking at the top display shown in Figure 14-7. It shows you how much time remains before a particular track is captured and the speed at which the CD is being ripped.

Incidentally, you can listen to the CD (or do other work) while ripping a disc. After iTunes has completed its mission, remove the CD by clicking Eject (the rightmost icon at the bottom of the screen). Copied songs are stored in the iTunes library.

Figure 14-7:
Ripping
a CD.

Importing other ditties

Songs previously downloaded from the Internet can be imported into iTunes by dragging them into your iTunes library. The assumption here is that you obtained those music files legally. If you did not, placing them inside iTunes will blow up your computer. (That's not really the case, but I urge you to play by the rules just the same. People's livelihoods depend on it.)

To import audio files from other applications or your desktop, choose File➪Add to Library and then select the file. Or drag the music into the Library, or the iTunes Dock icon.

Creating playlists

You listen to music under a variety of circumstances, such as entertaining at a dinner party, soothing a crying baby, setting a romantic mood, or drowning in your sorrows after a painful breakup. In the last situation, the last thing you'd want to hear is Barbra Streisand belting out "Happy Days Are Here Again," even if the song is otherwise a staple in your iTunes library. With a playlist, you can organize material around a particular theme or mood.

The simplest way to create a new playlist is to click the + button in the bottom-left corner of the iTunes window. You can also choose File➪New Playlist or press the keyboard tandem ⌘+N.

A new playlist with the inelegant name "Untitled playlist" appears in the source list. Type over that with the name of the playlist you have in mind (Jazz Crooners, Dance Mix, Corny Songs, or whatever). Then merely drag the songs from the library into the folder representing the new playlist.

If you're adding multiple songs into the playlist, hold down the ⌘ or Shift key to select a bunch of tracks. You can drag the whole batch over in one swoop.

To delete a song from a playlist, highlight it and press Delete. Don't worry, the original track remains in your library. Songs in playlists never really leave the library; the playlist merely functions as a pointer to those files. For the same reason, a particular song can show up in as many playlists as you want.

When playlists get smart

Putting together a playlist can be fun. But it can also take considerable time and effort. Using *smart playlists,* you can have iTunes do the heavy lifting on your behalf, based on specific conditions you establish upfront: how fast a song is (based on BPM, or beats per minute), the type of music, a song's rating, and so on. You can also limit the playlist to a specific length.

Choose File⇒New Smart Playlist. In the dialog box that appears, click Add (+) to choose the parameters you're basing the smart playlist on from pop up menus. Click the – button to remove a condition.

Take a look at the Smart Playlist Figure 14-8. It has iTunes looking for all songs with *Love* in the title that you haven't heard in a couple of months or heard more than 14 times. The song must have been encoded with a bit rate between 128 and 160 Kbps (see the "Compassionate compression" sidebar). The overall length of the playlist cannot exceed 2 hours. If you want iTunes to alter the smart playlist as songs are added or removed, select the Live Updating option.

Figure 14-8: Finding the love in a Smart playlist.

Loading tunes onto the iPod

Transferring your songs, playlists, and — as you'll also see — videos, audiobooks, and podcasts to an iPod is as simple as connecting the device to your Mac through USB or FireWire, depending on the iPod model. Each time you connect, the iPod automatically mirrors any changes to your songs and playlists in iTunes, unless you select Manually Manage Songs and Playlists under the iPod section of iTunes Preferences, found in the iTunes menu.

Compassionate compression

iTunes can sing to a variety of audio file formats. Most digital tracks imported into the iTunes database are compressed, or shrunken, so the music doesn't hog an inordinate amount of space on your hard drive. But there's generally a tradeoff between file size and sound quality. As you might imagine, larger files offer the finest sonic fidelity. At least in theory.

The best known of these compression schemes is *MP3,* a method in which files are squeezed to a reasonable size, even though the sound is perfectly acceptable to all but the most serious audiophiles.

Apple prefers an alternate compression method. On Macs with QuickTime 6.2 or later, Apple uses a default encoding scheme known as MPEG-4 AAC (Advanced Audio Coding), a compression format that rivals the sound quality of an audio CD, and one that Apple claims is equal if not superior to MP3s encoded at the same or a higher bit rate. (If you have an earlier version of QuickTime, MP3 is the default.)

The songs you purchase at the iTunes Music Store are also in the AAC format. According to Apple, the High Quality AAC setting produces files that take up less than 1 megabyte for each minute of music. But iTunes also recognizes other file formats: Apple Lossless, AIFF, and WAV. These last two flavors are uncompressed, so the music is of exceptional quality, but the files gobble up disk space. Apple Lossless is an audiophile format that matches AIFF and WAV in sound quality but takes up half the space. You can burn CDs in the Lossless or AIFF formats.

If you're inclined to mess with these file formats, visit iTunes Preferences, click the Advanced tab, and make your choice in the Importing section. You can set up the encoder to import using AAC, AIFF, Apple Lossless, MP3, or WAV, and also choose the stereo bit rate. In techie terms, 128 kbps is the default.

A connected iPod shows up in the iTunes source list. Click the little Eject icon next to the name of your iPod in the source list before removing the device from a USB or FireWire cable. (Connecting a photo-capable iPod also transfers pictures from iPhoto, the star of the next chapter.)

Burning audio CDs

Knowing how to create a playlist is a handy precursor to burning or creating your own CD that can be played in virtually any standard compact disc player.

To burn a CD:

1. **From the iTunes menu, click Preferences, and then click the Advanced tab.**
2. **Click Burning.**

3. **For the Disc Format, select Audio CD.**

4. **Choose the gap between songs (from 0 to 5 seconds).**

5. **If you want all the songs on the CD to play at the same volume, click Sound Check.**

6. **With those preliminaries out the way, choose the playlist with the songs you want to burn and make sure all the tunes you want have check marks next to their names.**

   Be mindful of the length of those tracks; regular CDs have room for about 74 to 80 minutes of music, or approximately 20 songs.

7. **When you're ready, click the Burn Disc button in the upper-right corner.**

8. **When instructed insert a blank disc.**

   Use a CD-R disc if you want to play the CD in almost any player. Although this type of disc can't be erased after you've recorded on it, it works in many more players than rewriteable CD-RW type discs, the kind that can be re-recorded.

9. **Click Burn Disc again.**

   Your CD burner chugs away. The entire procedure may take several minutes.

In this example, we burned an audio CD. Apple also gives you the option to burn an MP3 CD. The advantage is that you can store a lot more music (more than 12 hours, or 150 songs) on a typical CD-R disc. The rub: Fewer CD players can handle this type of disc.

Tuning into Internet radio

Listening to your own CDs and digital tracks is terrific. Presumably a lot of thought went into amassing your collection.

But at times, nothing beats the serendipity of radio: Not knowing what's coming next, hearing a nugget you haven't heard in decades, hearing a new jewel for the first time.

You don't have to leave your Mac to revel in this type of experience. In fact, when you click Radio in the source list, you'll have access to a heck of a lot more radio stations than you'll find on AM, FM, or even subscription-based satellite radio. These are *streaming Internet radio* stations, and you can choose from hundreds of them. Apple categorizes these by genre, as shown in Figure 14-9. Click the triangle next to a category name to see all the station options in that genre. Double-click to tune into a particular station. It starts playing in a few seconds, mercifully minus the static of regular radio.

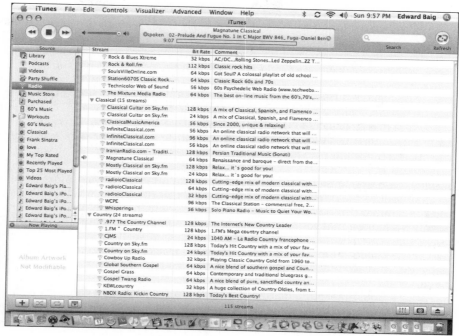

Figure 14-9:
You won't
find all
these on
AM or FM.

Pay attention to the *bit rate*. The higher the bit rate number, the better a station will sound, though you're at the mercy of your Internet connection. Dial-up users may want to stick with stations streaming at less than 48 kbps.

You can include Internet radio stations in a playlist. Of course, you must still be connected to the Internet to hear them. Recording Internet radio streams requires a third-party application such as RadioLover from Bitcartel Software. Download an evaluation version at www.bitcartel.com/download.html.

Finding Music Online

iTunes serves as a gateway to a delightful emporium for music lovers. It's the iTunes Music Store where hunting for songs is a pleasure for all but the most tone-deaf users. Don't believe me? How else to explain more than a billion downloads since Apple opened up the place? To enter the store, click Music Store in the iTunes source list.

Sadly, you won't find every song on your wish list in the iTunes Music Store because some performers or the music labels that control these artists' catalogues foolheartedly remain digital holdouts. They have yet to put their records up for sale in cyberspace. No Beatles songs are listed, and Madonna was a latecomer until she started appearing in Apple ads.

If you ask me, it smacks of greed. But then don't get me started.

Now that I have that rant off my chest, let's put a positive spin on buying music online compared to doing so in the physical world. For one thing, good as it is, your neighborhood record store isn't going to carry the more than 2 million tracks found in the iTunes Music Store. Moreover, every tune in the iTunes joint is always "in stock."

Shopping online for music affords you other privileges. Most notably, you have the opportunity to cherry-pick favorite tracks from an album, without having to buy the entire compilation. Note, however, that some record labels require that some tracks be purchased only as part of a full-blown album.

What's more, you can sample all the tracks for 30 seconds, without any obligation to buy. Most of the songs that you do choose to buy cost 99¢ a pop.

Then there's the matter of instant gratification. You can start listening to the music you buy inside iTunes mere seconds after making a purchase, as you'll see later in the chapter.

Seeking online music recommendations

In a real-life music store, you might find an adolescent clerk willing to recommend an album or artist. (Although why is it you have a sneaking suspicion this kid doesn't speak the same language you do, much less enjoy the same repertoire?) If you get really lucky, you may come across a Julliard graduate moonlighting between gigs. But more often than not you're browsing the shelves on your own, not that that's a bad thing; I love spending time in record stores.

But face it, we all need a little counsel now and then. You'll find plenty of it in the iTunes Music Store from Apple as well as from people like you who happen to adore music.

In some respects, the front page of the Music Store is like the window outside Tower Records. You'll see colorful album covers, promotions for particular artists, and more.

The page is laid out with new or recent releases, staff favorites, a list of top songs and top albums, a few exclusives, and other recommendations — presented in the main genre you select by clicking the drop-down menu under Inside the Music Store (on the left side of the screen).

Figure 14-10 shows the front page of the store when you've selected Children's Music as your genre.

Now suppose you click the banner where Julie Andrews is choosing her favorite Disney ditties. You're transported to a page like the one shown in Figure 14-11. In the bottom half of the screen is the list of songs in her compilation. Click any of these to hear 30-second samples. Now look above the song list. You'll find customer reviews and ratings.

Feel free to contribute your own reviews. In iTunes, everybody can be critic.

Figure 14-10:
Browsing selections for the kids in the iTunes Music Store.

Figure 14-11:
Choosing
songs with
help from
Mary
Poppins.

iMixes

In the last section, I mentioned that you can write your own reviews. In fact, you can go a lot further than being a critic. You can compile a list of songs for people with similar tastes. Throughout the Music Store, you'll come across top-rated *iMixes,* playlists created by ordinary music fans like you.

To contribute your own iMix for all the world to see in the iTunes Music Store, follow these steps:

1. **In the source list, click the little arrow to the right of a selected playlist.**

   If no arrow appears, select the Show Links to Music Store option, which is on the General tab in iTunes Preferences.

2. **Click Create iMix.**

3. **Enter a title and a description.**

   You might use a title such as "Ed's Sappy Love Songs" and a description such as "Great sentimental music to share with a bottle of a wine and a special friend." Apple won't let you use profanity.

4. **Click Tell a Friend to spread the word.**

Although your playlist can include tracks you've ripped from a CD, only tunes sold in the iTunes Music Store will appear in your iMix. Apple makes the iMix available for one year from its publish date.

You can rate other people's iMixes on a scale of 1 to 5 stars. Accordingly, they get to rate your compilation. If enough of them grade you favorably, your iMix may also be featured on the album pages of featured artists. By my way of thinking, that gives you as much credibility as any *American Idol* judge.

The search for great music continues

Check out the following list for other ways to stumble upon terrific music. Make sure you have time on your hands. The quest can be deeply addictive:

- ✔ **Search:** A great starting point in your exploration is to search for artists or song titles by entering the name in the Search Music Store box near the upper-right corner of the screen. You can put more weight behind your search by clicking Power Search from the Inside the Music Store list. It lets you search by several parameters simultaneously (song, artist, album, genre, and composer).

- ✔ **Browse:** If you're not starting out with a particular artist in mind, click Browse from the Inside the Music Store list. You see a window such as the one shown in Figure 14-12. Choose a genre in the column to the left, a subgenre in the column to its right, an artist in the next column, and so on, until you've narrowed the list down to tunes you want to own.

- ✔ **Top Artist Downloads:** If you happen upon an album page but aren't familiar with the performer's music, consult the Top Artists Downloads list and click to hear your 30-second sample.

- ✔ **Listeners also bought:** If you're impressed by what you hear from a given artist, you may also be attracted to other music purchased by fans of the artist's work.

- ✔ **Charts:** Consult Billboard's Top Charts for a list of the Billboard Hot 100, Top Country, or Top R&B by year. The Billboard Top 100 dates back to 1946, when in reality it was the Top 41. Perry Como anyone?

  You can also click Radio Charts to get lists of songs playing on radios station in cities ranging from Appleton-Oshkosh to Augusta, as you can see in Figure 14-13.

Figure 14-12:
Browsing
for music is
nirvana.

Figure 14-13:
What's
playing in
Oshkosh?

✔ **Hobnob with the stars:** Well not exactly hobnob. But an eclectic cast of the rich and famous — Liv Tyler, Ramsey Lewis, Blondie, Jay-Z, Kiefer Sutherland, Sharon Stone, Eurythmics, William Shatner, Bill Maher, Billy Bob Thornton, Carole King, B.B. King, Nicole Kidman, Russell Crowe, Heidi Klum, Sarah McLachlan, Jennifer Garner, Taye Diggs, Jackie Chan, Smokey Robinson, RuPaul, Andrew Lloyd Webber, Kanye West, Sting, Al Franken, Lance Armstrong, the Reverend Al Green, and many more — have put together lists of their favorite works. The artists usually provide brief descriptions of why they chose certain songs, as shown in Figure 14-14. Regrettably, purchasing songs from these celebrity playlists is not an automatic ticket to stardom.

✔ **Just For You:** Apple is testing a service called Just For You, which has personalized recommendations based on your past musical purchasing habits. It'll serve up suggestions such as "You own *Groovin'.* We recommend: Herman's Hermit's Retrospective." Or "You bought *Guero.* We recommend *Stand Up,* Dave Matthews Band." Under each suggestion you can click "Already Own It" or "Don't Like It." The idea is that as Apple learns more about what tickles your fancy, it will provide sharper recommendations over time. The company can also steer you to certain songs through its iTunes MiniStore, as the "MiniStore, minicontroversy" sidebar explains.

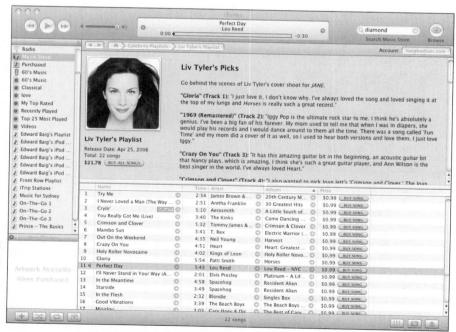

Figure 14-14:
Listen with Liv or other celebs.

MiniStore, minicontroversy

Apple initially took some grief when it rolled out the iTunes MiniStore as part of an iTunes software release in January 2006. The feature is meant to help you discover new music when you click items in your own library. As you do so, the MiniStore shows songs that relate to the material you're listening to, as shown in the figure. Citing possible privacy breaches, however, some critics went after Apple for failing to disclose what it was doing. In short order, Apple alleviated the concerns by turning the MiniStore off by default. Now you must opt-in by clicking the Show/Hide MiniStore button (labeled in Figure 14-4).

When you're ready to buy

So now that you have all these recommendations, you're ready to spend some money. First, though, you have to set up an account with Apple (assuming you haven't already done so) or use an existing AOL account. Here's how:

1. **In the Source List, click Music Store.**

2. **In the sign-in window, click Create New Account.**

3. **Fill in the requested credit card and other info.**

4. **The rest is easy. Find a song you want to buy and click Buy Song.**

To make sure you really mean it, Apple serves up the warning shown in Figure 14-15.

5. Click Buy to complete the transaction.

In a matter of seconds (usually) the song is downloaded to the aptly named Purchased playlist.

Figure 14-15: We're happy to take your money but...

Are you sure you want to buy and download the Song "Hey Good Lookin'"?

Your credit card will be charged for this purchase and your music will begin to download immediately.

☐ Don't ask me about buying Songs again.

Cancel   Buy

Once a week, you can download a free single handpicked by Apple (or sometimes even more than one). The freebies are typically from artists you've never heard of, though the music is usually quite good. The downloading experience is identical to buying any track except you're clicking Get Song instead of Buy Song.

Apple's generosity has a hidden cost. The company is taking the Lay's Potato Chip "bet you can't eat just one" approach. The expectation is that you'll stick around the Music Store for awhile and part with your hard-earned money at some point. Heck, less than a buck a track doesn't sound like much for those songs you just *gotta* have. But take it from first-hand experience, those 99¢ tunes add up quickly. To find out just how much you're spending, click the Account window, enter your password, and choose View Account. You can click Purchase History to check out your latest transactions.

If you click Manage Artist Alerts on the Account Information page, Apple will send you e-mail letting you know when artists whose music you've bought in the past have added new music to the Music Store. To do so, select the Send Me Artist Alerts for All Artists in My Purchase History option. Just another way to get you to part with your money.

Allowances and gifts

If you've bought one too many lame sweaters or neckties over the years as an 11th-hour birthday gift, iTunes may be your salvation. Click Gift Certificates to buy something truly valuable. iTunes Gift Certificates can be issued in amounts from $10 to $200. You can e-mail the certificate, print it, or have it go out through the U.S. Mail. The whole shebang takes a minute or so.

Digital rights police

When you buy a regular compact disc, you can pretty much do with it whatever you like. Pop the disc into as many CD players as you have access to. Copy the songs (via iTunes) onto your Mac. Fling the thing like a Frisbee for all anyone cares.

So what exactly do you own when you purchase a song electronically from iTunes? The rights to listen to that song on just five "authorized" computers. If you try to share music on a sixth machine, you're told you need to deauthorize one

of the previous five. To do so, make sure the computer is connected to the Net. Then under the Advanced menu in iTunes, click Deauthorize Computer. The five-machine limit applies to Macs as well as Windows machines. You can also deauthorize all five machines at once by choosing Deauthorize All on the Account Information page. Quick takeaway: If you're getting rid of an old machine, remember to deauthorize it.

In the list on the left side of the Music Store under Account, click Gift Certificates for the particulars. To redeem a certificate you've received, start out at the same place.

If you click Allowance instead, you can set up a regular monthly allowance (in the same $10 to $200 amounts) that gets automatically topped off on the first of the each month. If all goes well, Junior will learn a thing or two about fiscal responsibility. Unused balances are saved until your kid makes another purchase. Of course, should your son or daughter abuse any privileges, you can pull the plug on his or her iTunes allowance at any time by heading over to the Account Information page.

You can drag songs into a playlist and give them as gifts, even if you don't own the songs. You hear the 30-second previews; your recipients get the full treatment. Click the arrow next to the playlist and click Give Playlist.

You can also give an entire album inside the iTunes Music store by selecting Gift This Music on the Album page.

Sharing music with other computers

If your Mac is part of a local computer network (see Chapter 18), you can share the music in your library with other machines running iTunes version 4.5 or later. Go to iTunes Preferences, click Sharing, and select the Share My Music option. You can share the entire library or selected playlists. For added security, you can require users of other computers to enter a password. iTunes must remain open for other computers to access your music. Limits apply, as indicated in the "Digital rights police" sidebar.

iTunes: More Than Just Music

I'm wondering how long the iTunes Music Store will be known as, well, the iTunes Music Store? iTunes *Media* Store seems a more accurate descriptor because, as you know by now, you can purchase a lot more than just music, and share it on an iPod.

Listening to audiobooks

From Ernest Hemingway to James Patterson, you can fetch the iTunes equivalent of books on tape. You can sample 90-second previews, three times as long as music selections. Of course, audio books can go on for hours, compared to three or four minutes for your average song. Prices vary too. A 22-minute audio of Stephen Colbert's remarks at the White House Correspondents' Dinner costs $1.95; an 8½-hour audio version of "Papa" Hemingway's *A Farewell to Arms* goes for $25.95. Choose Audiobooks from the Inside the Music Store list and start prowling the virtual bookshelves for interesting titles.

Capturing podcasts

Podcasts are another form of Internet radio but very different from the radio I described earlier in this chapter. For one thing, some podcasts go beyond radio and show video. Moreover, instead of listening to live streams via the Net, podcasts are downloadable files you can listen to whenever you get around to it.

As you'll see after choosing the Podcasts genre inside iTunes, podcasts cover a broad range of topics (business, politics, sports, TV and film, technology, and so on) and are served up by experienced broadcasters, mainstream media outlets (National Public Broadcasting, *Newsweek, USA TODAY, Wall Street Journal*), as well as ordinary Joe's and Josephine's.

Podcasts are free to download and (typically) commercial free. You can fetch individual episodes by clicking Get Episode or subscribe to podcasts that arrive on a regular basis. As with audiobooks, you can click to hear a 90-second sample.

You can find the podcasts you've downloaded by clicking Podcasts in the Source list.

Choose the Podcasts tab under iTunes Preferences to manage your podcasts. Among other choices, you can instruct iTunes on how often to check for new episodes (such as daily or weekly) and how long to keep episodes you've downloaded (all unplayed, most recent, last two, last five, and more). You can also dictate which podcasts should be transferred over to an iPod.

You can submit your own podcast directly to Apple by clicking the Submit a Podcast link on the main iTunes page. You'll have to provide the podcast's RSS feed. Apple reserves the right to review podcasts before posting them. You can create a podcast through GarageBand software, as I elaborate on in Chapter 17.

Catching up on Lost and Desperate Housewives

Quick story. I had never seen the hit series *Lost* before downloading the pilot episode onto iTunes (and then an iPod). I was instantly hooked. I immediately understood the power of iTunes/iPod video.

Lost and *Desperate Housewives* were among the first handful of TV shows that Apple made available on iTunes. The number of programs quickly mushroomed to incorporate everything from *The Daily Show with Jon Stewart* to NASCAR highlights. Music videos and short films are also available.

Videos inside iTunes cost $1.99 apiece; as with audio tracks you can sample 30-second previews.

You can drag movie or video files you create yourself or obtain from other sources into iTunes.

Before you can transfer some videos to an iPod, you may have to convert them to a format iPod recognizes. Select the video, and choose Advanced⇨Convert Selection for iPod.

As video becomes even more prevalent, you'll see a lot of those earbud people gazing intently at their iPod displays.

Chapter 15

Taking an iPhoto Close-Up

Disruptive technology is a concept that has been floating around for nearly a decade. Loosely defined, it describes how a once dominant technology gets elbowed aside and eventually displaced by something new. The idea was coined by Harvard B-School professor Clayton M. Christensen, and those Ivy educators are pretty darn smart.

Disruptive technology is just what seems to be happening in the world of photography, where digital cameras have dramatically overtaken the film side of the picture-taking biz. Ever cheaper and more capable cameras are becoming so pervasive that they're even built into numerous mass-market cell phones.

For consumers, digital cameras afford lots of advantages over their film counterparts. Most notably, you can preview shots before you ever snap an image. (Try that one with your old man's Instamatic.) What's more, if you aren't pleased with the results after taking the picture — for goodness sakes, one kid is looking sideways and the other has her eyes shut — you can erase it on the spot with no harm done and without having to pay to get the shot developed.

With iPhoto, Apple brings its own special smarts to digital photography. The program is part digital shoebox, part processing lab, part touch-up artist, and more. Through this wondrous member of the iLife suite, you can import, organize, view, edit, and ultimately share your masterpieces with an adoring public (or, at the very least, family and friends).

Getting Pictures into the Computer

Taking pictures with most digital cameras is a snap. Taking *good* digital pictures is another matter entirely and beyond the — pun alert — focus of this book.

When you press your digital camera's shutter button, images are typically captured onto small (and removable) memory cards. Even as the price of memory declines, the capacity on these cards rises. You can now capture many hundreds of pictures on relatively inexpensive cards.

In the past, it was a challenge to get digital images onto your computer, where the real fun begins. iPhoto drastically simplifies the process. Take a gaze at Figure 15-1 to familiarize yourself with some of the program's main elements. There's a lot here, which we'll delve into throughout this chapter.

Connecting a digital camera

In most cases, you run a direct connection from the digital camera to the Mac by connecting the USB cable supplied with the camera. Turn the camera off and then plug one end of the cable into the camera and the other end into the Mac. Turn the camera back on.

iPhoto opens, assuming you clicked Yes when the program asked you whether you want to use iPhoto to download photos when a camera is connected. (This questions pops up the first time you launch the program.) The way iPhoto takes charge, you won't even have to install the software that came with your camera. Given how cumbersome some of these programs can be, that, my friends, is a blessing.

Information/calendar/keywords pane

Source list (rolls and albums appear here)

Viewer   Scroll guide

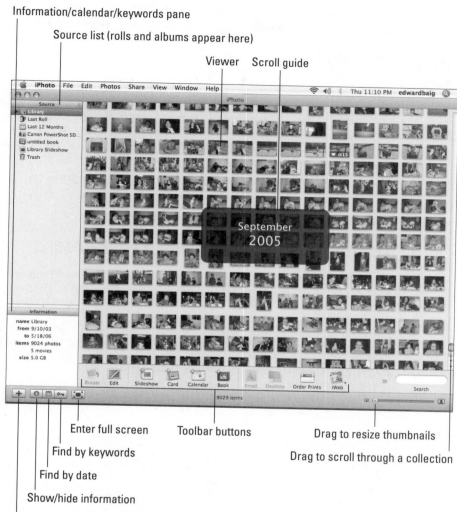

Figure 15-1:
Zooming in
on iPhoto.

Enter full screen   Toolbar buttons   Drag to resize thumbnails

Find by keywords   Drag to scroll through a collection

Find by date

Show/hide information

Click to create a new album, smart album, book, or slideshow

If everything went down as it should and iPhoto was called into action, skip ahead to the next section. If you ran into a problem, you can try the following:

✔ Check to make sure your camera is turned on and you have a fresh set of batteries.

✔ Because every camera is different, consult the instructions that came with your model to make sure it's in the proper setting for importing pictures (usually Play mode). Don't you just hate when that happens? You want an answer now, and here I am directing you to some manual that was likely translated into English from another language. Translated poorly, I might add.

✔ As a last resort, make sure your camera is compatible with OS X by visiting www.apple.com/macosx/upgrade/cameras.html.

Importing images from the camera

When you connect a camera and iPhoto comes to life, the main screen will indicate that it's ready to import images, as you can see in Figure 15-2.

Figure 15-2: Getting ready to import your pictures.

To transfer images, follow these steps:

1. **Type a Roll Name and Description for your photos in the appropriate fields.**

2. **Determine whether you want to erase the pictures from the camera after they have been copied onto iPhoto.**

   To do so, select the Delete Items from Camera After Importing option. If you're not sure, you can always delete images directly from the camera later.

3. **Click Import.**

   Your pictures are on their way to their new home inside iPhoto's digital shoebox; the process may take several minutes depending on how many pictures you're moving over. The time depends on a variety of factors, including the number and quality of the images being imported. You'll see the images whiz by as they're being copied.

4. **When the program has finished importing, click the eject button or drag the camera's name from the source list to iPhoto trash, at the bottom of the source list.**

5. **Turn off and disconnect the camera.**

Seeing double? If iPhoto detects a duplicate photo it will ask whether you're sure you want to copy it over again. Click Import to proceed or Don't Import to skip this particular image. To avoid getting this question for each duplicate image, select the Apply to All Duplicates option.

iPhoto will also copy over movie clips from your digital camera, provided they're compatible with QuickTime. These videos are automatically transferred in the same way as still images.

Importing images from other sources

Not all the pictures in your iPhoto library arrive by direct transfer from your digital camera. Some reach the Mac by the Web, e-mail, CDs or DVDs, flash drives, or memory card readers. Other pictures may already reside some place else on your hard drive.

To get these pictures into iPhoto, simply drag them into the iPhoto viewing area or onto the iPhoto dock icon. You can drag individual pictures or an entire folder or disk.

If you prefer, choose File⇨Import to Library and browse for the files you want to bring over. Then click Import.

iPhoto is compatible with JPEG and TIFF, the most common image file formats, as well as a photo enthusiast format (available on some digital cameras) known as RAW.

If you haven't bought a digital camera yet and are shooting 35mm film, you can still play in iPhoto's sandbox. Have your neighborhood film processor transfer images onto a CD or post them on the Web. Given where the film processing industry is heading, it'll be thrilled to have your business.

Finding and Organizing Images

Right from the outset, iPhoto helps you organize pics so you can more easily find the ones you want to view later. All the imported pictures are stuffed in the iPhoto library, which you can easily access by clicking Library in the source list on the upper-left side of the screen.

Your entire image collection shows up in a grid of *thumbnails,* or mini pictures, in the main viewing area on the right. If you're having trouble making out those thumbnails, drag the slider at the bottom-right corner and watch how those thumbnails grow. Cool, huh? Now drag the slider to the left to make the pictures shrink. You can peek at many more pictures in the viewing area that way.

Double-click a photo to make it larger. Click Done to return to the thumbnail view.

Movie thumbnails appear with a little camera icon and the duration of the clip. Clicking a movie thumbnail opens the QuickTime Player.

Oh, and don't worry about your photo library growing too large, no matter how prolific a photographer you may be. Version 6 of iPhoto can accommodate up to 250,000 pictures. To convince you that that's a very big number, Apple's marketers point out that you can take 1,000 snapshots a month for 20 years and still not bump up against the limit.

Of course, if all Apple did was drop all those pictures into one large digital dumping ground, you'd have a heck of a time finding that oh-so-precious shot of your proud kid getting her elementary school diploma. So how do you uncover the very images you want to admire over and over? Let us count the ways.

For starters, iPhoto organizes pictures into virtual *film rolls.* Remember when you imported pictures and were asked to fill in a Roll Name? You'd be wise to fill in something descriptive (such as Paris Vacation) because months from now collections called "Roll 07" or "Roll 359" won't be very revealing.

Apple automatically creates some rolls on your behalf. For instance, to help you locate the batch of pictures you just imported, iPhoto conveniently places them into a folder named Last Roll. If you click Last Roll in the source list, those are the only photographs you'll see.

If you're looking for the pictures you took during, say, the past year instead, click the Last 12 Months roll.

Go to Preferences under the iPhoto menu and click the General tab if you want to change what's shown in the source list from Last 12 Months to an album containing photos in the Last 1 to 19 months.

In the same section, you change the source list display from Last Roll to Last 2, 3, 4, all the way up to 25 rolls.

Navigating with the iPhoto calendar

Now suppose you want to display just the pictures you took around the time your little angel was born. Click the calendar icon at the bottom-left corner of the screen and scroll to the month and date in which you want to display pictures, as shown in Figure 15-3.

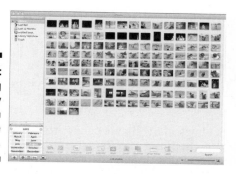 

Figure 15-3: Viewing pictures by the month and by the day.

iPhoto captures more than just photos when picture files are transferred over. Through captured *metadata,* the program knows the make and model of the camera used to take the image; the date and time the picture was taken and imported; the size in *pixels,* or picture elements; the aperture setting of the camera; whether a flash was used; and more. Such data is factored into Spotlight searches.

Navigating with the Scroll Guide

You can scan for pictures in your library taken during a specific period by dragging the scroll bar on the right edge of the iPhoto screen. As you do so, a floating translucent panel called *Scroll Guide* appears in the middle of the window showing you the date and (depending on preferences) title of each film roll.

Assigning keywords

Keywords may be the key to finding pictures in the future. These are labels, or tags, applied to a set of photos. Apple provides some keywords right off the bat: Favorite, Family, Kids, Vacation, and Birthday. You create your own keywords by selecting the Keywords tab under iPhoto Preferences (see Figure 15-4) and clicking the + (Add) button.

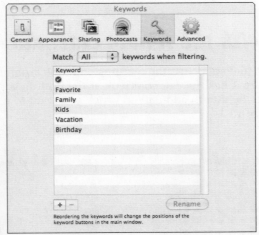

Figure 15-4:
The key to keywords.

Above the list of keywords is a check mark. Its purpose is to flag all the photos you may want to pull together for a specific project. The check mark shows up in the bottom-right corner of a thumbnail on selected images.

To actually assign keywords (or the check mark) to specific photos:

1. **Select the specific picture.**

2. **Choose Photos⇨Get Info.**

3. **Make sure the Keywords Tab option under Get Info is highlighted.**

4. **Place a check mark next to the keyword (or keywords) you want to use for the image.**

   As an alternative to Steps 2 to 4, open the keywords pane on the bottom-left corner of the screen by clicking the button that looks like, well, a key. Drag the photo onto the appropriate keyword.

Now that the underlying keywords are in place, how the heck do you put them into action? Open the keywords pane and click one or more of the keyword buttons. The clicked buttons turn blue, and the iPhoto viewer displays only those pictures that match the highlighted keywords.

Now suppose that you want to display pictures that match one keyword *or* another (Family or Vacation, for example). This time, click the keywords in question while also holding down the Shift key. The keys turn purple. Again, the viewer will show only the appropriate collection of pictures.

If you want to hide pictures with certain keywords — I won't ask, so don't tell — press Option on the keyboard while clicking the keyword or keywords you want to hide. The keyword buttons turn red, and pictures represented by those keywords are *not* shown.

Assigning ratings

You can also assign ratings to pictures on a scale between zero and five stars. There are several ways to do this with selected images:

- Choose Photos⇨My Rating and click the number of stars you have in mind.
- Open the Information pane by clicking the little circled *i* button near the bottom-left corner of the screen, and then click the representative dot next to Rating.
- While holding down the ⌘ key, press the 1, 2, 3, 4, or 5 key (representing the number of stars) on the keyboard.

Placing your work into albums

In the film age, really organized people took the time to methodically place prints into old-fashioned picture albums. I admire people like that because I lack this particular organizing gene.

Fortunately, the iPhoto equivalent of lumping pictures into albums is much simpler. The process is similar to creating playlists in iTunes (see Chapter 14). So you can place all the pictures from your ski trip in one album, pictures of the high school reunion in another, and so on. Here's the drill:

1. **Choose File⇨New Album, or click the + button at the bottom-left corner of the iPhoto screen.**

2. **Type a name for your album (Hawaii Honeymoon, Dance Recital, whatever)**

3. **Click Create.**

The name of your new album shows up in the source list. Now you have to populate that album with pictures, as follows:

✔ Drag individual photos onto the Album name or icon in the source list.

✔ To select a batch of photos to drag over, hold down the ⌘ key while clicking the pictures you want to include.

✔ To select adjoining photos, hold down the Shift key and use the arrow buttons.

✔ To select all the photos between two photos, hold down Shift and click the first image, then hold Shift and click the last image. All the pictures in between will be selected.

As you drag a batch of photos en masse to the album, a little red circle indicates how many pictures you're moving over.

If you want to select the photos *before* creating an album, select the pics and then choose File⇨New Album From Selection.

Although photos are lumped into albums, the pictures actually remain in the iPhoto library. The images inside albums are merely pointers to the original files. So you can place the same picture in multiple albums. You can also remove pictures from an album without fear that the images will be deep-sixed from the iPhoto library.

After you create a bunch of albums, you can group them into a folder. Choose File⇨New Folder. Give the folder a name (such as Vacations) and drag all the relevant albums into the folder. When you select the newly created folder, you'll see all the pictures stored in all the albums contained in that folder.

Creating a smart photo album

Just as you can create smart playlists in iTunes, you can sire *smart albums* in iPhoto based on specific criteria, such as keywords, photos you've rated highly, pictures taken with a particular camera, or the shutter speed. To create a smart album:

1. **Choose File⇨New Smart Album.**

2. **Type a name, just as you do with a regular album.**

3. **Select the conditions that must be met for pictures to be included in the Smart Album.**

   Click the + button to add matching criteria or the – button to remove criteria. As new pictures are imported to your library, those that match these conditions are added automatically to the smart album.

In Figure 15-5, I've set up a smart album seeking only highly rated pictures taken without a flash at the beach since the end of 2004.

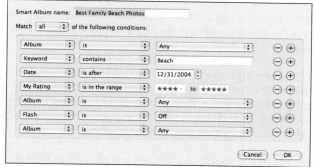

Figure 15-5: A very smart album.

Viewing pictures

In the main viewing area, photos are displayed in the order in which you imported them. If you want to change the order, choose View⇨Sort Photos, and then choose an option, such as By Film Roll or By Rating.

Under the View menu, you can also decide whether to display the titles, keywords, film rolls, and ratings of your photos.

Touching Up Your Photos

Here's a dirty little secret. The drop-dead gorgeous models gracing the covers of magazines don't really look like that. (Well maybe some do, but work with me here.) The unsung heroes are the touch-up artists, who remove a flaw from a picture here, a blemish there. We should all be so lucky to be able to put our own mugs in the best light. And lucky we are for having iPhoto on the Mac.

Now iPhoto is by no means a photo editing superstar along the lines of Adobe's Photoshop. But for the mainstream snapshooter, iPhoto comes with several handy editing tools for removing red eye or applying special effects.

We'll get around to these in a moment. But first let's examine a new majestic way to display your images in iPhoto that can help you take advantage of every last pixel.

The full-screen treatment

In iPhoto 6, Apple added a full-screen viewing option that takes advantage of today's large and beautiful computer displays. What's more, Apple lets you edit in this mode.

To enter the full-screen edit mode, select a photo from the main viewing area and click the full screen button (labeled in Figure 15-1). When you roll your mouse at the *top* of the screen, a strip of thumbnails called the *photo browser* (see Figure 15-6) slides in and out of view. Roll your mouse to the bottom of the screen to slide the various editing tools into view.

You can compare between two and eight photos in the full-screen view by holding ⌘ while clicking thumbnails in the photo browser. If you click the Compare button instead, the photo you choose is compared with the one to its immediate right.

If you prefer the full-screen view all the time, go to iPhoto Preferences and click the General tab. Under the Edit Photo drop-down list, select Using Full Screen.

Photo browser

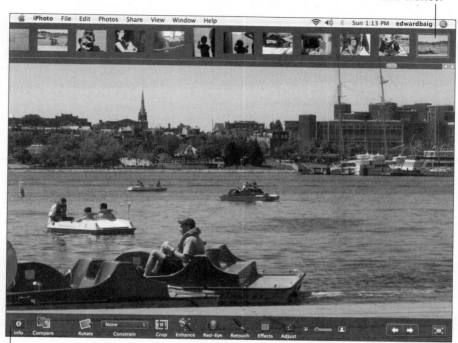

Figure 15-6:
Full-screen
editing
majesty.

Editing tools

To exit the full-screen mode, press the Escape key on the keyboard.

If you want to edit photos from the conventional view instead, double-click a thumbnail in the viewing area, and the same editing tools you see in the full screen view appear below the selected image. Alternatively, highlight a picture and click Edit in the menu bar.

Let's have a look at some of those editing buttons now.

Rotating an image

Sometimes the picture that turns up in the photo library is oriented incorrectly because of the way you rotated the camera when shooting the original. To fix the orientation in iPhoto, select the image and click Rotate on the editing toolbar, at the bottom of the screen. The image rotates counterclockwise by 90 degrees. Keep clicking until the picture is oriented properly. Press the Option key while clicking to make the picture flip the other way.

Cropping an image

Cropping means snipping away at the periphery of an image, so you can get up close and personal to the subject at hand while removing traces of that Yo-Yo in the background who is sticking his tongue out.

To crop an image:

1. **Click Crop on the editing toolbar.**

2. **Choose the cropping area:**

   • To choose your own cropping area, click None from the Constrain menu. Move your pointer over the image and drag it diagonally across the area of the image you want to keep.

   • To limit the crop area to a specific dimension, click Constrain and make a selection.

   Among the choices, select 4 x 6 for a postcard, 20 x 30 for a poster, or 4 x 3 if you plan on using the picture in a coffee table book, which I discuss later this chapter. iPhoto puts a translucent gray border around the potential cropping area.

3. **Use the mouse to drag the crop area into the proper position.**

4. **Click Crop and then Done to save your changes.**

 If you're unhappy with a newly cropped picture, choose Edit⇨Undo (or press ⌘+Z). And at any time, you can choose Photos⇨Revert to Original and pretend like nothing happened.

If you want to crop an image *and* keep the original, choose Photos⇨Duplicate. Give the cloned picture a name and use it to do your cropping.

Repairing blemishes

What do you do when that otherwise immaculate portrait is ruined by a small stain on your sweater? Or the sudden appearance on your face of the *zit that ate Cincinnati?*

Click Retouch on the editing toolbar to turn on iPhoto's high-tech spot remover or software airbrush. Hold down the mouse button and use the crosshair pointer to brush over the freckle, blotch, or pimple. iPhoto paints over these spots using surrounding colors. Use short strokes to avoid smearing an image and making the picture appear even more ghoulish. Click Retouch again when you're finished.

Retouching larger images is easier than smaller ones, making full-screen mode all the more valuable when editing thusly. Still (I hate to be the one to tell you this), getting rid of minor defects won't win you a modeling contract.

Press the Control key to toggle and compare your touch-up job with the original picture. As before if you're not pleased with the result, you can Revert to Original.

Enhance and adjust

The quick fix Enhance tool automatically brightens a faded or too-dark image or adjusts one that's too bright by correcting the image's color saturation and tint. Click the Enhance button once, and iPhoto does the rest.

In reality, the picture isn't always enhanced, but as usual you have a variety of undo options. And again, press and release the Control key to easily compare the new image with the old.

While iPhoto does all the work for you inside Enhance, Adjust puts the onus on *you.* Clicking Adjust brings up a palette like the one shown in Figure 15-7. Manually drag the sliders to adjust the brightness, contrast, sharpness, exposure, and other settings. If you get totally lost after mucking with these settings, click Reset Sliders to start from scratch.

Figure 15-7:
Getting
adjusted.

Reducing red-eye

Flash photography often results in *red-eye,* where it looks like your subject is auditioning for the lead role in *Rosemary's Baby: All Grown Up.* Fortunately, iPhoto, like Visine, can get the red out.

The operation is devilishly simple. Click the Red-Eye button and place the crosshairs pointer in the center of each red eye. Use the size slider to zoom in on each reddened pupil and click. Click the Red-Eye button again to complete the exorcism.

Special effects

Clicking the Effects button brings up a tic-tac-toe style panel with eight one-click special effects (a ninth button, in the center, brings the photo back to its Original state).

Black & White, Sepia, and Antique (an aging effect) affect the actual image. So do Fade Color, which lessens the color intensity in a photo, and Boost Color, which has the opposite effect. You can repeatedly click the mouse to lay on the effects even more. Clicking Matte, Vignette, and Edge Blur alter the edges of the picture.

Admiring and Sharing Pictures

Until now, we've been speaking of organizing and doctoring images. But enough of that. It's time to sit back and admire our handiwork. And then show off our Ansel Adams skills to everyone else.

Creating slideshows

If you're of a certain generation, you may remember having to sit still while your parents pulled out the Kodak Carousel Slide Projector. "There we are in front of the Grand Canyon. There we are in front of the Grand Canyon — *from a slightly different angle*."

The 21st-century slideshow, care of a Macintosh, brings a lot more pizzazz. Your pictures are backed with a soundtrack right out of your iTunes library. You can slowly zoom in and out of photos employing the Ken Burns Effect, named after the documentary filmmaker.

To create a slide show, follow these steps:

1. **Choose the album or groups of photos you want in your show.**

2. **Click the Slideshow button on the toolbar.**

3. **Select the order you want photos in the show to appear by dragging them on the photo browser.**

4. **Click Music to choose a soundtrack from iTunes, GarageBand (Chapter 17), or from sample music included with iPhoto.**

5. **Click Settings and make your selections.**

   You can choose how long you want to play each slide (3 seconds is the default) and choose a transition between slides (Dissolve, Page Flip, Twirl, and so on). Remove the check mark if you don't want to use the Automatic Ken Burns Effect. Add check marks if you want to scale photos to fit the screen, and show titles, ratings, and slideshow controls. You can also choose whether to repeat music during the slideshow or whether to adjust slide durations so they will play as long as the music plays.

6. **When you're satisfied with the settings, click OK.**

7. **If you want to tweak settings for individual slides, click Adjust.**

8. **To preview visual changes to slides in a smaller window without sound, click Preview.**

9. **Click Play to get on with the show.**

You can rotate and rate pictures in a slideshow on-the-fly or pause the show by moving your cursor onto the screen.

You can also burn your slideshow to a DVD or export it to a QuickTime movie. We'll talk more about burning DVDs in Chapter 16.

E-mailing pictures

To send pictures using e-mail, highlight an image in your library or in an album and click the Email button on the editing toolbar. Or hold down the ⌘ key to select a bunch of photos to e-mail.

You'll be asked to choose a size for the photo (small, medium, large, or actual size) in the dialog box that appears in Figure 15-8.

Figure 15-8:
Size matters
when
sending
photos via
e-mail.

Mail Photo

Photo

Size ✓ Small (Faster Downloading)
       ✓ Medium
         Large (Higher Quality)
         Actual Size (Full Quality)   Choose size for emailed photos

Include: ☑ Titles   ☑ Comments

Cancel   Compose

Smaller files are faster to send and download; the larger files boast superior quality but may not slip past your ISP's server size limitations.

Before clicking Compose, decide whether you want to include the titles and comments with your photo by selecting those options (or not).

Click Compose. Tiger's Mail program opens with the picture already attached (assuming Mail is your default e-mail application). Fill in the recipient's address, type a subject line, and add any additional prose before sending the picture on its merry way.

Visit iPhoto Preferences if you want to send e-mail through another Mail program such as AOL or Eudora.

You can also e-mail pictures as attachments through such Web-based e-mail programs as Gmail, Hotmail, and Yahoo! Mail.

Booking them

There aren't many guarantees in life. But one of them is that bound coffee-table photo books of the family make splendid presents. Apple makes it a breeze to design these professionally printed 8½-by-11-inch books. And when the grandparents see what *you* produced, don't be shocked if they ask how come you're not working in the publishing business.

From iPhoto, you choose the size and design of these books and of course choose the batch of photos to be included. Images are sent out over the Internet to a printing plant, which binds and ships the book (within days) on your behalf to its final destination.

As of this writing, Apple's hardcover photo books start around $30 (for 10 pages). Medium and large softcover versions start at $10 to $20, respectively. Small-sized 2.6-by-3.5-inch books (sold three books at a time) fetch $12.

Here's how to go about designing a photo book:

1. **Choose the photos you want in the book.**

2. **Click the Book button on the editing toolbar.**

   The Book Type dialog box appears.

3. **Select the size of your book, and whether you want double-sided pages.**

4. **Choose a book design.**

   Among your choices are Picture Book, Formal, Travel, Baby Boy, and Baby Girl. Some themes let you type text with your pictures. For detailed descriptions, click the Options + Pricing button

5. **Click Choose Theme.**

   You are now in *book view*. Figure 15-9 shows the current page of your book in the main iPhoto viewer, below a thumbnail strip of pictures you can manually drag onto photo placeholders in the page layouts.

6. **If you want to fatten your book, click Add Pages on the editing toolbar.**

7. **To determine the layout of pictures on a page and whether to add text, click Page Design.**

   If you want iPhoto to arrange your book for you (it's not nearly as much fun), choose Autoflow.

8. **When you're satisfied, click Buy Book to enter credit card and shipping information.**

Figure 15-9:
Publishing
the great
photo book.

You can also turn your book into a slideshow. Choose the book from the source list and click the Play button. Click Settings to change transitions, choose background music, and tweak other effects, as described with regular slideshows earlier in this section.

Cards and calendars

Choose the Order Prints button to — this isn't a trick question — order prints directly from Kodak. You can choose various sizes, of course. You need an Apple account with Enable 1-Click Purchasing. (You'll be taken through the account process the first time you order.)

You can design a customized calendar (up to 24 months) by choosing a Theme (some with text), a start date, and whether to add national holidays (from about three dozen countries). You can also import your iCal calendars as well as birthdays from your Address Book.

An 8-by-10-inch 12-month calendar costs around $20.

Photocasting

What if your first child was born recently and you want to share images of the adorable infant with *everyone*. It's not practical to invite them all over to your house to view albums (unless they're willing to take turns changing diapers). And e-mailing the pictures to your entire extended family isn't practical given your lack of sleep.

Lots of online sites let you upload pictures to share with others. But what if you could "publish" an album so that pictures instantly appear in other people's iPhoto 6 library? What if anyone with an RSS reader (see Chapter 11) who "subscribes" to your album could also view the pictures? And what if each time you add or alter pictures in the album, the people given access will also see those changes?

You now have an understanding of the power of *photocasting,* an especially nifty feature introduced with iPhoto 6. Think podcasting for pictures. For some of you, photocasting might be the single best reason to sign up for a .Mac membership.

Here's how this particular bit of magic works:

1. **Choose the Album you want to share.**

2. **Choose Share⇨Photocast.**

   The dialog box shown in Figure 15-10 appears.

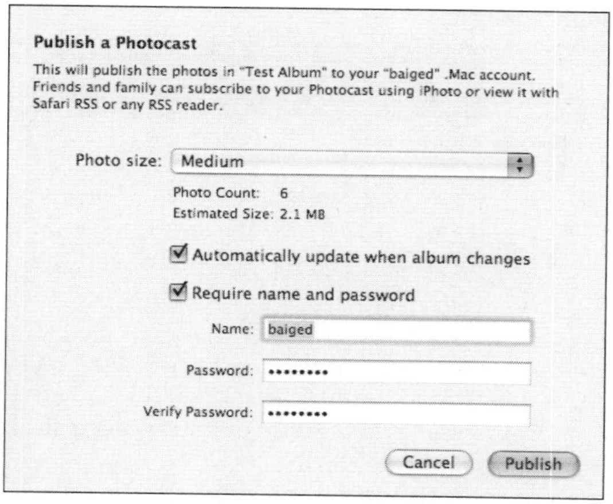

Publish a Photocast

This will publish the photos in "Test Album" to your "baiged" .Mac account. Friends and family can subscribe to your Photocast using iPhoto or view it with Safari RSS or any RSS reader.

Photo size: Medium

Photo Count: 6
Estimated Size: 2.1 MB

☑ Automatically update when album changes

☑ Require name and password

Name: baiged

Password: ••••••••

Verify Password: ••••••••

Cancel   Publish

Figure 15-10:
Publishing a
photocast.

3. **Choose a size for your photos (small, medium, large, actual size).**

4. **If you want the photocast to be constantly refreshed, select the Automatically Update When Album Changes option.**

5. **If you want to restrict access, select the Require Name and Password option and fill them in.**

6. **Click Publish.**

   A little circle turns up in the source list to let you know the photocast operation is underway. If your album contains a lot of pictures, the process may take awhile to complete. A dialog box appears with the URL or Web address to subscribe to your album.

7. **Click Announce Photocast to spread the word via an e-mail like the one shown in Figure 15-11.**

   The message tells your would-be subscribers how to proceed. An icon like the one shown here in the source list reminds you that your album is being photocast.

<table>
<tr><td>Send</td><td>Chat</td><td>Attach</td><td>Address</td><td>Fonts</td><td>Colors</td><td>Save As Draft</td></tr>
</table>

Announcing My New Photocast

To:

Cc:

Bcc:

Subject: Announcing My New Photocast

Account: Edward Baig <baiged@mac.com>   Signature: Signature #2

Hello,

I've published a Photocast using iPhoto that I'd like to share with you. To subscribe, just click on the following link:

http://photocast.mac.com/baiged/iPhoto/test-album/index.rss

If you have iPhoto 6, this Photocast will appear in your iPhoto Source list and you can use its photos just like any other photos in your library: for slideshows, your desktop, custom photo books, etc. And, whenever you are connected to the Internet, iPhoto will automatically update this Photocast so you see the latest photos I've added. (Requires Mac OS X version 10.4 or later)

If you don't have iPhoto 6, you can view the photos in this Photocast with Safari RSS or any compatible RSS reader on Mac, Windows or other computers by using the link above. Just click on the link or copy it into the URL field of your RSS reader and bookmark the URL to return to the photos in the future. Learn more about iPhoto 6 at www.apple.com/iphoto.

Note: If this Photocast is password protected, please contact me for the username and password.

Edward Baig
baiged@mac.com

Figure 15-11: Inviting subscribers to your photocast.

You can pull the plug on your photocast by returning to the Share menu, clicking Photocast and choosing Stop Publishing. This action removes the photos from your .Mac account but not from the iPhoto library.

If you can't recall how many albums you're publishing, visit the photocast section of iPhoto Preferences to consult the list.

Subscribers need not have iPhoto 6, or even a Mac, to admire your photocasts. However, they must have an RSS reader and must enter the URL you shared with them in your e-mail. Subscribers can drag photocast pictures into their own albums, books, calendars, and cards, but they can't erase or edit your pictures.

.Mac members can publish to iDisk a slideshow that others can view over the Internet. Choose Share⇨.Mac Slides and click the Publish button in the dialog box that appears. Then click Announce Slideshow to send an e-mail instructing folks on how to view the show.

Under the Share menu, you can also export a slideshow to iDVD, an application you get to know better in Chapter 16.

iPhoto Meet iWeb

As you know, the iLife applications are meant to work together. iPhoto gets along quite nicely with the newest member of the iLife suite, iWeb, Apple's clever Web page and blog creator.

iWeb is built around predesigned *templates* and placeholders for, among other things — you guessed it! — pictures. You can export photos from iPhoto to iWeb and then drag those pictures on top of placeholders, to replace images that had been warming up the spot. Just follow these steps:

1. **Select the photos you want to export.**

2. **Choose Share⇨Send to iWeb, and click either Photo Page or Blog.**

   iWeb opens (if it was not open already). You can also click the iWeb button in the iPhoto toolbar.

   Apple recommends sending 3 pictures max to a blog. You can add up to 99 pictures to a Web site.

3. **Inside iWeb, choose the template to which you want to add pictures and drag them onto the placeholder.**

If you choose a blog, iWeb creates a new blog entry for each picture. Type text explaining what the picture is all about.

Eventually you'll publish the whole shebang on .Mac — if you're a member, of course.

Sharing pix on your network

You can stream pictures to other computers connected to your local network. In iPhoto Preferences, click Sharing and then select the Share My Photos option. Add a password if desired. In Preferences, the other computers should select the Look for Shared Photos option. Although these other machines can display your images, they can't add pictures from the original machine to their library or albums. All the computers involved in sharing must have OS X version 10.2.6 or later and iPhoto 4 or later.

Preserving Your Digital Shoebox

I've already warned you I'm going to take every chance I get to ensure that you back up precious files. And what's more precious than keepsake photographs?

iPhoto makes it simple to burn CDs and DVDs. Per usual, select the photos you want to copy (individual pix, albums, or your entire library). Choose Share⇨Burn and insert a disc into your CD or DVD burner. Depending on the size of your collection and whether you have a CD or DVD burner, you may be able to archive your entire collection onto a single disc.

If you burn pictures inside iPhoto, they can be viewed later only in iPhoto. To create a disc that can be viewed also on a Windows machine or elsewhere, choose File⇨Export and then choose a file format such as JPG. Next, choose a location inside Finder. Quit iPhoto and open Finder. Make sure you have a CD or DVD in your burner and drag the folder with the photos you exported onto the disc icon. After the files have been copied, choose File⇨Burn Disk and then click Burn.

Whether you burn CDs or DVDs, you'll thank me if you ever have to retrieve photos from these discs. Losing a lifetime of memories is just the kind of disruption everyone seeks to avoid.

Chapter 16

Shooting an iMovie Screen Test

*H*ooray for Hollywood. Hooray for iLife. Apple's digital media suite, specifically through iMovie HD, provides the video editing and other software tools you need to satisfy your *auteur* ambitions. Then when the movie is in the can, you can find an audience with help from iDVD.

"I'd like to thank all the people who made this award possible. The wonderful cast and crew, my loving family, my agent. And a special thanks to Steve Jobs . . ."

Of course, even if your filmmaking aspirations are of a more modest nature — producing slick highlights of Johnny or Gillian's soccer games, rather than anything with genuine box office appeal — iMovie and iDVD are still a director and producer's best companions.

In this chapter, I'm working with version 6 of both iMovie and iDVD, available with the rest of the iLife '06 upgrade for $79.

Okay, then, let's get on with it. Places everyone. Ready? Action!

Tape, hard drive, and DVD camcorders

Not all digital camcorders sold today are simpatico with iMovie. Popular *MiniDV* camcorders make nice with Apple. These compact models, from such leading manufacturers as Sony, JVC, Panasonic, Canon, and Samsung, start at less than $300 and can fetch well into the four digits; prices for the MiniDV cassettes that you record on have dipped below $3.

Sony is the only maker of *Digital8* camcorders, whose main benefits are low prices and the ability to handle analog 8mm and Hi-8 tapes. Consider this camera if you have a sizable library of analog media. But there are few Digital8 models to choose from, and the cameras are bulkier than their MiniDV compadres.

If you intend to edit in iMovie, steer clear of another Sony camcorder type, *Micro MV.* The cameras and tapes are appealingly small, but they are pricey and aren't compatible with iMovie. Two other types of digital camcorders are also not well-suited for iMovie. These are camcorders that capture video directly onto miniature DVDs and hard drive models such as the expensive JVC Everio models.

In scary movie tech-speak, iMovie accepts imported video in the high-definition formats HDV 720p and 1080i (a discussion for later), as well as MPEG-4 and 16:9 cinematic widescreen. Basic footage is captured in NTSC and PAL, differing standards used around the world.

Shooting Your Oscar Winner

Legendary filmmaker Alfred Hitchcock is said to have asked, "What is drama but life with the dull bits cut out?" So before sitting in front of the Mac, you have to go out and capture some of that life on video. Trimming the dull stuff and converting your raw footage into worthy home cinema comes later.

Alas, I can't train you to become Hitchcock or Orson Welles or Steven Spielberg. Heck, if I could do that I'd be sipping martinis in Cannes right about now (or at least authoring *Filmmaking For Dummies.*) But I do know enough to send you off to Oz with the right gear. And that gear pretty much consists of a digital camcorder.

Using a digital camcorder

Sony is credited with producing the first camcorder, the 1983 Betamovie. It used a Betamax cassette. Through the ensuing decades, camcorders handled a variety of media: VHS tapes, VHS-C, 8 millimeter, Hi-8. These *analog* camcorders more than served their purpose for years. But as in almost every other corner of technology, camcorders too have gone digital. And why not? Video shot with a digital camcorder doesn't deteriorate when it's copied. Pristine sound is also preserved.

iMovie can exploit only video footage in digital form. The good news for consumers is that prices for most digital camcorders have plummeted in recent years. The most common type of digital camcorder makes use of matchbook-sized 60-minute *MiniDV* tapes. But you also have a lot of other choices, as shown in the "Tape, hard drive, and DVD camcorders" sidebar.

I advise searching online for camcorder options. Apple will be happy to sell you models at the store on its Web site, at www.apple.com. You can generally find excellent prices and a wide selection at www.bandhphoto.com. I also recommend a visit to www.camcorderinfo.com and a sister site for beginners at www.easycamcorders.com. These terrific resources feature reviews, ratings, and primers.

When you purchase a camcorder, make sure you also get the proper FireWire cable (4-pin-to-6 pin variety) to connect to your Mac. Just to confuse you, FireWire also sometimes goes by the name i-Link or IEEE 1394.

Using an iSight camera

Of absolutely no surprise to anyone, iMovie HD works fine with video captured by Apple's own iSight cameras, be it the standalone version or versions built in to iMacs, MacBook Pros, MacBooks, and late model PowerBooks. You must have iChat AV to use iSight with iMovie.

iSight and most of the consumer camcorders sold today deliver excellent results. But they're not HD (see the sidebar titled "The lowdown on high definition").

The lowdown on high definition

You might have guessed that the HD in iMovie HD stands for high definition, just like on increasingly popular (and affordable) HDTVs. Video produced in high definition boasts rich color and vivid detail: the ripples in a duck pond, the freckles and pores on a human face, each blade of grass on the ball field. Everything's in widescreen. Sound is equally superb. As this book was being published, prices for high-definition consumer camcorders would set you back at least $1300. Conveniently, they use the same MiniDV cassettes as standard definition digital camcorders, though any video you shoot in high definition, even on that same cassette, can't be played back through a standard camcorder.

From Here to Eternity: Camcorder to iMovie

Whether in high definition or not, you've shot scene after scene of amazing footage (what could be more dramatic than junior's first steps?). But remember Hitchcock's creed about getting rid of the dull bits? iMovie can help you do just that. First, though, you have to dump what you've captured into the computer.

When you open iMovie for the first time, most likely by clicking its dock icon, you're greeted with the window shown in Figure 16-1. Because this is your starting-off point, click Create a New Project. Later you can choose between Open an Existing Project or Make a Magic iMovie, a terrific let-the-Mac-do-most-of-the-work shortcut I'll get to later in the chapter.

Figure 16-1: You oughta be in pictures.

Importing from the camcorder

As you begin your project, these are the steps to follow:

1. **Type the name of your project and choose a destination folder on your hard drive.**

   Movies is the default folder.

2. **Select a video format from the pop up menu.**

   For now choose DV, the format used with most camcorders.

Of course, you can also select DV Widescreen, which results in a cinematic 16:9 *aspect ratio,* referring to the ratio of the width to the height of a picture. (Lots of state-of-the-art TVs can display video in widescreen.) You can also select iSight, MPEG 4, or high def formats HDV 1080i or HDV 720p.

3. Click Create.

The iMovie screen that appears resembles a director's clapper board. One view of the iMovie program is shown in Figure 16-2.

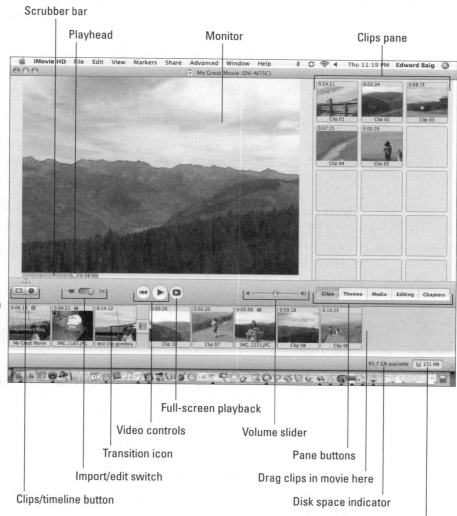

Scrubber bar

Playhead   Monitor   Clips pane

Figure 16-2:
The iMovie
program in
all its glory.

Full-screen playback

Video controls   Volume slider

Transition icon   Pane buttons

Import/edit switch   Drag clips in movie here

Clips/timeline button   Disk space indicator

Deleted footage goes in the trash

4. **Set the camcorder to VTR or Play or VCR mode, depending on the model.**

5. **If you haven't already done so, connect the camcorder to the Mac with a FireWire cable. Make sure the camera is turned on.**

6. **Back in iMovie, set the import/edit switch, which is below the monitor window, to the capture position.**

   Click so that the switch is to the left by the movie camera icon rather than on the right next to the scissors icon.

7. **If you have a machine with iSight, or have more than one camcorder connected, choose the camcorder you are using for the project at hand from the camera mode pop-up menu list.**

   You can now control your camcorder through the Mac by clicking iMovie's play, pause, stop, rewind, and fast-forward buttons.

8. **Use iMovie to rewind the tape to just before the footage you want to grab.**

9. **Click the Play button.**

10. **When you arrive at the precise section of the tape where you want to start capturing, press the spacebar or click the Import button in the iMovie monitor.**

    You can watch the video in the monitor area. At the same time, iMovie detects scene breaks and splits them off into *clips*. These land in the Clips pane to the right of the monitor.

11. **When you have all the footage you want, click Import or press the spacebar again.**

12. **Disconnect the camcorder.**

If you prefer, arrange to place clips directly on the movie timeline, whose advantages are discussed later in this chapter. Choose iMovie HD⇨ Preferences, click the Import tab, and make sure Movie Timeline is selected rather than Clips Pane.

Inside iMovie Preferences, you can also check whether you want to start a new clip at each scene break (the default) and whether you want to set designated time limits for your scenes.

Importing videos from other destinations

You may have video you want to use in your final blockbuster that's already on your hard drive. Or perhaps you want to incorporate video that's on a CD or DVD. Choose File⇨Import and browse for the videos (or still photos and audio for that matter) that you want to include.

All is not lost if you have an MPEG 4 camcorder with a USB connector instead of FireWire. Connect the camera through USB; the camera will appear as a hard disk icon on your desktop. Open the icon and drag the video onto your desktop or right into iMovie.

iMovie doesn't automatically break these videos into clips. Nor can you use the program's capture controls to import video or control the USB-connected camcorder.

This may be about the time you say a little prayer of thanks that you splurged for an extra-roomy (or additional) hard drive. Video consumes about 13 gigabytes for every hour of footage (and I'm not even talking high definition). After you finish your movie and put in on a DVD to share with family and friends, discard the unneeded footage so you'll have plenty of space for the sequel. iMovie is mindful of the available space on your hard drive; you'll see an indicator at the bottom-right corner of the screen.

Mastering Post-Production

Your raw footage is in place. In this section, you find out how moviemaking really gets accomplished: by arranging scenes and adding music, pictures, titles, transitions, and more. Get ready to unleash your creative juices. Assembling a movie is where the real joy begins.

Dragging, renaming, and rearranging clips

Adding a clip to your movie is as simple as dragging it from the Clips pane to the clip viewer or storyboard track. As Quentin Tarantino films prove time and again, movies do not *have* to be linear. Feel free to drag clips in any order and change them at will. Chronology be damned. When you drag a new clip between two existing scenes in the clip viewer, whichever clips are already there will step aside to make room.

Because the clips in the Clips pane take on such illuminating names as Clip 03 and Clip 08, you may want to rename them to something a tad more revealing, such as Alex Scores Goal or Leslie's Big Monologue. Double-click the clip, and type that more enlightening name over the old one in the Clip Info window that appears.

The cutting room floor

It's isn't likely or desirable that all the scenes currently in the Clips pane will make it into your final movie. All smart filmmakers shoot a lot more footage than they can possibly use. (*Gotta* have options, my friend.) A good first step is to watch the clips you've assembled by highlighting them in the Clips pane and clicking Play. The idea here, of course, is to inspect scenes with a critical director's eye.

You can watch clips in the monitor or full-screen by clicking the Play Full Screen button, labeled in Figure 16-2. (I love names that tell you what something does.) To return to the smaller monitor view after going full-screen, click anywhere on the screen or press the Esc key.

From the get go, some clips are obvious candidates for the trash: the ones with blurry close-ups, pictures of your shoes (when you forget to turn off the camcorder), or grandma hamming it up for the camera. Select the clips you want to discard, and either press Delete on the keyboard or choose Edit⇨Cut.

Such clips are dumped into the iMovie trash can, where they remain until you empty it. To do that, click the trash can icon at the bottom-right corner of the application, and then click Empty Trash in the iMovie Trash window that pops up.

To shed unwanted footage in a scene you otherwise want to keep, try *cropping* it. Just like cropping a photograph, you are keeping only a specific portion of the video and snipping away at its edges:

1. **Select the scene in question.**

2. **Drag the playhead in the blue scrubber bar below the monitor to the precise point where you want your scene to commence.**

3. **Click underneath the playhead, leaving a little crop marker (it looks like a triangle).**

4. **Drag the playhead to the right.**

   As you do so, that section of the scrubber bar turns gold.

5. **Now choose Edit⇨Crop.**

   Only the highlighted gold portion of the bar is retained.

You can drag each crop marker apart to highlight the portion of a scene you want saved. When you click a crop marker and press either the left or right arrow keys on the keyboard, the crop marker moves a single frame at a time. Hold down Shift while pressing either arrow key to make the crop marker skip ten frames.

To trim just the beginning or end of a clip, drag the crop markers where you want them and choose Edit⇨Clear.

Sometimes you want to split up a single clip to add titles, images, or clips. Move the playhead to the point where you want to break up the clip and choose Edit⇨Split Video Clip at Playhead.

If after all you're cropping and trimming you're not pleased with the results, you can go back to the original clip as imported from your camera. Control-click the clip and select Revert Clip to Original.

Adding still pictures to a movie

Interspersing still photos inside your movie is a great way to show off your artistic prowess. To do so:

1. **Click the Media pane button.**
2. **Click Photos at the top of the Media pane.**

   You now have your entire iPhoto library at your disposal, as shown in Figure 16-3.

3. **Select the picture you want to add.**
4. **In the Photo Settings window, drag the sliders to zoom in and out of the picture and select the duration for your photo to remain on-screen.**
5. **If you want to add panning and zooming to a photo as explained in the previous chapter, select the Ken Burns Effect option.**
6. **Drag the photo to the clip or timeline viewer to add it to your flick.**

To add a slideshow inside your movie, select multiple pictures in Step 3. You can do so in several ways. Here are two: To select all the pictures, choose Edit⇨Select All; for a range of pictures, hold down the Shift key while you click the first and last pictures you want to include.

Figure 16-3:
An iPhoto cameo.

Adding the perfect soundtrack

What would your epic be without an award-winning score? Or a James Earl Jones or Gene Hackman voiceover (you should be so lucky)? Click the Media pane button, as in the preceding section. But this time, click Audio at the top of the pane.

As will immediately become apparent, you have several audio sources to choose from:

✓ **iTunes:** All the music in your iTunes library (Chapter 15) is at hand. If you have thousands of songs in the library, type the name of an artist or title you're looking for in the search box. (Entering *Bell,* for example, would bring up works from Joshua Bell or Patti LaBelle or titles such as *Jingle Bells* or *Wedding Bell Blues.*) If a song you want for your movie isn't in iTunes yet, pop in a CD to copy it.

- ✔ **Your own composition:** You can also import music from GarageBand, the subject of Chapter 18. Suffice to say for now that GarageBand is the recording studio inside iLife for producing your own hit records.

- ✔ **Canned sound effects:** Apple has compiled dozens of cool audio effects. Under Skywalker Sound Effects, you can check out and ultimately apply the sound of Electricity, Film Projector, Heartbeat, Squeaky Door, Ticking Clock, and many more. Standard Sound Effects include Bubbles, Cartoon Boing (a personal favorite), Crickets, Footsteps, and Jet Fly By. You'll find animal sounds (Cow Moo, Rooster Call), sports sounds (Bowling Strike, Tennis Serve), and common sounds around the office (Fax Machine Tones, Telephone Busy Signal).

  If you really want people to think you've produced something special, consider adding one of the Clapping or Cheering Crowd effects to the end of your movie. If you have a low opinion of your work (or a warped sense of humor), apply the Booing Crowd effect.

- ✔ **Voiceovers:** Since Jones and Hackman were already booked, record your own narration by clicking the red microphone button. (Your Mac likely has a built-in microphone, but if it doesn't you can buy one.) Before proceeding, move the playhead on the scrubber bar to the spot where you want to begin.

So what exactly do you do with all this marvelous music and sound? How do you make sure the soundtrack matches the video rolling on the screen? For the answers, let's take a closer look at the timeline viewer.

Time (line) is on your side

The clip viewer, where we've mostly been hanging out, is great for rearranging clip sequences. In the timeline view, though, you get a more detailed look at the building blocks of your movie. Individual clips or scenes are represented by horizontal bars of lengths that correspond to their relative duration in the movie, as you can see in Figure 16-4. You get to the timeline by clicking the little clock icon on the clips/timeline view switch (labeled in Figure 16-2). Press ⌘+E to quickly toggle between the clips and timeline views.

The timeline is comprised of three tracks; the top is reserved for your video (and pictures), and the bottom two are for audio. Having more than one audio track grants you flexibility to play with sound and music. You might use narration on one track and music in another. You can have sound effects and music going on simultaneously.

Figure 16-4:
The timeline
view.

To add music, highlight the song in question, move the playhead to the frame where you want the soundtrack to kick in, and click Place at Playhead.

Alternatively, drag the song or effect or narration directly onto one of the two audio timeline tracks (or drag audio from one track to the other). You may have to slide the entire audio track in either direction so it lines up properly with the video. Audio tracks are represented by a colored ribbon and (if Show Audio Waveforms is selected in View) displayed graphically by the intensity of the sound.

Sound is captured along with video when you import clips into iMovie from a camcorder. Determining volume levels for your video and audio tracks, so that one doesn't drown out the other, can be a challenge.

Following are some of the things you can do with sound:

✔ Mute an entire track by selecting or unselecting the box to the track's far right.

✔ Adjust levels so that some parts of a track are louder. Choose View➪Show Clip Volume Levels. A volume level bar stretches across the track. Drag the bar up or down like a rubber band to raise or lower the volume in that portion of a scene.

- Adjust the volume level of selected sound effects by dragging the volume slider near the bottom-left side of the iMovie window.

- As with a video clip, tinker with the length of an audio clip by dragging its edges. Hold down the Option key as you drag the end of a clip to hear its sound.

- Drag one clip on top of another in the same audio track to hear both at the same time. This is a helpful trick if you feel constrained by having just three iMovie tracks.

- Separate the audio track from a video clip. Select the clip and choose Advanced⇨Extract Audio.

Adding transitions

Clips are arranged as you want them, the soundtrack is in place. Now you just need a smooth bridge from one scene to the next.

In movie-speak, those bridges are *transitions,* and iMovie gives you more than a dozen to choose from, found when you click the Editing pane button and then click Transitions at the top of the pane.

You may not know the names of all these transitions, but you've undoubtedly seen ones such as Fade Out and Cross Dissolve in movies and television. It's kind of a hoot to preview others by clicking their names in the list, even if you'll never use them in your movie. In the Push transition, for example, the new scene entering stage left pushes the existing scene out of the way. As Figure 16-5 shows, the new scene arriving with the Ripple transition makes an entrance in a giant transparent bubble, vaguely reminiscent of the Good Witch Glinda's appearances in *The Wizard of Oz.*

When you choose the transition you want, use the speed slider to determine how long the transition should take. Then just drag the name of the transition style between the two scenes you want to bridge. iMovie will take several seconds to *render,* or process, the transition; a red progress bar lets you know how long the rendering will take place.

You can't place certain long transitions between two short scenes. If you try, a dialog box will clue you in as to how long clips must be to use that particular transition. Note also that the Fade and Wash effects are the only transitions you can use at the beginning or end of a movie.

Sound off

Howling wind. A grinding camera motor. The bark of a neighbor's dog. Not all the sounds picked up by a camcorder's microphone are appropriate to your scene. iMovie can help you muzzle unwelcome audio. After you've selected the clip you want to hush, click the Editing pane button and then click Audio FX. Select Noise Reducer and click Preview. As you watch the clip in the monitor, drag the slider between Less and More until you detect sound levels you can live with. Click Apply to make the change.

While in Audio FX, check out other sound options. Click Reverb and you can choose among Room, Club, Cathedral, Atrium, Arena, and Plate. Select Pitch Changer and you can drag a slider between Monsters and Chipmunks. You can also choose Delay, Highpass, Lowpass, Bandpass, and Graphic EQ, a master control for bass, midrange, and treble. You're not expected to know what any of these sound like — try 'em out. Go crazy, you Foley Artist you! (That's the film crew member who is often responsible for sound effects.)

Figure 16-5: The Ripple is one of several iMovie scene transitions.

To employ the same transition throughout your movie, click Add after you've selected all the clips in your film.

Adding special effects

If you thought transitions were a blast, try applying special effects to individual scenes or the entire film. Once again, click Editing. Now click Video FX at the top of the pane.

You can choose an effect that makes it look like your scene was shot in rain or fog (even if in reality it was a bright sunny day). Effects can turn a color movie into black and white. Two of my favorites are Aged Film and Glass Distortion.

If you have the time, check out all the effects. When you click an effect, use the sliders to determine how quickly to usher an effect in and out. Different sliders appear for different effects. For example, in the N-Square effect shown in Figure 16-6, drag the Squares slider to increase or decrease the number of squares that show up on screen. When an effect is to your liking, click Apply and wait for iMovie to process your request.

Figure 16-6:
Hollywood Squares through the N-Square effect.

Then feel free to submit your resume to Lucas film's Industrial Light & Magic. You're ready for the big time.

The title track

Every good movie needs a decent title to hook an audience — even if the film is all about your recent vacation and the only people watching are the ones who took the trip with you. But c'mon, we've gone this far. Don't quit on me now. While we're at it, add closing credits too. You're the person who put this darn thing together and you want kudos.

Besides, selecting titles is as easy as everything else you've performed in this chapter:

1. **Click the Editing button.**

   You ought to have this down by now.

2. **At the top of the pane, click Titles.**

3. **Scroll down the list and choose an effect for your title.**

   As usual, you have lots of possibilities (such as Flying Letters, Scrolling, Spinning, and Video Terminal). Select one to preview it.

4. **Enter the name of your title in the text fields.**

   Some titles include more fields than others and include + and - buttons for adding more lines of text. You can also adjust the font, typeface, size, and color.

5. **Use the speed slider to determine how long the title (and your name) will be in lights — at least figuratively.**

6. **If you want a black background in your movie when titles are displayed, select the Over Black option.**

   The Over Black option is shown in Figure 16-7. Otherwise the title will appear on top of your video.

7. **Click Add.**

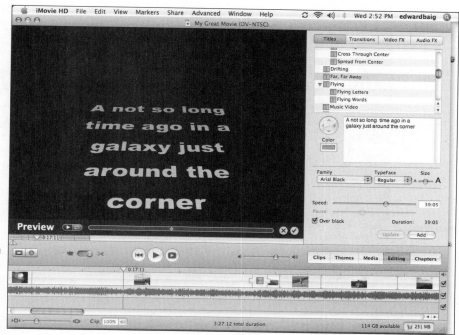

Figure 16-7:
The Far Far
Away title
over black.

Using themes

You may have noticed another pane button called Themes. A *theme* is a collection of professionally produced and coordinated motion graphics, titles, overlays, transitions, and background effects to add zing to your motion picture.

To take advantage of themes, you'll need OS X version 10.4.4 or later.

Let's put these effects into action:

1. **Click the Themes button.**

2. **From the pop-up menu at the top of the pane, click to choose a theme.**

   Examples are Travel, Road Trip, and Pass Through.

3. **Select Theme Elements to display in the iMovie monitor, as shown in Figure 16-8.**

Figure 16-8:
Movies
come alive
through the
use of
themes.

4. **Add titles to the appropriate field.**

5. **Click the Clips button and drag clips to the drop zones in the window that appears.**

   These are placeholders for your content. You can drag pictures onto drop zones also by selecting Media and then clicking Photos.

6. **Click Themes.**

7. **Click Apply.**

   A new clip is added to the end of your movie.

8. **Drag the clip wherever you want it to appear in the film.**

Making a Magic iMovie

Let me try an analogy on you. Students still learn the basics of arithmetic in grade school, even though today's math problems can be solved with any simple calculator. So now I'm going to tell you that we spent all this time learning how to produce a movie in iMovie. And yet iMovie can pretty much do it all for you.

Actually, your crash course in moviemaking does help. Besides, as the head of your very own Macintosh studio, you still have a few executive decisions to make.

You have to connect your camcorder with a FireWire cable to import the footage at the core of your Magic iMovie; USB won't cut it. Here's how to proceed, after your camcorder is connected:

1. **Choose File⇨Make a Magic iMovie or select the same from the opening iMovie HD window.**

   The window in Figure 16-9 appears.

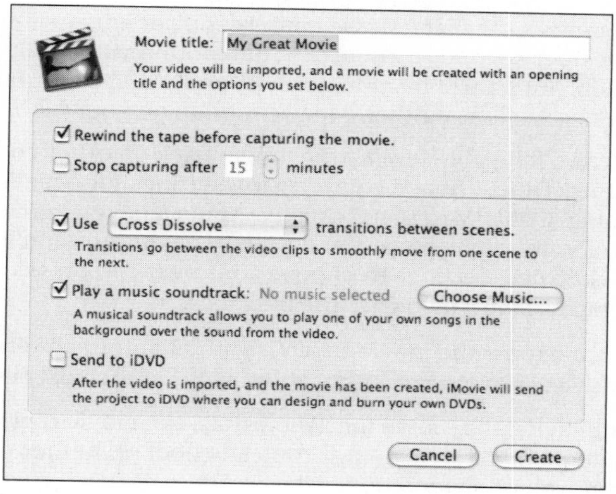

Figure 16-9: The Magic iMovie window.

2. **Fill in a movie title.**

   See, that's an important decision.

3. **Determine whether to rewind the tape before capturing the movie, and whether to stop capturing after a designated time.**

4. **Choose the transitions between scenes or let iMovie randomly choose on your behalf, by selecting that option from the pop-up menu.**

5. **Click the Choose Music button and drag songs you want added to the movie.**

6. **Decide whether to send the project to iDVD to design and burn your own DVD.**

7. **Click Create.**

And that is pretty much it. The rest, as they say, is (i)magic.

Sharing Your Blockbuster

What good would *The Godfather* be if nobody could watch it? So it goes for your classic. Take one last look at the movie you've produced so far. Watch it in full-screen on your Mac. If you're convinced it's a wrap, it's time to distribute it to an audience. Start by visiting the iMovie Share menu, which has the following options. (Note that each menu option has a Share Selected Clips Only option. So instead of the full movie, you can send selected clips from the timeline or clips viewer.)

✔ **Email:** Although you can send a movie as an e-mail attachment, this option is impractical with large files. Consider e-mailing only one- or two-minute movies. At that, iMovie compresses, or squeezes, the flick to just 10 frames per second (by contrast, full-motion video is 30 fps) at a low resolution. Sound will be monaural rather than stereo. You can send the movie using Mail or another e-mail program on your Mac.

✔ **QuickTime:** You'll be able to play the movie back on other computers that have QuickTime. Choose compression settings for e-mail, the Web, Web streaming, CD-ROM, and full quality. Apple lets you know the estimated size of your movie file at the designated compression level. You can also click Expert Settings to choose your own compression settings. The less compression, the bigger the file.

✔ **iDVD:** You can export the movie to iDVD with chapter markers you create in iMovie. I have more to say about iDVD in the next section.

✔ **iWeb:** Compressing the movie for iWeb brings the movie down to 12 fps, with medium-quality stereo sound. You can choose whether to share the movie on the Web or a video podcast.

If you choose a video podcast, your movie is compressed to 30 fps with better quality stereo. But you have to deal with a much larger file size. iWeb adds a Subscribe to Podcast button on your main blog page so that visitors can click to receive new episodes downloaded to iTunes on their computers. The movie adheres to an industry standard for video known as H.264. The 44.1 kHz sound conforms to AAC stereo audio. I know, I know, this is a lot of technical mumbo-jumbo.

✔ **GarageBand:** By sending your movie to GarageBand, you can add another score.

✔ **Bluetooth:** Using this short-range wireless technology, you can transfer your movie from a Bluetooth-equipped Mac to a compatible Bluetooth device.

✔ **iPod:** If you have a video-capable iPod (Chapter 15), you can format the movie for the iPod, send it to your iTunes library, and use iTunes to copy the "film."

✔ **Video camera:** Yes, after all the effort of getting video out of your camera, you can put it back in. Of course, what you're delivering is (presumably) a polished, well-edited movie. Connect the camera to the Mac through FireWire, insert a blank tape into the camcorder, and switch it to VTR mode. Add the number of seconds of black you want at the beginning and end of the movie. When the transfer is complete, you can connect the camcorder to a TV and watch.

When iMovie and iDVD Get Together

iDVD is a program for *authoring,* or designing, a DVD. iDVD is tight with iMovie (and, for that matter, with iTunes and iPhoto). As with iMovie, you can exploit Hollywood-style themes and click a Media button to add pictures and music.

When you're ready to burn DVDs, you'll need a Mac with a SuperDrive or at least a compatible third-party DVD burner. (Apple works with many.) All recent vintage Macs include CD burners, but not all have DVD burners.

Chapter markers

The movie DVDs you buy or rent at places such as Blockbuster are divided into *chapters* so you can quickly find specific scenes throughout a film (and I use that word loosely because no film is actually involved). The chapters are accessed through the main DVD menu.

You can add chapter markers to your movie too from inside iMovie. Click the Chapters pane button, move the playhead to the point where you want to start a chapter, and then click Add Marker. Type a title for your chapter in the indicated field. If you change your mind, click Remove Marker.

You can also create chapter markers in iDVD. Visit the Advanced menu in iDVD and select Create Chapter Markers for Movies.

iMovie automatically adds a chapter to the beginning of your movie. Don't add a chapter marker within a transition, or within a second of a transition or other chapter marker.

When you export a video from iMovie to iDVD, the iDVD program opens. It recognizes whatever chapter markers you added. If you created a Magic iMovie and selected the option to send your movie to iDVD, you already have a completed project inside iDVD ready for the final DVD treatment.

If you're starting in iDVD from scratch, the dialog box that appears gives you several options: Create a New Project, Create a Magic DVD, and Open an Existing Project or OneStep DVD (more on that soon).

If you choose Create a New Project, you need to set the encoding quality that iDVD will use to prepare the project to be burned. Under the iDVD menu choose Preferences⇨Projects and select either Best Quality (takes longer to burn) or Best Performance. If you choose Best Performance, you can also select the Enable Background Encoding option. (The feature is accessible also in the Advanced menu.) This option lets you continue to work while iDVD does its thing.

Choosing a theme

Just as you can choose a theme in iMovie, you can do so in iDVD. In this context, a *theme* is a menu design for your DVD, with differing background images, buttons style, fonts, music, and animations.

Each new theme includes three coordinated menus — main menu, chapter selection menu, and slide show menu — that are consistent across the entire disc. (You an also customize your own theme.)

Click the Themes button and scroll through the list on the right to choose a theme that meets your requirements, such as the Travel theme displayed in Figure 16-10. Themes with a circled walking man icon on the bottom-right have motion. Note that you're not limited to the default themes; you can purchase third-party themes online.

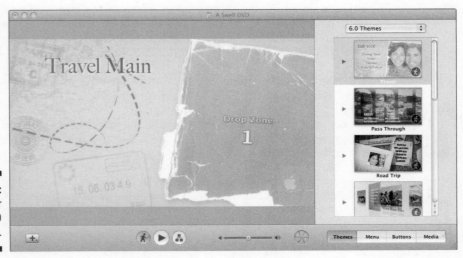

Figure 16-10: A theme for your iDVD movie.

The newest themes delivered in iDVD 6 can exploit the widescreen 16:9 aspect ratio available on HDTVs (and some analog TVs). These latest themes also work in the standard (4:3) format. You can also choose themes from prior versions of iDVD.

As with the themes in iMovie, you can drop content into designated drop zones. To add a movie to a drop zone, drag it from the Media pane or elsewhere on the Mac. If you add a movie with chapter markers, iDVD automatically creates scene selection submenus with a left-pointing arrow that serves as a Back button.

Menus can hold up to 12 buttons. If you want to go above a dozen, you need to create submenus to hold them. To do so, click the + (Add button) at the bottom-left corner of the iDVD screen and choose Add Submenu.

An iDVD slideshow

Want to create a DVD slideshow presentation? Follow these steps:

1. **In the main iDVD window, click the + button and select Add Slideshow.**

2. **Double-click the My Slideshow button that now appears in the main iDVD window.**

   That window is replaced with a drop zone requesting that you *Drag images here.*

3. **From the Media pane, drag an iPhoto album or individual pictures.**

4. **From the drop-down lists at the bottom of the screen, choose the duration your slides will appear and a transition to move smoothly between slides.**

5. **Click Settings.**

6. **Select the options you want to add to the slideshow.**

   If you want slides to repeat, select Loop Slideshow. If you want to display navigation arrows, select that option. You can also choose to add image files to a DVD-ROM, and show titles and comments.

7. **To add a soundtrack, choose Audio in the media pane and drag the song you want onto the audio well, shown in Figure 16-11.**

   The Slide Duration pop-up changes to Fit To Audio. That way, the slides and music start and end together. If you prefer, return to a duration of your choosing.

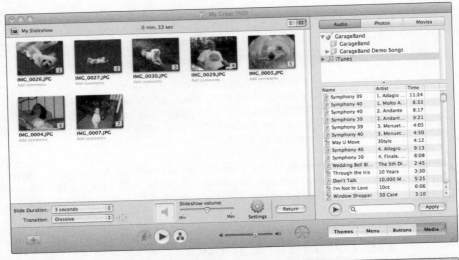

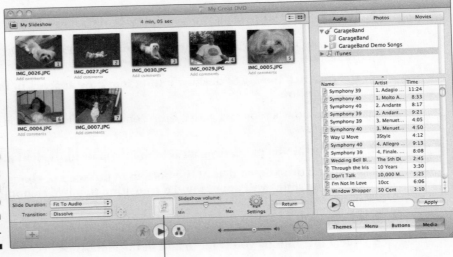

Figure 16-11:
Dragging
audio to
add a
soundtrack.

Audio well

Altering menus

Although themes come with their own menu screens, you can alter the look
of text on menus by clicking the Menu button, sandwiched between the
Buttons and Themes. You can change the font type, size, and color of the title
(by clicking the color box). You can click Edit Drop Zones to change the background, audio, and photos. To change things back to their initial state, click
Reset Text.

To make sure your menus and submenus will show up on television, choose View➪Show TV Safe Area. iDVD will place a red rectangle around the area of the screen that will be visible on the tube.

Altering buttons

DVD buttons are also meant to fit a particular theme. But if your ideas clash with Apple's, you can change the look of buttons by clicking the, um, Buttons button. Buttons come in different shapes and sizes and customizable colors. Buttons can be text-only or display video. A movie button is created when you drag a movie from the Media pane onto the DVD menu screen.

Take a look at the scene selection buttons in Figure 16-12. When you select a button in the main iDVD window, you can change its shape by clicking one of the button alternatives in the upper portion of the Buttons pane. Scroll up and down the list to find button choices you like. The T selection creates a text-only button.

The DVD jungle

Technologists just can't help themselves, which leaves consumers in the lurch. Take the confusing muddle that represents DVD media types. Although the following disc types work with iDVD 6, it's a good idea to double-check the types of media that your burner can handle. Go to the System Profiler (found under Applications inside the Utilities folder) and choose Disc Burning.

✔ DVD-R and DVD+R (the latter is pronounced "DVD plus R"): No do-overs. You can record these "write-once" discs only one time, so if you make a mistake, you have to use a brand new blank disc. On the positive side, these can play back on most conventional DVD players. As with all the discs mentioned here except the double-layer disc, these hold about 4.3 gigabytes.

✔ DVD-RW and DVD+RW: The good news is these "rewriteable" discs can be recorded over and over. The bad news is they won't play back in all DVD players.

✔ DVD+R DL: This double layer (write once) disc can store nearly twice as much stuff as the single-layer discs. But older DVD players can't handle this type of disc.

Meanwhile, two other incompatible, rival high-definition disc types have emerged recently: Blu-ray discs and HD-DVD discs. Macs were not equipped to handle either nascent format at the time of this writing, though that may have changed by the time you read this. Apple is one of the companies publicly supporting Blu-ray, but it is also a member of the DVD Forum, the group backing HD-DVD.

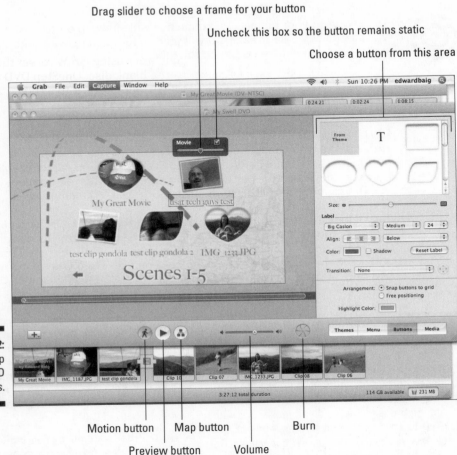

Drag slider to choose a frame for your button

Uncheck this box so the button remains static

Choose a button from this area

Figure 16-12:
Button up
your iDVD
menus.

Motion button   Map button   Burn

Preview button   Volume

Buttons representing video normally display the first frame in a particular scene. If you want a different frame as the face of the button, click the actual button so that a slider appears. Drag the slider until the frame you want appears. If the button you click has a movie playing in it, uncheck the box (labeled in Figure 16-12) so that the image will remain static.

Map view editing

Click the Map button at the bottom of the screen (labeled in Figure 16-12) to switch to iDVD's Map view, sort of a bird's-eye view of your project. You can quickly see how menus and buttons are laid out and connected to one another, and double-click the chart to jump to a particular scene.

OneStep DVD

Back when you first opened iDVD, you had the opportunity to click OneStep DVD. To use it, connect your digital camcorder using FireWire, set the camcorder to VCR mode, click OK, and insert a blank disc. OneStep DVD automatically rewinds the tape, imports your video, and burns it to a DVD.

Making a Magic iDVD

Just as you can make a Magic iMovie in iMovie, you can make a Magic iDVD in iDVD. For the latter, choose a theme and drop the movies and photos you want included onto strips in the main iDVD window, as shown in Figure 16-13. iDVD takes charge from there, adding a main menu with buttons for your flick, slideshows, and so on. Drop zones are autofilled with your stuff. You can edit the Magic iDVD before going on to burn the project to a disc.

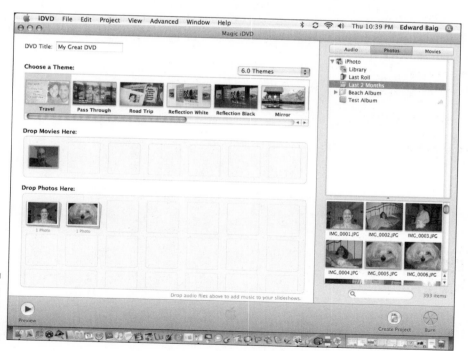

Figure 16-13: Creating a Magic iDVD.

Burn Baby Burn

You have reached a truly exciting moment. You are almost ready to burn your DVD. To make sure everything is perfect, click Preview to see what your DVD will look like. A little on-screen remote control functions like a regular DVD remote so you can simulate the post-burning experience.

I also recommend checking out the Project info window. It's the first selection under the Project menu and is a wealth of information. You can make sure you've gone with the right aspect ratio (standard or widescreen.) You can see your encoding choice (best performance, best quality). And you can see the duration of your project, the number of tracks and menus you're using (you get up to 99 each), and so on.

Satisfied? Click the Burn button and insert a blank DVD, though as "The DVD Jungle" sidebar indicates, which disc to use isn't always clear cut. The burning process takes awhile depending on the speed of your burner and the Mac itself. A progress bar lets you know how the operation is going before the disc finally pops out. Don't bother staring at the screen — you probably have better things to do with your time. Like maybe writing your Oscar acceptance speech.

Chapter 17

The Show Must Go On

Do you fancy yourself the rock icon? Your face plastered on the cover of *Rolling Stone* and *Entertainment Weekly*? Groupies stalking you wherever you go? Your band's very own tour bus? *"Why Ed, it has nothing to do with such perks. To me it's all about the music."* Whatever's driving you, GarageBand 3 is iLife's digital recording studio for making records, creating podcasts, and scoring movies produced in iMovie.

If you're inclined to skip this chapter because you can't distinguish an F-sharp from a B-flat, take note: You need not read music, play an instrument, or possess a lick of musical talent to compose a ditty through GarageBand.

Sure, having a good ear helps. And if you can belt out a tune, tickle the ivory, or jam with the best of them, all the better. Connect a microphone, piano keyboard, or electric guitar to the Mac, and exploit GarageBand to the max.

Forming a GarageBand

When you first launch GarageBand, you can choose to open a New Music Project, New Podcast Episode, or New Movie Score. For now, we'll stick with music. I address podcasts and movie scoring later:

1. **Launch GarageBand.**

   The program is located in the Applications folder. Or click the dock icon shaped like a guitar.

2. **In the dialog box shown in Figure 17-1, enter a name for your song and choose a location for the file (GarageBand is the default).**

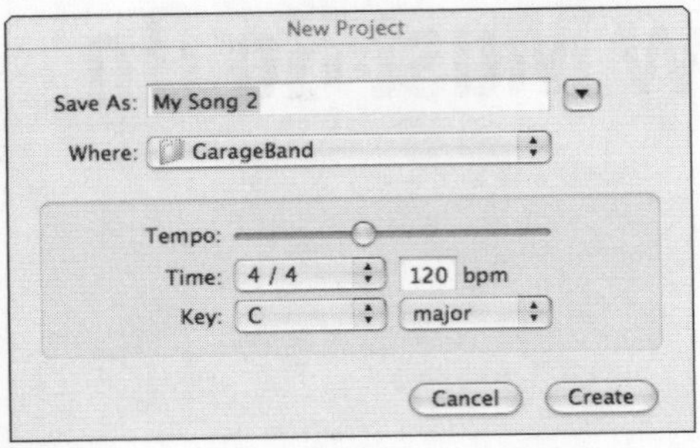

Figure 17-1:
And a one
and a two
and a three.
Creating a
new project.

3. **Set a *tempo*, or constant speed, by dragging the slider anywhere between 40 and 240 beats per minute, or *bpm*.**

4. **Choose a Time signature and a scale, or *key*, from the pop-up lists.**

   Don't fret if you don't know what any of these musical designations mean. Just stick with the defaults. You'll learn as you go and can change them later.

5. **Click Create.**

   The window that opens will look something like Figure 17-2.

Keeping on track(s)

Mastering GarageBand is all about getting comfortable with tracks (discussed in this section) and loops (see the next section).

Most musical compositions consist of several *tracks,* or layers of individual parts recorded by different instruments. You can connect instruments to your Mac through one of the methods mentioned in the "Connecting real instruments" sidebar or take advantage of numerous digitally sampled *software instruments,* heard as you play a small on-screen keyboard by clicking its keys with the mouse. You can choose a wide variety of software instruments, in all the major instrument families (percussion, brass, and so on).

When you open a new project, GarageBand introduces you to the first of these software instruments, a grand piano. It appears by default in the tracks list. It's the instrument you will hear when you play that miniature keyboard.

Tracks   Mixer   Playhead   Timeline

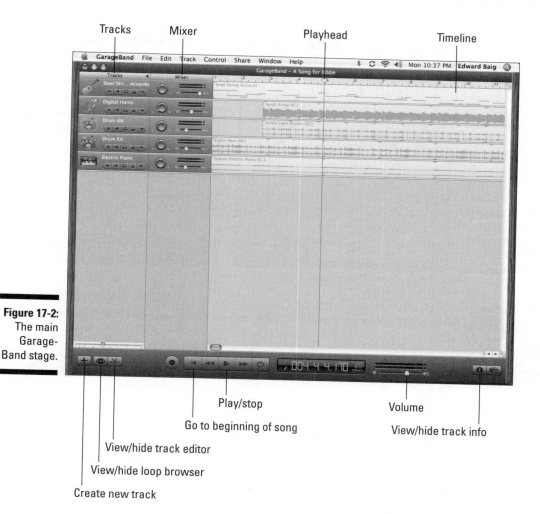

Figure 17-2:
The main
Garage-
Band stage.

Play/stop   Volume

Go to beginning of song   View/hide track info

View/hide track editor

View/hide loop browser

Create new track

To add a new track:

1. **Click the Create a new track (+) button at the bottom-left corner of the program, or choose Track⇨New Track.**

2. **Select Software Instrument or Real Instrument.**

3. **Click Create.**

   A new track shows up in tracks list, accompanied in the header by its icon, name (Grand Piano until you change it), and several tiny controls. Among other functions, these controls let you mute the track, lock it to prevent editing changes, make it a solo, and permit or disable a recording.

In the Track Info pane (see Figure 17-3) you can change your instrument selection from Grand Piano to any other available instrument. To do so, choose an instrument category from the left column of the Track Info pane (Guitars in this case) and an actual instrument in the right column (Classical Acoustic).

Figure 17-3: Adding software instrument and real instrument tracks.

You can open the Track Info pane anytime by clicking the little *i* icon at the bottom-right corner of the screen. Alternatively, choose Track⇨Show Track Info.

If you selected a real instrument in Step 2, choose an Input (stereo or mono, channel 1 or channel 2), depending on how the instrument is connected to the Mac. Select Monitor from the drop-down list to be able to hear the instrument as you play it. If the real instrument you're choosing is your own voice, choose Vocals and the instrument that most closely matches your style, such as Epic Diva, Helium Breath, or Megaphone.

Getting loopy

Don't let the heading scare you, I'm not advocating alcohol. I'm merely suggesting you might become artistically intoxicated experimenting with GarageBand *loops,* the professionally recorded (and royalty-free) musical snippets at the very foundation of your composition.

Loops supply drum beats, rhythm parts, melody lines, bass sections, and so on. Apple includes more than 1,000 loop files with GarageBand. You can add thousands more by purchasing optional $99 Jam Packs (covering Remix Tools, Rhythm Section, Symphony Orchestra, and World Music).

Click the button that looks like the famous CBS eye logo to open the *loop browser* across the bottom portion of the screen. You can view the loop browser by columns, buttons (as shown in Figure 17-4) or podcast sounds.

Figure 17-4:
In the loops.

Loops ‡						Name
Reset ⊗	All Drums	Piano	Rock/Blues	Single	Ensemble	Ambient Beat 01
Favorites ✐	Kits	Elec Piano	Urban	Clean	Distorted	Ambient Beat 01
Bass	Beats	Organ	World	Acoustic	Electric	Club Dance Beat 013
Guitars	Percussion	Synths	Electronic	Relaxed	Intense	Club Dance Beat 013
Strings	Shaker	Brass	Country	Cheerful	Dark	Club Dance Beat 018

Scale: Any ▾   Q▾   79 items   Club Dance Beat 018 / Club Dance Beat 022

Search for loops inside the browser by instrument (Bass, Guitars, Strings, and so on) genre (Rock/Blues, Urban, Country), mood (Relaxed, Intense, Dark), or combinations of these. Incompatible loop buttons are dimmed. For example, you wouldn't be able to find loops that are relaxed *and* dark.

The list of loop possibilities shows up on the right side of the browser. Click one of them to check it out, conveniently in the project's key and tempo. Most usefully, you can audition loops while the rest of your project is playing to hear how all the tracks blend. If the loop passes muster, drag it onto the timeline. Individual tracks and loops make up the rows of the timeline. To add a new loop, click Reset in the loop browser and make another selection.

The musical patterns in loops repeat (why do you suppose they're called loops anyway?). You can also tug on the right edge of a loop to lay down a track for the entire song. Loops don't have to start at the beginning of a track; and if you want to change the mood midstream, you can add a second loop onto the same track. If you want more than one loop to play in a song (which is typical), create multiple tracks.

The *beat ruler* above the timeline serves as a guide; it displays beats and *measures,* the latter is how the units of musical time are, um, measured.

If you go by the name, I *dunno,* Bono or the Boss, you can create loops from your own performances. Select a Real or Software instrument in the timeline. Choose Edit⇨Add to Loop Library. Then type a name for the loop, choose a scale and genre (from the pop-up menus), and choose an apt Mood Descriptor. Click Create when you're finished.

Building an arrangement

Adding loops or recording your own musical pearls (with real or software instruments) creates a *region* in a track. Regions are color coded as follows:

- ✔ **Purple:** Real instrument regions you record
- ✔ **Blue:** Real instrument regions created by loops
- ✔ **Orange:** Real instrument regions from imported audio files
- ✔ **Green:** Software instrument loops from recordings or loops

Connecting real instruments

If you'd rather not use the on-screen music keyboard to control software instruments, you can connect a real MIDI keyboard through a USB cable (on most newer gear) or a MIDI adapter (on older equipment). MIDI is geek shorthand for Musical Instrument Digital Interface, a standard that has been around for years. You can connect other MIDI instruments, including guitars, woodwinds, and drums, and record onto a real instrument track in GarageBand. Click the red record button when you're ready to rock.

Move the playhead to just before where you want to start jamming.

If the high-quality instrument you have in mind is your own singing voice, connect a microphone (in lieu of the Mac's built-in microphone) to the *audio input* port on the computer. Open System Preferences, Click Sound, Input, and select Line In. Drag the Input volume slider to an appropriate level. Good microphones are especially useful when you're recording podcasts, as discussed later in the chapter.

Regions can be cut, copied and pasted, or resized to play as long as you need them to. You can also move regions to another track or another area of the timeline.

Mix it together, maestro

Easy as Apple makes it to lay down tracks and add loops, you won't become Quincy Jones overnight. Fact is, even when you match tempos and such, some music just doesn't sound good together. I didn't have much success blending a Classic Rock Piano with a New Nashville guitar. Mixing or balancing all the parts so that one track doesn't drown out another is a challenge in its own right. You can find various mixer controls and level meters under the Mixer, labeled in Figure 17-2.

If you make a mistake fiddling with any of the controls you encounter in GarageBand, just call on that old standby, the Undo command, at the top of the Edit menu. Or press ⌘+Z.

You may want to display your composition with standard notes, clef signs, and so forth. To do so, select a software instrument region and open the Track Editor by clicking the button at the lower-left corner of the screen. Click the notation view button (it has a musical note on it) in the lower-right corner of the editor's header area and start composing. Notation view is displayed in Figure 17-5.

Figure 17-5:
Follow the
score in
Notation
view.

Creating Podcasts

Podcasts are like your own Internet radio or TV show, with music (from iTunes or elsewhere), pictures, sound effects, video, or some combination of these. Fans can download your podcasts over the Net (or find them in iTunes) and subscribe to receive them on a regular basis. Podcasting was introduced with GarageBand 3, so don't try the steps in this section with an earlier version of the program.

Here's how to put a polished podcast together.

1. **From the opening GarageBand 3 screen, click New Podcast Episode.**

2. **Type a name for your podcast.**

   The main screen looks like Figure 17-6. It's a little different from the GarageBand screen you were using for music. At the top of the tracks list you'll notice a special Podcast Track to drag photos or other artwork from your iPhoto library, accessible through the GarageBand media browser. Next are tracks to optimize for a male or female voice, plus Jingles and Radio Sounds.

3. **If you haven't already done so, plug in your microphone.**

4. **Choose an audio track (Male or Female) and click the red record button. Start gabbing in your finest radio voice.**

   You can apply editing tweaks later.

5. **To add a radio-style jingle to your podcast, open the loop browser (again by clicking the button that looks like an eye) and select Jingles. Choose one that seems appropriate for your podcast and drag it onto the timeline.**

   More than a hundred jingles are included. If you're delivering news commentary, for example, one of the Broadcast News jingles (Long, Medium or Short) might fit the bill.

6. **To add extra audio effects, choose Sound Effects from the loop browser.**

   As with any other loop, drag Sound Effects onto the timeline.

Figure 17-6:
Your
podcast
broadcast
studio.

You can open a sound effects instrument to add sound effects while you record your own voice. Choose Window⇨Musical Typing. When you press the key on your keyboard corresponding to the key in the radio sounds instrument, shown in Figure 17-7, you add that sound to your podcast. Make sure the red enable recording button is highlighted on your audio track and Radio Sounds track.

7. **To add artwork to your podcast, drag pictures from the Media browser onto the podcast track.**

A chapter marker is added for each picture in a window near the bottom center of GarageBand.

Your very own talk show

A podcast doesn't have to be just about you. You can host a talk show. Start an audio or video chat through iChat, and click the Record button. You'll be asked whether you want to record the conference. Click OK. GarageBand creates a real instrument track for each person in your audio or video gab fest. If it's a video chat, GarageBand adds a new region to the podcast track each time that person starts to speak and grabs a still image from the iSight camera. That mug is displayed as artwork.

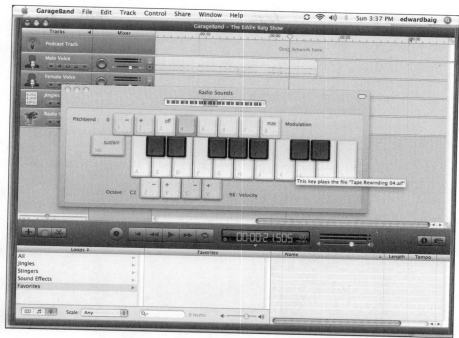

Figure 17-7:
The Sound
Effects
Instrument.

Folks who listen to your podcast on iTunes or photo-capable iPods can see the images. You can add URLs to those pictures. To add a visual title to your podcast, drag the artwork to the Episode drop zone in the bottom-left corner of the GarageBand program.

Ducking

At times you want to decrease the volume of your background tracks so you can hear spoken dialogue. The answer is a, um, quack-pot solution called *ducking*. (Sorry. Couldn't help myself. Feel free to call the pun police on me — again.)

Choose Control⇨Ducking. In each track's header, an arrow control appears. Select the up arrow to make a track a *lead* track and the down arrow to make it a *backing* track. When ducking is on, the sound on backing tracks is lowered whenever sound is detected on a lead track. You can adjust the amount of ducking by displaying Track Info. Choose Track⇨Show Track Info, click Details, and drag the Ducking Amount slider.

Sharing your podcast

When you're ready to share your podcast, you have a few options, each appropriately found under the Share menu. Click Send Podcast to iTunes to do just that. Or click Send Podcast to iWeb to do that. In iWeb, the podcast automatically becomes a blog entry.

From iWeb, you can publish your podcast to .Mac. Then visitors who click the Subscribe to Podcast button can receive any new episodes.

You can also submit your podcast to the iTunes Music Store. Your podcast is available free to your awaiting public:

1. **Click Inspector in the iWeb toolbar (it's to the bottom right of the screen), and then click the RSS button to open the Blog & Podcast button, shown in Figure 17-8.**

Figure 17-8: Using iWeb Inspector with your podcast.

2. **Add the Series Artist name and Contact Email.**

   Your e-mail address will not show up in iTunes.

3. **In the Parental Advisory pop-up, indicate whether your podcast is Clean or Explicit.**

4. **Select the Allow Podcast in iTunes Music Store option.**

5. **Choose File⇨Submit Podcast to iTunes.**

6. **Enter copyright information, a category for your blog, the language, and again indicate whether it is Clean or Explicit.**

7. **Click Publish and Submit.**

You are responsible for owning or getting permission for any copyrighted material associated with your podcast. Apple maintains the right to pull the plug.

Scoring an iMovie

Most memorable motion pictures also have great soundtracks. GarageBand 3 makes it a relative breeze to score the epic you created in iMovie. From iMovie, choose Share⇨GarageBand. This opens GarageBand and sends your movie there. The GarageBand media browser appears on the right side of the screen, with thumbnails of your iMovie projects.

If you double-click the thumbnail of the movie you have in mind, it plays inside the media browser. To start scoring the flick, drag it onto a video track. In a few seconds after a conversion takes place, the video track is laid out with individual scenes in the timeline. A real instrument track called video sound is added automatically, as shown in Figure 17-9.

When you click Play, the movie plays in the video preview window to the right of the timeline. Everything is synchronized with the music timeline, so you can add new loops, instruments, effects, and so forth, and arrange and mix them as with any GarageBand project. Move the slider at the bottom left to see more of the movie on the timeline.

When the video track is highlighted and you click Track Editor, you can add
markers to the movie. Just move the playhead along the timeline to the correct spot and click Add Marker. Type a chapter title and URL if desired. If so,
select the Displays URL option. Chapters are useful if you intend to burn a
movie onto a DVD. If that is indeed your poison, choose Share⇨Send Movie
to iDVD and let your DVD burner take over from there.

Remember, the show must go on.

Part V
The Creepy Geeky Section

The 5th Wave   By Rich Tennant

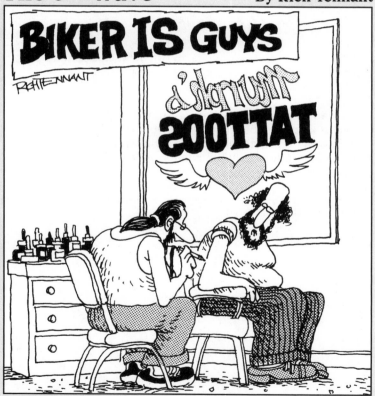

"Remember, I want the bleeding file server surrounded by flaming workstations with the word, 'Motherboard' scrolling underneath."

In this part . . .

Sooner or later I was going to run the technical mumbo-jumbo by you. Fortunately, it's not nearly as painful as you might think.

So read on about the virtues of wired and wireless networking. Find out how to turn your Mac into a, gosh, Windows PC. Figure out what to do when your Mac behaves irrationally. Within limits, you too can become a Mac fixit man or woman.

Chapter 18

Networking Madness

*I*n some ways a treasured Mac is like a baby. The machine is loved, pampered, even spoiled. But the reality for most of us is that our chosen computer is but one among many. It may very well have siblings, um, other computers in the house. Or your Mac may reside in a company or dormitory, where it almost certainly has to get along with other computers. If you've bitten into one Apple, you've perhaps bitten into others. For that matter, chances are quite good that the Mac must share quarters with a Windows machine. It's such a brave new world that your Mac may even sit next to a computer that runs the operating system known as Linux.

In the ideal computing environment, the various machines can share files, data, music, printers, an Internet connection, and other resources. That's what *networking,* or the practice of connecting multiple computers, is all about. Although networking topics are as geeky as any you'll come across, Apple, in customary fashion, simplifies it as much as possible.

Read on for a basic introduction to computer networking.

Networking Done Right

There's no right or wrong way to network computers. In this day and age, you can set up a wired or wireless network or, more than likely, a combination of the two.

Two or more interconnected machines in the same proximity form what geeks commonly refer to as a *local-area network, LAN* for short. Contrast that with a *wide-area network,* or WAN.

I'll start with the traditional tethered approach to cobbling a network together. You'll be that much happier when you're liberated from wires later on.

The wired way

If the Macs you intend to network are almost always going to stay put in one location, the wired approach is arguably the best way to proceed. Wired networks are zippier, more secure, typically less expensive (notwithstanding the cost of lengthy cables), and perhaps the easiest to set up (though you may get an argument there, too), unless dealing with a mess of wires becomes, well, a real mess.

In Chapter 2, I introduce you to Ethernet, the data cable whose end looks likes an oversized phone plug. Such cables also go by the names Cat 5, 10BaseT, or 100BaseT. What's more, not all Ethernet cables are created equal, as the "Crossing over" sidebar explains.

Up for more geek terminology? The connector at the end of an Ethernet cable is called *RJ-45,* not to be confused with *RJ-11,* the connectors that are put to use in telephones. RJ stands for Registered Jack, which is probably only useful if asked in a game of *Trivial Pursuit.*

To get started with a wired network, plug one end of the cable into the Ethernet port included in all modern Macs. The other end typically goes into an inexpensive network *hub, switch,* or *router,* which in turn is connected to the box feeding your Internet connection, usually a broadband cable modem or DSL.

Although there are technical distinctions between hubs, switches, and routers (and routers usually contain built-in hubs), I'll use the terms interchangeably here. In any case, routers contain multiple jacks, or *ports,* for connecting each Mac (or other computer) or printer that becomes part of your network.

Crossing over

You can directly connect one Mac to another sans hub using a special kind of Ethernet cable called a *crossover* cable. This cable is a dead ringer for a standard Ethernet cable, so be sure and ask which one you're getting at the store and label it when you get home. Such a cable is required to directly connect older Macs but isn't necessary when connecting newer machines, which can automatically detect when a crossover cable is used. For a list of Apple products that do or do not require the use of a crossover cable, consult `http://docs.info.apple.com/article.html?artnum=42717`.

Cutting the cord

Certain benefits of technology are so obvious they practically explain themselves. Wireless is one of those liberating technologies. By eliminating cables, you can

- Wander around with a laptop and still hold on to a connection.
- Drastically reduce the tangle of cables and cords, so that the area behind your desk won't be nearly as untidy.
- Easily add on to the network later, without worrying about connecting cables.
- Access other wireless networks outside your home or office, through public or private *hotspots* (found in numerous coffeehouses, airports, libraries, parks, and elsewhere). Accessing these hotspots may or may not be free.

Landing safely at the AirPort

All the Macs introduced during the last few years are capable of exploiting wireless networking through radio technology that Apple brands AirPort. Most of the rest of the computing world refers to the core technology as Wi-Fi, as outlined in the "ABCs of Wi-Fi" sidebar.

If your Mac doesn't have built-in wireless but does have OS X version 10.27 or later, you can install an optional $79 AirPort Extreme card. Also note that AirPort Extreme is not compatible with Power Mac G5 Dual and Power Mac G5 Quad computers introduced in October 2005.

Macs with built-in wireless communicate over the air — even through walls and at times considerable distances — with a compatible router or *base station*.

As of this writing, Apple sells two versions of the AirPort base station, the $199 AirPort Extreme, shown in Figure 18-1 and described in this section, and the portable $129 AirPort Express addressed later.

Courtesy of Apple

Figure 18-1:
The flying saucer—shaped AirPort Extreme base station.

Apple grounded the first-generation AirPort base station model and cards, though you can still find them on eBay. The cards may be your only hope if you hope to go wireless on an older Mac.

Although Apple would love to sell you an AirPort base station, wireless-capable Macs can tap into routers produced by the likes of Belkin, D-Link, Linksys, and Netgear, even if you previously set those up to work with a Windows network. Windows machines can also take advantage of an AirPort base station.

Under ideal, and frankly rarely met, conditions, AirPort Extreme provides maximum ranges of 50 feet at around 54 Mbps (which is plenty fast) and 150 feet at 11 Mbps (still plenty fast enough for Web surfing). The range and speed of a wireless network is affected by all sorts of factors, including interference from other devices, concrete, and metal walls.

A combination of up to 50 Macs or Windows PCs can simultaneously share a single AirPort Extreme base station.

To set up AirPort Extreme:

1. **Plug the AirPort Extreme to a power outlet.**

   See not *all* cords are eliminated in a wireless scenario. There's no power switch; status lights are your only immediate clue that your AirPort has taken off.

2. **If you're using a cable modem or DSL, connect an Ethernet cable to the LAN port on the base station. With a wired Ethernet network, connect to the WAN port.**

   You can also connect a regular phone line to the modem port.

3. **Run the AirPort Setup Assistant software, found in the Utilities folder inside the Applications folder.**

4. **For advanced security and other settings, run the AirPort Admin Utility software, also found in the Utilities folder.**

 You can determine the signal strength of your wireless connection by examining the radiating lines icon in the menu bar pictured here.

Boarding the AirPort Express

It looks kind of like a power adaptor that might come with an Apple laptop, right down to its built-in plug (see Figure 18-2). But the rectangular near 7-ounce AirPort Express device is a versatile little gadget. This portable hub has just three ports on its underbelly: Ethernet, USB, and line-out.

ABCs of Wi-Fi

The underlying technology behind AirPort is called Wi-Fi, the friendlier moniker applied to the geekier *802.11* designations. "Eight-oh-two-dot-eleven" (as it's pronounced) is followed by a letter, typically *b* or *g*. These letters indicate the speed and range you can expect from your wireless configuration. Alas, the geek alphabet makes little sense. Indeed, a few years ago, products that met a wireless standard called 802.11*a* hit the market *after* those based on 802.11*b*. And here you thought you had learned your ABCs by kindergarten?

AirPort Extreme measures up to the modern 802.11*g* standard, nearly five times faster than the *b* standard that the original AirPort met when it debuted in 1999. As this book was being published, products based on an even faster

standard, 802.11*n,* were emerging, though none had been introduced yet by Apple. (That may well have changed by the time you are reading this.) In any case, the newer standard is *backwards compatible,* meaning products based on it will work with older gear, though not to its fullest potential.

Keep in mind that when it comes to Internet downloading and uploading speeds, the limiting factor is your Internet provider, not the maximum networking speeds that your Wi-Fi gear is capable of. Faster networking speeds refer to how swiftly files are delivered from one computer to another device on the network, which is important if you want to transfer, or stream, sizable video files. But you won't surf the Net any faster than the signal coming in from your ISP.

Figure 18-2:
The portable base station, AirPort Express.

Courtesy of Apple

If you plan on using AirPort Express as a router, plug the device into an AC outlet and connect an Ethernet cord to your cable modem or DSL. You'll use the same AirPort software as the Extreme base station.

There's no on-off button; status lights clue you in on how things are going. A steady green status light tells you that you've connected with no problem. Flashing amber means the device is having trouble making a connection, and you may have to resort to other means, including (as final resort) taking the end of a straightened paperclip and holding down a "reset" button for 10 seconds.

Here's what AirPort Express can accomplish:

- Connect it to your cable modem or DSL and use it as a wireless 802.11g router, just like its larger sibling.

- Use it as a wireless *bridge* to extend the range of an existing AirPort network beyond 150 feet.

The process, known as creating a *WDS* for *Wireless Distribution System,* has a potential downside: It could impair the performance of your existing network. Open the AirPort Setup Assistant software and following the on-screen instructions.

- ✓ Connect a printer to the AirPort Express USB port to share that printer with any computer on the network.

- ✓ Connect a cable from the broadband box in a hotel room, and you can roam around the room and surf wirelessly.

AirTunes

One more clever feature is available, and it involves the aforementioned line-out port. If you connect AirPort Express to your home stereo receiver or powered speakers, you can pump the music from your Mac (or Windows) iTunes library through your stereo system. You can use either a mini-stereo to RCA-type cable, or what's called a mini-digital, fiber-optic Toslink cable, if your stereo can accommodate that kind of connector.

Either way, iTunes detects the remote connection. Through a small pop-up menu, you can click Computer to listen to music through your Mac (or whatever speakers it is connected to) or you can listen through Express and whichever speakers or stereo it is hooked up to. Apple refers to this wireless symphony as *AirTunes*.

Apple will sell you these optional (Monster brand) cables for $39. For about $60, Apple will also sell you a Keyspan Express remote control. Absent such a remote, you'd have to race to the Mac with iTunes to determine which songs will play through the stereo. The Keyspan remote control's "receiver" connects to the USB port on the AirPort Express device.

Testing your network

With all your equipment in place it's time to make sure everything works as it should. Fortunately, testing your network is as easy as opening Safari and seeing if you can browse.

If you run into problems, click the signal strength icon in the menu bar and make sure an AirPort network or other router is in range.

If you're still having trouble, open System Preferences under the menu and choose Network. Click the Assist Me button, and then click Diagnostics in the dialog box that appears. You can check the status of AirPort and Network Settings, your ISP, and so on.

If you live in an apartment building or are right on top of your neighbors, their routers may show up on your Mac's list. In some instances, the signal will be strong enough so that you may piggyback on their setup, not that I'm advocating doing so. Let this be a lesson that they should have implemented their security settings (requiring robust passwords) and that in setting up your own Wi-Fi network, you should do the same.

Let's Share

Responsible parents teach kids how to share toys. When the youngsters grow up and their toy of choice is a Macintosh, they may still be in that sharing frame of mind.

Anyway, with your networking gear in place, do the following:

1. **Choose ➪System Preferences:**

2. **In the Internet & Network section, click Sharing.**

   The pane shown in Figure 18-3 opens. You may want to change your computer name at this point. Calling it *Edward Baig's Computer,* as I do, makes it sound like "it's my computer and you can't play with it." Naming it say *Basement iMac* would help you distinguish the computer from, say, *Bedroom MacBook Pro.*

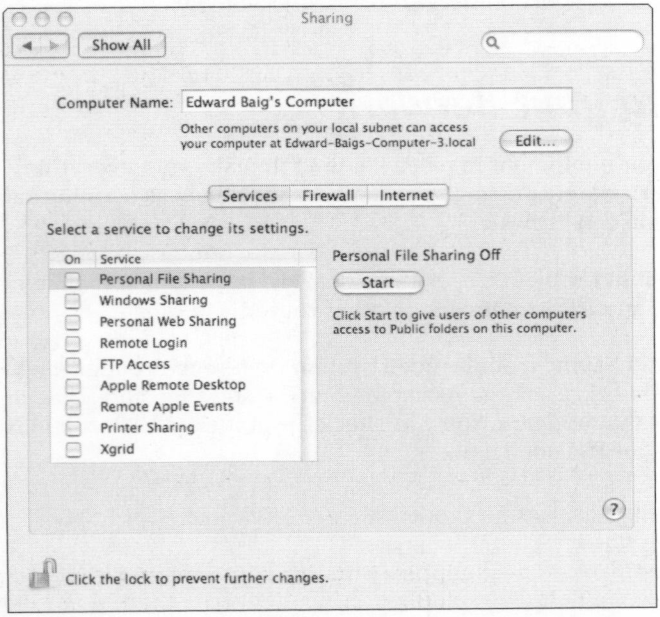

![Sharing preferences pane. Computer Name: Edward Baig's Computer. Other computers on your local subnet can access your computer at Edward-Baigs-Computer-3.local. Tabs: Services, Firewall, Internet. Select a service to change its settings. On/Service list: Personal File Sharing, Windows Sharing, Personal Web Sharing, Remote Login, FTP Access, Apple Remote Desktop, Remote Apple Events, Printer Sharing, Xgrid. Personal File Sharing Off. Start button: Click Start to give users of other computers access to Public folders on this computer. Click the lock to prevent further changes.]

Figure 18-3:
It's polite to share.

3. Click the Start button, under Personal File Sharing Off.

After several seconds, users of other machines can access any Public folders on the Mac. If you change your mind about sharing — you may feel uncomfortable that anyone on the Net can read those publicly available files — click the button that now says Stop.

Other Mac users can access your machine by choosing Go⇨Network in the Finder.

If you select the Windows Sharing option, you can let Windows users in on the fun too. You'll have to take the additional step of entering the password of each account you may want to share.

Brushing Up on Bluetooth

Of all the peculiar terms you come across in the tech world, *Bluetooth* is probably my favorite. The name is derived from tenth-century Danish monarch, Harald Blåtand, evidentially the wireless networking champ of his time. Blåtand was considered a peacemaker in warring Scandinavia, and isn't networking after all about bringing people — or things — together? In any case, Blåtand apparently translates to Bluetooth in English.

Fascinating history, Ed, but I thought I bought Macs For Dummies *not* European History For Dummies. *What gives?*

Fair point. Here's the drill: Bluetooth (the technology, not the Viking king) is a short-range wireless scheme that lets your Mac make nice with a gaggle of compatible gadgets, from up to 30 feet away.

Among the tricks made possible with Bluetooth:

- Connect the Mac to a Bluetooth cell phone at a distance of 30 feet. If you don't have access to a Wi-Fi hotspot, you may be able to use the phone as a modem to connect wirelessly to cyberspace.
- Wirelessly print through a Bluetooth printer.
- Exchange files with another Bluetooth-ready Mac or other computer or gadget.
- Schmooze via iChat through a Bluetooth headphone.
- Synchronize data with a Palm-based handheld device.
- Control a wireless Bluetooth keyboard or mouse.

Some newer Macs come equipped with Bluetooth capabilities. Companies such as Belkin and D-Link sell Bluetooth adapters in the $35 to $40 ballpark.

Getting discovered

The path to a meaningful Bluetooth experience starts in System Preferences. Click Bluetooth under the Hardware section, and you're taken to the area shown in Figure 18-4.

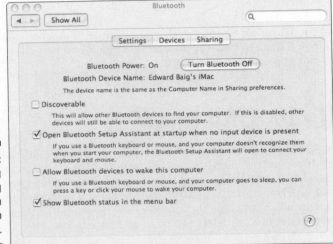

Figure 18-4:
Controlling
everything
through
Bluetooth
Preferences.

Before the Mac can communicate with a Bluetooth device, or in turn that device with your Mac, the machine's Bluetooth feature must be powered on. To help other devices find your Mac, select the Discoverable option.

Similarly, you'll want your other Bluetooth devices to be placed in a Discoverable mode so that your Mac can communicate with them. But be wary. If you're out in public, you may want to turn off Discoverable mode for security or privacy reasons.

You can control how the various devices share files with your Mac. Click the Sharing tab in Bluetooth Preferences and turn Bluetooth File Transfer On or Off as desired. Inside this important area, you can also choose to permit Bluetooth File Transfer, Bluetooth File Exchange, and Bluetooth-PDA-Sync.

You can also determine the Public or other folders that Bluetooth devices are permitted to browse on your computer. As one other key measure of security, select the Require Pairing for Security option (described next), which means a password will be required before files can be transferred.

Pairing off

To pair, or set up, Bluetooth devices to work with your Mac, follow these steps:

1. **Choose Bluetooth in System Preferences.**

2. **Select the Devices tab and click Set Up New Device.**

   Alternatively, if the Bluetooth status icon appears in Tiger's menu bar, click the icon and click Set up Bluetooth Device. Either way, the Bluetooth Setup Assistant appears.

3. **Select the types of devices you want to set up, such as a mobile phone.**

   Choose Any Device if the device you have in mind is not on the list. Make sure the given device is within 30 feet of the computer.

4. **Make sure Bluetooth is turned on in the selected device.**

   If Bluetooth is not turned on, you may have to dig through the device's menus to find the control that wakes up Bluetooth.

   With any luck, the Mac should find it. As shown in Figure 18-5, my Bluetooth setup found a Palm device.

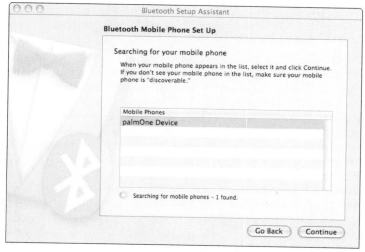

Figure 18-5:
Two devices are about to share Bluetooth heaven.

5. **Click Continue.**

   The Mac will spend a few seconds gathering whatever intelligence it can about the chosen device to determine how to interact with it.

6. **Click Continue again.**

The device will ask you to enter a passkey.

7. **Enter the passkey.**

The pairing process is complete, and the gizmo and the Mac can share a Bluetooth connection.

You may want to take a few more steps and click Devices under Bluetooth Preferences. From there, highlight the device in question and then click the Configure button to set up any other supported Bluetooth services on the device.

To send files wirelessly from the Mac to the device in the future, click the Bluetooth menu icon and choose Send File. Then select the file you have in mind from the Finder window. Click Send. Remember to turn on Bluetooth in the other device.

By now you should be pleased your baby is playing so well with others.

Chapter 19

Surviving in a Windows World

*I*f it weren't for the fact that their darling computers are so darn special, you might expect loyal Macintosh users to have an inferiority complex. But there's absolutely nothing inferior about the Mac operating system, save its teeny-tiny market share.

Apple has had only modest success through the years getting Windows users to switch to the Mac camp. However, the runaway success of the iPod and the move to Intel processors may help Apple lure more Windows defectors. (I sure don't know many people who actively choose to go from Mac to Windows, unless business requirements dictate otherwise.)

That said, this is, for better or worse, a Windows dominated world. More times than not, the Apple user has to adapt to the Windows environment rather than the other way around. From time to time, the Mac user encounters programs and Web sites that get along only with the Windows platform.

The Apple-Intel pairing demonstrates, however, that this is a topsy-turvy world. Intel and Microsoft have been a couple for so long it still seems unlikely that Intel would seek alliances elsewhere, especially with Apple.

What's more, as we'll see in this chapter, you can actually transform the newest Macs into fully functioning Windows computers. That bears repeating: *You can actually transform the newest Macs into fully functioning Windows computers.*

What Mac and Windows Have in Common

For all their differences, Mac and Windows are more alike than you may initially grasp. Sometimes, it's only a matter of semantics. Okay, it's more than that. But this chapter is about harmony, so common ground is as good a place as any to start:

- ✔ Macs and Windows PCs can share the same printers, scanners, digital cameras, mice, keyboards, and other peripherals.

- ✔ Both systems are fluent in the common file types, including PDFs, JPEGs, and text.

- ✔ Microsoft produces a version of Office for both platforms. So you can work in programs such as Word, Excel, and PowerPoint with little difficulty. The Mac and Windows versions of Office have used the same files since Office 97 for Windows came onto the scene.

- ✔ The Mac can read Windows PC–formatted CDs and DVDs.

- ✔ Both sides can easily communicate by e-mail or the AIM (AOL) instant messaging service.

- ✔ You can access a .Mac account (Chapter 12) — including documents, pictures, and movies stored in iDisk — from a Windows PC.

- ✔ Versions of the Windows Media Player, QuickTime Player, and RealPlayer work on a Mac.

- ✔ As noted in Chapter 18, the two systems can be on the same wired or wireless network. If file sharing is turned on in Windows, the computers can share files.

- ✔ And as you already know, Intel is now inside both computers.

Making the Switch

Okay, so you've read enough of this book to satisfy your curiosity about the Mac and you're ready to defect to the Apple side — or at least get a Mac to play alongside a Windows machine.

But frankly, you've invested a lot of time and energy over the years in getting your Windows files and preferences just as you like them. You have a lengthy list of Internet Explorer bookmarks and favorite background pictures too. Within certain limits, this section describes ways to replicate your Windows environment on a new Mac.

Move2Mac Software

The $50 Move2Mac program from Detto Technologies does most of the heavy lifting of moving to a Mac from Windows. You create a profile of settings and files that you want to move over from the PC, and let the software take over from there.

Move2Mac combines software you load on both your Mac and PC with a special cable to connect the two. For pre-Windows XP systems, get the version of Move2Mac with a Mac-USB-to-PC-parallel cable. For an XP machine, get a USB-to-USB cable.

The software is smart enough to put files in the right place. So My Music files in Windows go into the Music folder on the Mac, My Pictures into the Pictures folder, and My Videos into the Movies folder.

Move2Mac can't do everything. Applications are not ported over from the PC, nor does Detto's program convert PC files to a Mac format. That's no big deal with a program such as Office because the Mac can read files produced in the Windows version of the program.

When a company produces versions of its software for both platforms — such as Intuit and its Quicken personal finance software — you have to convert files produced in Windows to the Mac format before you can access your data.

It takes about 15 minutes to migrate 500MB of data. You can move data off a single PC (to any number of Macs), unless you pay for extra software licenses. Check out www.detto.com/move2mac/ for more information.

Help from Apple

When you buy a new Mac at the Apple Store, you qualify to have a certified Mac technician, not so modestly known as a Genius (see Chapter 19), transfer all your data for free. If you purchased your Mac online or at another retailer, a Genius will still transfer your data, for a fee starting at $50.

The PC must be running Windows 95 or later, and you need to bring your Windows installation disks, any appropriate cables, and the PC keyboard and mouse. Under this free scenario, you have to configure settings on your own.

Burning a disc

Because your Mac can read CDs or DVDs formatted for Windows, you can burn your important files onto a disk and copy them onto your Apple. You may not have to burn all your files onto a disc, but a good place to start is in your My Documents folders (which may include photos and videos) on the Windows machine.

External hard drives

You can exchange files on external USB or FireWire-based hard drives, USB "thumb" drives, and Iomega Zip drives.

You can even use an iPod as an external drive by setting it up for disk use. Temporarily dump songs off the iPod to create more room (then add the music back later). Visit docs.info.apple.com/article.html?artnum=300173 for a detailed explanation.

Using an existing network

Another way to get files from Windows to a Mac is by using a network. Make sure file sharing is turned on in Windows. I won't walk you through all the steps in Windows, but start by double-clicking My Computer, then click Tools, Folder Options, View and make sure the Use Simple File Sharing option is selected.

Add your Mac to your wired or wireless network (if it's not already part of it) and exchange files as outlined in Chapter 18.

The KVM switch

If you just bought a Mac but are holding on to your Windows computer for awhile, consider a *KVM* (keyboard-video-mouse) switch. This device uses USB to let the two machines share the monitor and various peripherals. A Belkin KVM switch with all the necessary cables costs around $70.

Enlisting in Boot Camp

In the preceding section I touched on various strategies for allowing *separate* Mac and Windows machines to coexist. But if you own one of the newer Intel-based Macs, you can run OS X *and* Windows XP on one machine.

It may seem like divine intervention. In fact, it's been possible to run Windows on a Mac for some time — with agonizing limitations. Macs loaded with Microsoft's Virtual PC emulation software can do Windows, too, but the program is painfully slow, can't work with any of the latest Apples, and is not compatible with all Windows programs on older Macs.

In the spring of 2006, two clever paths to a WinMac machine emerged. I address the first, from Apple itself, in this section. I weigh in on another method from a Northern Virginia startup named Parallels in the next section.

Boot Camp, Apple's near-finished beta software, shook up the computing public upon its apocalyptic arrival in early April. After loading the software onto my iMac, it instantly became the fastest (among the many) Windows machines in my house.

Although Boot Camp is still in beta as of this writing, Apple announced that it will be featured in the next major release of OS X (dubbed Leopard), which is expected early in 2007. In the meantime, you can download a version of the software at www.apple.com/macosx/bootcamp. It includes Boot Camp Assistant software, stored in the Utilities folder under Applications.

Boot Camp itself is free, but you have to supply your own single-disc, full-install version of the Windows XP CD with Service Pack 2 ($199 on up). An XP upgrade disc won't cut it.

Other requirements follow:

- An Intel Mac with OS X version 10.4.6 or later — if need be, run Software Update
- At least 10GB of free space on the startup disk
- A blank recordable CD or DVD

If you don't run into snags, the entire installation (including Windows) should take about an hour.

But because snags *are* possible, back up all your important information on the Mac's startup disk. Remember too that when you transform your Mac, it becomes as vulnerable to viruses and spyware as any other Windows PC.

Basic training

Here are the steps you must take to get through Boot Camp:

1. **Run Boot Camp Assistant (in the Utilities folder under Applications) to make sure you have the latest *firmware* on your computer.**

   You'll find any updates at `www.apple.com/support/downloads/`. Follow any on-screen instructions if you are updating the firmware.

2. **Click Burn a Macintosh CD, and insert a blank recordable CD or DVD.**

   Boot Camp Assistant guides you through burning a Macintosh Drivers CD, as shown in Figure 19-1. You need these software drivers later on to instruct Windows.

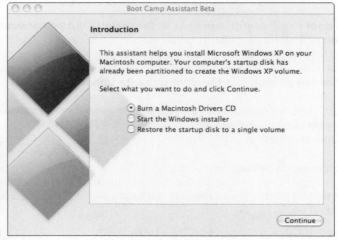

Figure 19-1: Getting through Boot Camp drills.

3. **Create a partition for Windows XP.**

   You are essentially carving out an area of your hard drive for the XP operating system. This partition must be at least 5GB and can swell as large as the total free disk space on hand minus 5GB. If you don't plan on doing much in Windows, keep the XP partition small; if you plan on running graphics-heavy games and a lot of Windows programs, you might devote a more generous chunk to Windows. Drag the divider to set the partitions for both OS X and XP.

4. **Insert the Windows XP CD. Click Start Installation.**

5. **When asked to select a Windows partition, select only partition C:.**

    Failure to do so could wipe out your entire Mac OS X startup disk.

6. **Format the partition in either NTFS or FAT.**

    FAT provides better compatibility between the two operating systems; NTFS is more reliable and secure.

7. **After Windows is installed, use the Mac Drivers CD you created in Step 2 so that AirPort, Bluetooth, the Eject key on the Mac keyboard, networking, audio, and graphics are recognized by the XP operating system.**

    A Startup Disk control panel for Windows is also added. You have to eject the Windows XP CD to install the Mac Drivers CD; to eject the CD, go to My Computer, select drive D:, and click Eject This Disk in the System Tasks list.

8. **When you see the message that the software "has not passed Windows Logo testing," click Continue Anyway.**

    Don't cancel any driver installers. The computer will restart.

9. **Follow any Found New Hardware instructions.**

As with any new Windows computer, Microsoft requires that you activate your XP software with 30 days.

Not everything in Windows may run smoothly (or at all) off the bat. For instance, many PC manufacturers include DVD decoders that help your machine recognize and play discs. But a DVD decoder is not included with a retail copy of XP. You'll have to separately add a DVD decoder for XP or merely watch those movies in Tiger.

As of this writing, certain peripherals and features were not supported under Boot Camp, including built-in iSight cameras, Apple's Bluetooth wireless keyboard and mouse, the Apple remote, the Apple USB modem, and keyboard backlighting on the MacBook and MacBook Pro notebooks.

Which raises the question? How do I return to OS X?

Switching operating systems

You can go back and forth between Tiger and XP, but you can't run both simultaneously under Boot Camp. Instead, you have to boot one operating system or the other, thus the name *Boot Camp.*

Here's how: Restart your machine and press down the Option key until icons for each operating system appear on the screen. Highlight Windows or Macintosh HD and click the arrow to launch the operating system you want for this particular session.

If you want OS X or Windows to boot every time, choose ⌘⇨System Preferences and click Startup Disk. Choose the OS you want to launch by default.

You can perform the same function in XP by choosing Start⇨Control Panel, and then choosing (under Category View) Performance and Maintenance. Next, click the Startup Disk control panel, and click either the Macintosh HD or Windows icon, depending on your startup preference.

A Parallels Universe

As we've just seen, Boot Camp's biggest drawback is its requirement that you reboot your computer every time you want to leave one operating system for a parallel universe. Can anyone spell *hassle?*

A remedy is available from a Virginia startup, Parallels, Inc., in the form of a *virtual machine.* Parallels Desktop for Mac (around $80) simulates a Windows machine inside its own screen within OS X. Or, if you feel like it, go full-screen with Windows. The faux machine behaves just like the real deal. You can add software, surf the Web, and listen to music (though I had trouble ejecting disks until I returned to the Mac environment).

You can even apply this virtualization stuff with versions of Windows dating back to Windows 3.1 as well as Linux, Solaris, OS/2, MS-DOS, and other operating systems.

Parallels differs from Boot Camp because you can run any OS *while* you run Tiger, without having to restart, as shown in Figure 19-2. What's more, you can share files and folders between OS X and Windows and cut and paste between the two.

Figure 19-2:
Entering a
Parallels
Windows.

There is a downside: Parallels spits out just enough technical jargon to ward off some users who might otherwise be attracted to such a program. Fortunately you can get the hang of Parallels quickly and ignore most of the scary terminology.

Here's how to fetch the program:

1. **Download a trial version at** `www.parallels.com/en/download`.

2. **Click Continue in the Downloads window on the Parallels-Desktop XXXX-Mac.dmg file.**

3. **Click the Parallels-Desktop.pkg icon.**

   A Welcome screen appears.

4. **Click Continue, and follow the instructions on all the other screens that appear.**

5. **Open the installed program from your Applications folder.**

6. **You'll have to choose and configure a virtual machine. Go with the recommended Create a Typical VM when asked how to proceed.**

7. **Specify the *Guest* operating system you have in mind.**

   In our exercise, it's Windows XP.

   8. **Enter a trial or permanent activation key, depending on whether you buy the program.**

   9. **Install Windows (or the OS of choice), typically by inserting a CD or DVD into the Mac.**

   You have to activate your copy of XP.

   You may be wondering, how do I control two operating systems with one mouse and keyboard? Clever of you to ask. Use the CD-player-like controls on the right edge of the Parallels Desktop window to turn on, stop, or pause your virtual machine, as shown in Figure 19-3. First turn on your virtual machine (by clicking the right-facing arrow), then click inside the Guest OS console, and your mouse belongs to Windows. Press Ctrl+Alt to release the mouse back into OS X's custody.

   By installing Parallels Tools under the VM menu, you can use the cursor in Windows without pressing any keyboard combinations.

Stop virtual machine (Windows)

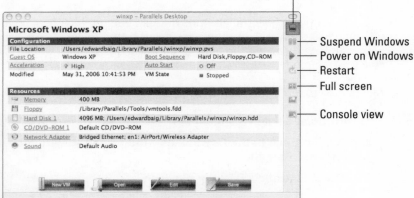

Suspend Windows
Power on Windows
Restart
Full screen

Console view

Figure 19-3:
Controlling
your virtual
machine.

   Virtual or not, you are running Windows on or inside your Mac. So take all the usual precautions of loading antivirus and other security software.

   Comforting, isn't it, to know that your Mac can do very nicely in a Windows world?

Chapter 20

Handling Trouble in Paradise

I'm reluctant to morph into Mr. Doom-and-gloom all of a sudden, but after reading about all the wonderful things Macs can do, it is my unpleasant duty to point out that bad @#$& happens. Even on a Mac.

Fortunately, most issues are minor. A stubborn mouse. Tired hardware. Disobedient software. Under the most dire circumstances, your computer or a key component within is on its last legs. A Mac, like any computer, is a machine after all.

That said, rarely is a problem beyond fixing. So stay calm, scan through the pages of this chapter, and with any luck you'll come across a troubleshooting tip to solve your problem. If not, I provide recommendations on where seek help.

A Cranky Computer

Your Mac was once a world-class sprinter but now can barely jog. Here are four possible explanations, and a fix to go with each one.

✔ **Your Mac needs more memory.** The programs you're running may demand more RAM than you have on hand. I always recommend getting as much memory as your computer (and wallet) permit. Adding RAM to the recent class of Mac machines isn't difficult (check your computer's documentation for specifics), though it does involve cracking open the case and making sure you're buying the right type of memory.

✔ **Your Mac is running out of hard drive space.** This is an easy one: Remove programs or files you no longer use. There must be something you can live without. But if every last bit is indispensable, purchase an additional drive.

✔ **Your Mac's processor, or CPU, is overtaxed.** If you suspect this might be the case, open the Activity Monitor, which is shown in Figure 20-1, by choosing Applications➪Utilities. Activity Monitor reveals a lot about the programs and processes currently running on your machine. Click the %CPU header to display the applications exacting the heaviest workload on your CPU (*central processing unit*). The most demanding are on top. Quit those you don't need at the moment.

✔ **The Mac may be trying to save energy.** If you're using a laptop, the Mac may be slowing the processor purposely. Choose ➪System Preferences and click Energy Saver. Click Options, and use the Processor Performance pop-up menu to switch from Reduced to Highest.

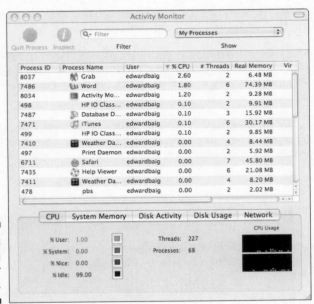

Figure 20-1:
Monitoring
your
activities.

A Frozen Computer or Program

Mentioning beach balls to anyone but a Mac maven usually conjures up pleasant images of the surf, sand, and a glorious summer afternoon. Now Mac people love a day at the beach as much as anybody. But the site of a colorful spinning beach ball is less welcome on your Apple, at least when that ball never seems to leave the screen. A beach ball that spins — and spins, and spins some more — is a sign that a cranky Mac has turned into a frozen Mac or that at least one of the programs on the machine is throwing a high-tech temper tantrum. (It isn't often that a frozen program will crash the entire system, but it does happen.) Those of you familiar with Windows can think of this as the Mac equivalent of the hourglass that lingers on-screen.

Your first instinct is to stick a pin inside this virtual *spinning beach ball of death,* if only you knew how. If you're a model of patience, you can attempt to wait the problem out and hope the spinning eventually stops. If it doesn't, consider the options described in this section.

Force Quit

Force Quit is the Mac's common way of telling an iced application "I'm as mad as hell and I'm not going to take it anymore." (If you're too young, that's a reference to the 1976 movie *Network,* as in television network.)

Choose ➪Force Quit or press ⌘ +Option+Esc. A window like the one in Figure 20-2 appears. Click the name of the deviant application (*not responding* probably appears next to its name). Under Force Quit you typically won't have to reboot your computer.

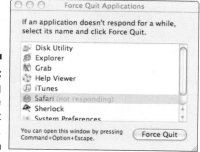

Figure 20-2:
Bailing through the Force Quit command.

Because you will lose any unsaved changes, Apple throws up a little admonition before allowing you to Force Quit. Alas, you may have no choice.

TIP

Ctrl-clicking a dock icon brings up a pop-up menu whose bottom item is Quit. If you hold down the Option key, Quit becomes Force Quit.

When a program quits on you

Sometimes, for reasons known to no man (or woman), a program keels over. Just like that. You could reopen the app and hope this was a one-time aberration caused by mischievous space aliens en route to the planet Vista. Or you might have a chronic ailment on your hands.

When programs suddenly drop, you may see dialog boxes with the word *unexpectedly*, like the ones shown in Figure 20-3. The box on the left appears the first time you experience this issue; the box at right shows what happens if the problem persists. If so, you may want to click Try Again to safely relaunch the fussy program. OS X restores the application's default settings (thus setting aside newer preferences settings), in case something you did (imagine that?) caused the snafu.

Figure 20-3:
When an application unexpectedly quits . . . and quits again.

Assuming everything went swell from there, you'll be given the option of keeping the new settings upon quitting the program. Your old preferences are saved in a file with a *.saved* extension, in case you ever want to go back. If that is the case, move the newer and current preferences file from its present location and remove the .saved extension from the older file.

If you feel like doing a good deed and sharing your experience with Apple (doing your itty-bitty part helps them make things right in the future), you see a screen like the one in Figure 20-4. Kindly note Apple won't directly get in touch with you about the issue.

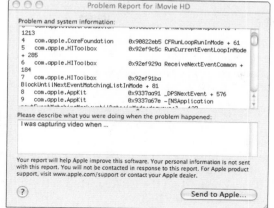

Figure 20-4:
Helping
Apple
trouble-
shoot.

If the problem continues, it may be time to visit the library. No, not that kind of library. A Preferences folder lives inside your Library folder, which in turn resides in your Home folder. Whew!.Got it? (And the ankle bone's connected to the shin bone, and the shin bone's connected to the . . .)

These preferences files have the *.plist* suffix and typically begin with *com.* followed by the name of the program, as in *com.microsoft.Word.plist.* Try dragging a .plist file with the name of the troubled application out to the desktop. If the program runs smoothly, trash the corrupted preferences file.

Now just to keep you on your toes, a separate Preferences folder resides inside a separate Library folder inside your Macintosh HD folder (which you can click on the left side of the Finder.) You may have to repeat this drill there.

Forcing a restart

Force Quit will usually rescue you from a minor problem, but it's not effective all the time. If that's the situation you're in now, you'll likely have to reboot. The assumption here is that your frozen computer won't permit you to start over in a conventional way by choosing ⌘⇨Restart.

Instead, try holding down the power button for several seconds or press Ctrl+⌘ and then the power button. If all else fails, pull the plug (or remove the battery from a laptop), though only as a last resort.

Safe boot

Starting up Tiger in *Safe mode* activates a series of measures designed to return your computer to good health. It runs a check of your hard drive (see the next section), loads only essential *kernel extensions* (system files) while ignoring others, trashes what are called *font cache* files, and disables startup and login items.

To start in Safe mode, press the power button to turn on your computer, and press and hold the Shift key the instant you hear the familiar welcome chime. Release Shift when the Apple logo appears. You'll know you've done it correctly because the words *Safe Boot* appear in the login window. (Prior to Tiger, the words *Safe Boot* appeared on the OS X startup screen; this feature was not an option before OS X version 10.2.)

Because of its under-the-hood machinations, it will take considerably longer to boot in Safe mode. This is perfectly normal. So is the fact that you can't use AirPort, a USB modem, or your DVD player, you can't capture footage in iMovie, and you can't use certain other applications or features.

If the Safe boot resolved your issue, restart the Mac normally next time, without pressing Shift. If not, it might be time to check your warranty or call in an expert, as noted later in this chapter.

Disk Utility

Just about every championship baseball team has a valuable utility player to fill nearly every position. The versatile *Disk Utility* tool on your Mac serves this purpose for all things hard drive–related. At a glance, it gives you a summary of your drives, including disk capacity, available space, and number of files and folders.

I'll concentrate on two of the main tasks Disk Utility performs: repairing damaged disks and fixing bungled *permissions,* as shown in Figure 20-5. Read the "Don't try (most of) this at home" sidebar for a peek at Disk Utility's other stunts.

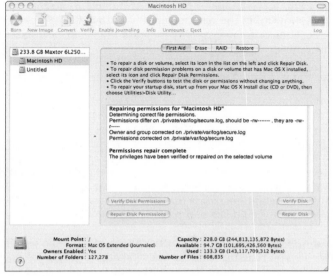

Figure 20-5:
Disk Utility
can fix
permissions
and repair
your hard
drive.

Permissions granted

As the computer's administrator, you have the right to open, view, and modify programs, folders, and files on your drive at will. Other user accounts on your system (as described in Chapter 5) are given varying privileges to read and change stuff. To regulate who gets to do what, the Mac has established a complex set of permissions.

Sometimes, because of new software you installed or a power glitch, these permissions get messed up, resulting in programs that freeze or fail to open. Disk Utility may be your salvation. Frankly, you may want to run the following steps anyway, as preventive maintenance, particularly if you installed a major operating system update or a new application:

1. **Open Disk Utility in the Utilities folder under Applications, and click the First Aid tab.**

2. **In the panel on the left, click to highlight the name of your hard drive.**

3. **Click Verify Disk Permissions to test permissions without changing anything (even if a permissions screw up is ultimately revealed) or click Repair Disk Permission to test *and* set things straight.**

Don't try and make heads or tails out of the log of puzzling messages that may show up in the results window as Disk Utility goes about its business. They don't necessarily indicate that your permissions were actually amiss.

Incidentally, you can only repair permissions on the disk you use to start OS X.

Repair job

If you suspect your hard drive is actually damaged (even a reboot doesn't seem to do much good), run Verify Disk to uncover any errors. If there are any, you must be an administrator to authorize a repair. You can't repair (or even test) *write-protected* disks and non-recordable CDs and DVDs.

But the most important restriction is this: Although you can use Disk Utility to test the drive you're using (and, as we've seen, fix permissions) you can't actually repair it until you boot from another disk. This is most likely your Mac OS X installation CD or DVD, which I hope you can easily lay your hands on. With that in mind, it's a good idea to make a copy of your install disc right now when you're thinking about it, and stash it in a safe place.

After booting with this other disc, open Disk Utility, select your startup disk, and click Repair Disk.

Incidentally, booting from the other disc is somewhat tricky. To do so, hold down the C key and wait until OS X boots. Make a language selection and select Disk Utility from the drop-down menu.

Get S.M.A.R.T.

After booting from the install disc, you may want to get really S.M.A.R.T. — as in Self-Monitoring Analysis and Reporting Technology. When you select a hard drive in Disk Utility, the S.M.A.R.T. status appears at the bottom of the window. If the status shows Verified, your disk is in okay shape.

If About to Fail appears in red, you have a ticking time bomb on your hands. Immediately back up your disk (or, at the very least, critical files) and replace the disc pronto.

Be aware that you can't check the S.M.A.R.T. status of all external drives.

Don't try (most of) this at home

Some of Disk Utility's other capabilities are downright scary for the novice user but worth mentioning just the same. For instance, you can use Disk Utility to erase your disks so that files can't be recovered. Unless you're a world-class spy, *you do not want to do this.*

The program can *partition,* or break up, your drive into separate volumes that Tiger treats as discrete disks.

Disk Utility can also create *disk images,* which are electronic files that store other files and folders and can be used for multiple purposes, such as backing up, hauling files from one Mac to another, and e-mailing files.

And here's a techie mouthful if ever there was one: Disk Utility can also create a *RAID scheme,* geek talk for Redundant Array of Independent Disks. It's a method of using several separate hard drives as a single volume.

Startup Problems

I just discussed a few ways to get you out of a pickle. But what if you can't even get the computer to start?

This is a very unusual circumstance. You probably have no power because the plug came loose (blame it on the dog or cat), the switch on the power strip is off, your battery ran out of juice, or there's a blackout in your neighborhood. Did you even notice that the lights went out?

On some laptops, you can tell if a battery needs recharging by pressing a small button on the battery. Lights on the battery let you know how much strength the battery has.

Here's another thing to try: Press power and hold down the ⌘, Option, P, and R keys and wait until you hear the startup chime a second time.

If you've added memory, installed an AirPort Card, or installed another component and the machine fails to start, make sure these are installed properly and try again. If your computer still can't be revived, try removing the memory or card you just installed and then give it another shot.

After that, if you still can't restart, you may have to seek warranty service, as discussed later in this chapter.

Reinstalling OS X

If a problem has truly brought your computer to its knees, it may be time to reinstall your favorite operating system. It's bad enough that you have to suffer through the hassle. (Remember that lengthy interrogation way back in Chapter 2?) Moreover, you're understandably panicked about retaining files and user settings.

Remain calm. Then do the following:

1. **Insert the OS X installation disk in your CD or DVD drive.**

2. **Double-click the Install Mac OS X icon and go through the usual installation drill.**

3. **When asked, choose your current OS X disk as your destination disk (which in all likelihood is your only option anyway).**

4. **Click Options.**

   You've arrived at an important point in the process.

5. **If you want to salvage existing files and settings, select Archive and Install and then Preserve Users and Networks Settings. If you prefer starting anew, select Erase and Install, keeping in mind that you can't undo it.**

6. **Click Continue.**

7. **To install certain parts of OS X, click Customize. To perform Apple's recommended basic installation, click Install.**

8. **Because the OS X disk you have may not have all the latest tweaks, pay a visit to Software Update (found in the menu) to bring Tiger up to date.**

A retail version of OS X may differ some from the version that was loaded on your computer.

Reinstalling OS 9

Reinstalling OS 9 or, for that matter, running so-called Classic apps, is no longer an option under Intel Macs (see the "Turn-of-the-century Macs" sidebar). But if you have an older machine, you can install a Mac OS 9 System folder with an OS 9 install CD or OS X installation discs. If the former, hold down the C key as your Mac restarts. This will let you start from the disc in your optical drive. If using an OS X disc, insert the Additional Software & Hardware Test disc. Then double-click Install Additional Software and you'll be guided on-screen from there.

Turn-of-the-century Macs

Back in 1999, people fretted about Y2K. Bill Clinton was acquitted in his impeachment trial. Lance Armstrong captured the first of his Tour de France titles. During the fall of that year, Apple introduced OS 9, the beginning of the end for what came to be known as the *Classic* Mac operating system. OS 9 finally yielded to something new and better in 2001, the more robust OS X, our Mac playground throughout this book. (Before the fact checkers come after me, OS X was available as a public beta in 2000.)

The very next year, Steve Jobs presided over a mock funeral for OS 9 at a conference. Apple's boss mournfully lifted an OS 9 box out of a casket and quipped, "He's now in that great bit bucket in the sky." OS 9 was still breathing,

though. Macs sold early in the 21st century could start in the new operating system through an OS 9 *simulator* called Classic mode. Macs sold after January 2003 would start only in OS X, though folks could continue to use older software through OS X's Classic environment.

This too would not last. In 2006, with the introduction of the Intel Macs, Apple announced that Classic would no longer be supported. OS 9 finally entered the history books. There's not much to running Classic apps (if your computer is capable). Double-click an OS 9 program, and the Classic environment kicks into gear. If visible, you can also click the number 9 icon in the OS X menu bar and choose Start Classic.

Common Fixes to Other Problems

Your computer won't have to visit the emergency room or undergo major surgery. But a little first aid is probably in order here and there. In this section, I consider some minor snags.

A jumpy mouse

Real mice live for dust and grime. And so for a long time did computer rodents. But the optical-style mice included with the most recent Macs don't get stuck like their ancestors because this kind of critter doesn't use the little dust-collecting rolling ball on its underbelly.

Be aware that optical mice don't particularly like glass or reflective surfaces, so if you find your mouse on one, use a mouse pad or slip a piece of paper underneath.

If your mouse doesn't respond at all, unplug it from the USB port and then plug it in again, just to make sure the connection is snug. If you have a wireless mouse, make sure the batteries are fresh.

Meanwhile, if you want to change the speed of your on-screen mouse pointer or want to change clicking speeds, visit Keyboard & Mouse under System Preferences, as described in Chapter 4.

A stuck CD

It's really cool the way most Macs practically suck up a CD. Here's what's not cool: when your mouse won't spit out the disc.

Take a stab at one of these fixes:

- ✔ Quit the program using the disc and then press Eject on the keyboard.

- ✔ Open a Finder window, and click the little eject icon in the sidebar. Or try dragging the disc icon from the Mac desktop to the trash.

- ✔ Log out of your user account (under the menu) and then press Eject on the keyboard.

- ✔ Restart the computer while holding down the mouse button.

My Mac can no longer tell time

If your computer can no longer keep track of the time and date, its internal backup battery may have bit the dust. You can't replace the battery yourself, so you'll have to contact the Apple store or an authorized service provider.

The wrong program answers the call of duty

The Mac makes certain assumptions about which application ought to open a particular file when summoned. For example, Preview is Tiger's document viewer of choice and routinely handles JPEG graphics and PDF documents, while DOC files are the province of Microsoft Word. But say you want the Adobe programs Photoshop and Reader to be responsible for JPEGs and PDFs, and Mac's own word processor, TextEdit, to take care of DOC duties?

Here's what to do:

1. **Highlight the icon of the program you want opened by a different application and press ⌘+I.**

2. **In the Get Info panel that appears, click the right-facing triangle next to Open With and choose the application to handle the document from here on out, as shown in Figure 20-6.**

   In this example, I've taken a DOC file that would otherwise open in Word and put TextEdit in charge. Incidentally, if you want to open the file from a different parent than Apple suggests, choose Other from the drop-down list.

Figure 20-6:
Letting a
different
application
open your
file.

Alternatively, access the Open With command by highlighting the file icon in question and choosing File⇨Open With. You can also bring up the Get Info pane from the same menu. Still another way to get to Open With: Press control while clicking the icon (or right-click if your mouse has two buttons).

3. **If you want the application to open each and every file you beckon in the future, click Change All.**

Kernel clink

Out of the blue, you are asked to restart your computer. In numerous languages, no less. Your machine has been hit with a *kernel panic*. The probable cause is corrupted or incompatible software. (One of these panics can also be induced by damaged hardware, although that is highly unlikely.)

The good news is that a system restart usually takes care of the problem with no further harm. If not, try removing any memory or hardware you've recently added. Of if you think some new software you installed may have been the culprit, head to the software publisher's Web site and see whether they've issued a downloadable fix or upgrade.

SOS for DNS

If you're surfing the Web with Safari or another browser and get a message about a DNS entry not being found, you typed the wrong Web address or URL, the site in question no longer exists (or never did), or the site is having temporary problems. DNS is computer jargon for *Domain Name System*. Similar messages may be presented as a *404 not found on this server* error.

Curing the trash can blues

In the physical world, you may try and throw something out of your trash but can't because the rubbish gets stuck to the bottom of the can. The virtual trash can on your Mac sometimes suffers a similar fate: A file refuses to budge when you click Empty Trash under the Finder menu.

Try junking the files by holding down the Option key when you choose Empty Trash.

There are a few possible explanations why a file refuses to go quietly. For starters, you can't delete an item that is open somewhere else on your computer, so make sure it's indeed closed. Moreover, you may be trying to ditch a file to which you do not have sufficient permission. The other most likely explanation is that a locked file is in the trash. You can unlock it by choosing File➪Get Info and making sure the Locked box is unchecked.

After a program unexpectedly crashes, one or more Recovered Files folders may appear in your trash after a restart. Temporary files are often used and disposed of by your applications, but during a crash these may not get disposed. If any of these files are valuable, drag them out of trash. More often than not, however, it is safe to discard them with the rest of the garbage.

Useful Routine Maintenance

Your computer can use some TLC every so often. Here are a few tips for helping it out.

Purge unnecessary files and programs

If you've had your Mac for awhile, you've probably piled on programs and files that no longer serve a purpose. Maybe they're drivers associated with a printer you replaced a couple of years ago. Maybe it's software you fell out of love with. Even if these files aren't slowing the system down, they're hogging disk space. These programs may even be agitating in the background. The Activity Monitor I mentioned earlier in this chapter may clue you in.

Bottom line: It's time to send these files and programs off to retirement for good (with a generous severance package, of course). You already know how to trash files. But it's not always obvious *which* files to dispose of. Some programs leave shrapnel all over your hard drive.

Type the name of the application you are getting rid of inside a Finder search box and do your best to determine whether files shown in the results are associated with the application you want to blow off.

Don't delete files that you know little or nothing about. The consequences aren't pretty if you accidentally trash a crucial system file. If you do throw unfamiliar files in the trash, wait a day or so until you're satisfied that you don't need them.

Backing up your treasures

I know I've beaten you on the head with this throughout the book. Consider this the final nag. Back up. Back up. Back up. Whether you use Disk Utility, Mac's Backup, third-party software, or another method, JUST DO IT. SOONER THAN LATER. There, I've finished shouting.

Repair permissions

For information on repair permissions, see the "Disk Utility" section, earlier in this chapter.

Updating software

As a matter of course, visit Software Update under System Preferences or in the menu, or arrange to have your Mac check regularly for updates. I update weekly, but you can have your computer do it as often as every day or as infrequently as monthly (which I don't recommend). If you're passing through System Preferences for any other reason, you can always go to Software Update and click Check Now.

Head over to the support areas of the Web sites of the publishers of other software on your computer to see whether they've updated their programs. The download is typically free.

Summoning Outside Help

Pretty much everything I've described in this chapter up to now is something you ought to be able to handle on your own. But eventually you'll run into situations beyond your expertise, especially if you face a serious hardware issue. Or perhaps you merely lack the time, patience, inclination, or confidence. I understand your reluctance. Fortunately, you can find help in plenty of places, though the help is not always free.

Third-party software

For all the fine troubleshooting tools included on a Mac, you may at times want to look to outside software. In this section I describe some of the programs that may bail you out of a jam or help with routine maintenance Prices and version numbers are subject to change. If you have an Intel Mac, make sure you get the Universal version.

- ✔ Alsoft DiskWarrior for OS X, at www.alsoft.com. An $80 repair utility that warns you of impending drive failure.

- ✔ Cocktail, at www.macosxcocktail.com. An inexpensive $15 shareware utility.

- ✔ OnyX 1.7.1, at http://www.titanium.free.fr/pgs/english.html. A free downloadable program from Titanium Software, shown in Figure 20-7, that can run a variety of maintenance tasks.

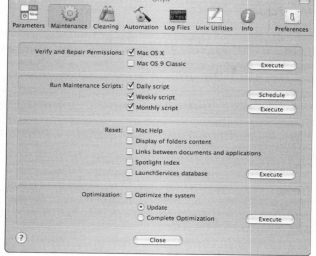

Figure 20-7:
OnyX
proves
useful third-
party
programs
can be
obtained for
free.

✔ Prosoft Data Rescue II, at www.prosofteng.com. A $100 program designed to help you recover files from a corrupt hard drive.

✔ SpringCleaning 8.0, at www.allume.com. Aims to boost performance by helping to eliminate stray files. The $50 utility is from Allume Systems.

✔ TechToolPro, at www.micromat.com. A problem solver billed as a "repair shop in a box." The $98 program is from Micromat.

AppleCare

Your Mac comes with 90 days of free telephone support and a year of free support at an authorized Apple retailer. The extended warranty program called AppleCare lengthens the time you can get free phone support to three years (from the day of purchase).

AppleCare covers the computer itself plus AirPort Express and Extreme base stations and Apple RAM (used with the Mac, of course). Certain models, including Mac Mini, let you also cover one Apple display if purchased at the same time.

Fees depend on the gear you're covering: AppleCare for an Apple display is $99; Mac Mini, $149; iMac or eMac, $169; MacBook, Power Mac, $249; PowerBook or MacBook Pro, $349. Extended warranties are like any form of insurance — a crap shoot, but a crap shoot worth taking for some folks.

Consulting Einstein

One of the features of the Apple retail store is the Genius Bar. Apple's in-store experts can answer questions about your Mac and, if need be, install memory and handle repairs (for a fee). My own experience leads me to believe that these (mostly) young men and women are quite knowledgeable about the subjects you're likely to hit them with. Judging by blog posts, however, not all of them are ready for Mensa. Now the bad news. You can't exactly mosey up to the Genius bar. Which leads me to . . .

Making a reservation

Meeting up with an Apple-branded Genius requires an appointment. Go to www.apple.com/retail and click the Apple store near you. Look for Apple Store Concierge and click Make a Reservation. You'll have to sign in as a Guest or ProCare member (see the next section). You can stake a claim on the next available opening.

If you're already in an Apple store and it's not crowded, make a reservation on the spot using one of the Macs in the store.

While in the store (or perusing the Web site), you may want to check the schedule of free classes, including various workshops in iLife, iWeb, and OS X.

Consulting a pro

As a ProCare member, you can book an appointment with a Genius at the store of your choice up to a week in advance. At $99 a year, ProCare isn't cheap, but you get the following princely privileges: priority repairs, a free hour of one-on-one training on topics you choose, admission to creative Studio classes in certain stores, an annual computer tune-up (systems diagnostics, a cleaning for your display and keyboard, and more) and help setting up a new machine.

Help, I need somebody

It sounds like a cliché, but free (or low-cost) help is all around you:

- ✔ The geeky next-door neighbor, your cubicle-mate, or the friends you didn't know you had on the World Wide Web.
- ✔ At a social networking site such as Meetup.com, you can search for and perhaps find a Macintosh user group meeting in your neck of the woods.

✔ Get referrals from Apple at `www.apple.com/usergroups`. You'll find a national and local events calendar, and you can enter your Zip code to find a group close by.

✔ For free online answers, poke around the newsgroups and computer bulletin boards, as described in Chapter 11.

✔ Check out the knowledge base of searchable troubleshooting articles at `www.apple.com/support`.

✔ Before leaving a chapter on troubleshooting and the geek section of this book, I'd be remiss if I didn't mention one other avenue for help. It's the Help menu found with most every program you use. To be sure, not every one of your questions will be answered or answered satisfactorily. But before heading on a wild goose chase in search of an enlightening response, give the Help menus a try. They've been right there all along.

Part VI

The Part of Tens

The 5th Wave   By Rich Tennant

© RICHTENNANT

THE PODCAST "LAMP TALK" WAS ABOUT TO BECOME "EXPLICIT."

"Sometimes these sockets need cleaning. First, make sure the lamp is unplugged, and then..."

In this part . . .

I'm always volunteering my top ten movie lists for a given year or genre, but then this isn't *Movie Appreciation For Dummies*. I guess it's not appropriate for me to serve up a list of my top ten favorite songs of all time either.

In this part, I meet my "lists of ten" *For Dummies* quota with ten top Apple- and Mac-related Web sites, ten nifty dashboard widgets, and ten more neat stunts your machine can adeptly handle, with a helpful assist from you.

(Pssst keep it quiet, but there's *The Godfather, Citizen Kane* . . .)

Chapter 21

Ten Clever Dashboard Widgets

*T*hink of the Dashboard widgets of Chapter 6 fame as a reflection of our busy lives. We're all distracted, pressed for time, going every which way. We generally know what we want, and we want it now. In this fast food society, snack software seems inevitable.

In this chapter, I present in alphabetical order a list of ten yummy widgets. With more than 2,000 widgets available as of this writing, you can easily come up with a menu of ten more widgets, and ten more after that. And so on. To find them, head to www.apple.com/downloads/dashboard.

Cocktail

Can you mix an, um, Apple Martini? Kamikaze? Or Piper at the Gates of Dawn? The free Cocktail widget from Seven lets you impress buddies with your bartender skills. Just type the drink you have in mind. Cocktail's database includes nearly 7,000 drink recipes. Click "Feelin Thirsty?" for a random selection. With its martini-glass icon, shown in Figure 21-1, Cocktail has one of the better-looking widgets too.

Figure 21-1:
I'll have a
Cocktail
with that
widget.

Countdown Plus

Hmm. Steven Chaitoff's simple Countdown Plus widget tells you how much time is remaining until a specified date, such as the newborn's due date, your next vacation, your anniversary, or the day you'll be paroled.

Gas

I loath paying a small ransom at the pump. Gas from Interdimension Media might help you save a few pennies per gallon. The widget promises updated information from GasPriceWatch.com. You can sort results by Regular, Plus, Premium, or Diesel and find stations within 20 miles of a designated Zip code. What's more, click the address of the gas station of choice, and the widget fires up Google Maps on your browser.

The Gas widget is free, but its producers hope you'll donate some of your savings to them (via PayPal). You can display the widget with a pole, as shown in Figure 21-2, or without.

Hurricane Tracker

If you live or expect to vacation in an area affected by hurricanes, Hurricane Tracker from Travel Widgets is a useful resource (see Figure 21-3). Roll the mouse pointer over the widget and click the little *i* on the bottom-right corner of the screen. That takes you to the back of the widget, where you can choose the location you're monitoring (such as Atlantic, Gulf of Mexico, or Northeast Pacific). Or choose how you want satellite images to appear (Visible, Infrared, Water Vapor).

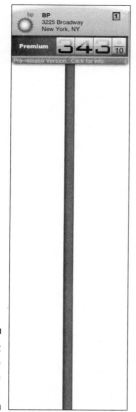

Figure 21-2:
A widget to find cheap gas.

Figure 21-3:
Tracking storms.

Morse Code Translator

.../—/... SOS is about the only thing I recall about Morse code from my Boy Scout days, but that doesn't matter thanks to Morse Code Translator, shown in Figure 21-4. This nifty widget teaches you the Morse alphabet and converts text to Morse code and Morse code to text. Just remember to have the Mac handy when you have to send a distress signal from your yacht.

Figure 21-4:
"Dot dot dot, dash dash dash." The Morse Code Translator widget.

Oh, and you may also want to memorize the following dots and dashes:

-/.-.//..-/-/-/.-./..-././/.-././.-/-/.///...//.-//.-././.-/

That's Morse code for *my computer won't start.*

Reverse Phone Lookup

The Reverse Phone Lookup is a handy widget for anyone who has ever written down a phone number on a scrap of paper and forgotten to jot the person's name or sees a number but no name on Caller ID. Type the area code and phone number; if the listing is public, you'll see the name and address.

pearLyrics/Sing that iTune

Sad refrain. One of my favorite widgets, pearLyrics, is no longer available, apparently over legal disputes with some in the music industry. I included pearLyrics because it still works on my machine and the idea behind it is so appealing to any music fan who has ever wanted to sing along but can't remember the words. Besides, you can still download a similar widget called Sing that iTune.

The two widgets display the lyrics of songs you're listening to in iTunes, at least some of the time. Unlike Sing that iTune, pearLyrics does not display album cover art. But in my experience, it uncovered lyrics far more often and delivered them more quickly than Sing that iTune.

If no lyrics are found, you could click directly onto the pearLyrics widget to initiate a Google search for the words. Moreover, if you click the lyrics displayed inside the widget, they are copied to your clipboard. Who knows, maybe pearLyrics will return by the time you read this. In the meanwhile, check out Sing that iTune.

Send SMS

SMS stands for Short Message Service, a popular global standard for dispatching text messages to cell phones. This widget from Alco Bolm Software lets you send text messages to a mobile phone from your keyboard. You type your missive in the area provided on the front of the widget, and then click to flip it over to enter a recipient and a phone number.

Your first purchase totals $15 (you can pay through PayPal) and covers the $10 annual fee and first 50 SMS messages ($5).Or check out a free alternative such as Keaka Jackson's SMS, found at `http://keakaj.com/sms.htm`.

Wikipedia

With the free collaborative Wikipedia encyclopedia, which I describe in Chapter 11, you can search on most any topic imaginable. Or try clicking the little "?" button next to the search field to display an article randomly, on subjects ranging from the Danish parliamentary election of 1975 to Modern Kung Fu. Keep in mind that anyone can contribute to a Wikipedia entry, so the information you uncover may be open to interpretation and possibly inaccurate. Click the Wikipedia button in the widget to jump to the full Wikipedia site.

Word of the Day

I'm feeling rather *sedulous*. After all, I'm diligent in my application or pursuit and steadily industrious. Besides, sedulous is my Word of the Day, delivered by a widget of the same name. Definitions (like the one provided in the sentence before this one) are supplied by Dictionary.com.

Apparently lots of folks are seeking to bolster their vocabulary. In requesting a PayPal donation, developer haym37.com says about 100,000 people refresh or load the widget daily, placing an enormous strain on the company's servers.

Chapter 22

Ten Indispensable Mac Web Sites

. . . .

. . . .

*I*n my line of work, I often get the "how come you didn't" e-mail or phone call, as in "how come you didn't write about my company or product?" So I won't be shocked to hear folks asking about this chapter, "how come you didn't choose my favorite Macintosh Web site?" Limiting any list to ten is exceedingly difficult. Especially when it comes to Web sites about your trusted computer. Please know that I know there are terrific sites that are not on this list. With that, here goes.

Macrank

www.macrank.com

You might say I was a tad defensive at the top of this chapter, alluding to all the Web sites I would *not* mention. Well, chances are you'll find your favorite cyberdestinations at Macrank, which ranks the top 100 sites for the Mac and iPod. Visitors to Macrank can rate sites from 1 (lowest) to 10 (highest) and add a comment.

MacFixIt

www.macfixit.com

When something has gone wrong and you're still seeking answers despite my best efforts in Chapter 20, check out MacFixIt. This troubleshooting site tackles a gaggle of issues, though you'll have to pay $24.95 a year for full access to more than a decade of content. Among the many topics I came across were making banking sites work with Safari; unresponsive keyboards; iMovie: "Disk Responded Slowly" alerts; and "Trackpad button clicks not registering" in the MacBook.

MacOSX Hints

www.macosxhints.com

At the MacOSX Hints site, you can learn to create a partitioned RAID setup, convert PowerPoint graphic metafiles, and secure e-mail with digital certificates. As you can see, some of the searchable hints can get pretty technical.

MacRumors

www.macrumors.com

Apple is one of the most secretive outfits on the planet. Seldom does the company spill the beans on new products in advance. That doesn't prevent numerous Apple watchers from speculating on what might be coming out of Cupertino. Besides, who doesn't love a juicy rumor now and then? Is Apple merging with Nintendo? Is Apple coming out with a higher quality iTunes? Head to MacRumors for the latest dirt.

MacSurfer

www.macsurfer.com

MacSurfer is a wonderful resource for the Apple news junkie. MacSurfer's Headline News sports links to articles on all things Apple, including traditional

media, Web sites, Apple itself, and bloggers. Links are segregated by Apple/
Macintosh, OS X, General Interest/Potpourri, Apple Hardware/Software,
Reviews/How-To/Tutorials/Tips, Analysis/Commentary/Editorial/Opinion,
Press Releases/Products/Public Relations, Computer Industry, Finances, and
more.

Macworld

www.macworld.com

It's all here at Macworld: news (via MacCentral.com), troubleshooting through
blogs such as Mac 911, product reviews, and current and past articles from
Macworld magazine.

The Unofficial Apple Weblog

www.tuaw.com

The Unofficial Apple Weblog (tuaw) is an enthusiast's blog that lets people
comment on Apple articles and reviews written by the likes of yours truly in
USA TODAY. (Sure it's a shameless plug for me and my paper, but we are near-
ing the end of the book. And there are plenty of links to articles by lots of
other journalists.)

Think Secret

www.thinksecret.com

Did I mention that Apple keeps things close to the vest? Think Secret digs for
inside Apple dope and often finds it. In fact, in 2005, Apple sued the 19-year-old
running Think Secret (claiming theft of trade secrets). Think Secret correctly
reported on what became the Mac Mini and iPod Shuffle, prior to the launch of
those products. (Apple came after two other sites at the time, PowerPage.org
and Apple Insider.) For all the leaking coming out of Washington, obviously
Silicon Valley has its moles too.

VersionTracker

www.versiontracker.com

VersionTracker is a repository for downloadable shareware, freeware, and updates to Mac software. Click a name to learn more about what a program does and to eyeball ratings and feedback.

And Last but Not Least, Apple.com

www.apple.com

Apple may seem like an obvious place to go. Heck, you probably already landed there just by opening Safari the first time. And you may not love the full blitz of Mac and iPod advertising and promotions, even if you already drank Apple's Kool-Aid. But presumably most of you already have sweet feelings for the company's products.

As I hinted at in Chapter 20, www.apple.com is full of helpful resources, especially for, but not limited to, newbies. You can download software updates and manuals, post questions in discussion forums, read press releases, and consult the knowledge base. Mostly, I think, you'll walk away with a renewed sense of good will for the company responsible for the computer most of you fancy so much.

Chapter 23

Ten Things to Leave You With

So here we are hundreds of pages into this book and there's still more to tell. Truth is, I could probably go on for hundreds more pages and still not do justice to everything your Mac can accomplish (with more than a little help from you, of course.) So even though the programs, functions, or capabilities covered in this chapter didn't quite make it into the book elsewhere, don't consider them unloved or an afterthought.

At the risk of tossing another well-worn cliché your way, last is most definitely not least.

Remote Madness

Roughly the size of a Bic disposable lighter or an iPod Shuffle, the simple iPod-white Apple remote, which the company has started including with recent Mac models, has minimal buttons: play/pause, volume up/down, fast-forward, rewind, and Menu. It's main purpose is to control the friendly icons and menus that make up the new Front Row interface (mentioned in Chapter 4) that lets you listen to music, and view photos, DVDs, and videos from across the room. But the multitalented Apple remote can also help you listen to an iPod, provided it has what's called a Universal Dock connector.

But suppose you have more than one Mac that's compatible with the remote control or an Apple accessory such as iPod Hi-Fi. You may want to *pair* the remote with a specific computer or other gear so that pressing the button doesn't make all the machines in one room bump heads. Here's how: Move the remote within three or four inches of the Mac and press and hold the fast forward and Menu buttons at the same time for five seconds. A little chain link symbol appears onscreen to tell you the pairing has been completed.

The Apple remote adheres to an iMac through a small magnet on the bottom right side of the computer. This arrangement makes it convenient to stow away. But wouldn't you know, there's a warning in the iMac manual to avoid putting an external hard drive, iPod, memory card, or other magnetic media too close to the magnet. I'm not sure any company can write a manual these days without putting in such warnings to satisfy lawyers. Because I'm pretty sure I've placed my iPod near the magnet without causing any damage. That said, follow or ignore this advice at your own risk.

If Math Moves You

I don't pretend to know a Conchoid (Figure 23-1) from a Lorentz's Attractor; the mathematics are frankly lost on me. But the Grapher bundled with Tiger and accessed through the Utilities folder (under Applications) lets you graph two- and three-dimensional mathematical equations. Moreover, the program's animations are pretty darn cool. And if you're curious about what the aforementioned Conchoid, Lorentz's Attractor, and other 2D and 3D formulas and equations look like, click the names in the Grapher Examples menu.

Speaking Another Language

Way back when you first set up your computer, you selected the language you wanted to use. But circumstances change. You suddenly have the opportunity to run your company's Rome office, and now you must immerse yourself in Italian.

To change your computer's preferred language, choose System Preferences from the menu and select International. Click the Language tab, as shown in Figure 23–2. Drag the language you want to use for application menus, dialog boxes, and so forth to the top of the language list.

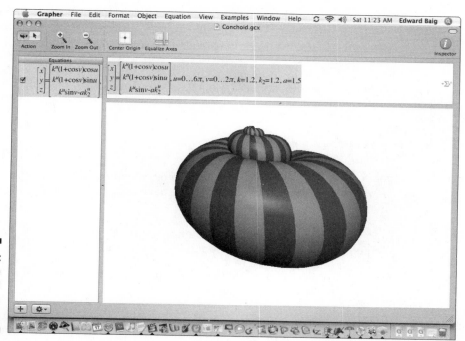

Figure 23-1:
Graphing a
Conchoid
through
Grapher.

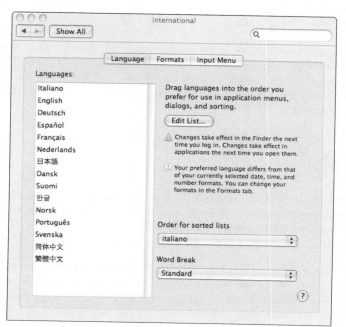

Figure 23-2:
The Mac is
multilingual.

Next, click the Formats tab under International to choose the region you live in, customize dates, time, and native currency, or decide whether to go metric or use the U.S. system of measurement.

If you also click the Input Menu tab, you can choose a different keyboard layout, such as the Japanese Kana Palette or the Korean Hangul.

Zip It in the Bud

Files you download off the Internet are often compressed or zipped — and for good reason. Zipped files take up less space and arrive much faster than files that haven't been squeezed down.

Compressed files are easily identified by their extensions, such as *.zip* (a common standard used in OS X and Windows) and *.sit*. Such files must be unzipped before you can read them. Prior to Tiger, Apple included a program for this purpose called StuffIt Expander from Allume Systems. But Tiger lets you decompress .zip files sans StuffIt.

StuffIt still comes in handy, though, for opening other types of compressed files, notably the .sit or .sitx compressed types. Go to `www.stuffit.com/mac/index.html` to download a free version of the software or to splurge for the Deluxe version (around $80, though I've seen it discounted for much less). In addition to shrinking files to a fraction of their size, StuffIt Deluxe lets you encrypt and back up files.

 Meanwhile, you can archive or create your own .zip files through Tiger. Right-click (or Ctrl-click) files you want to compress inside Finder and choose Create Archive Of. The newly compressed files carry the .zip extension. The archive is created in the same location as the original file and is named *originalfilename*.zip.

FYI on FTP

FTP, or *File Transfer Protocol,* sites are typically set up by companies or individuals to make it easy to exchange sizable files over the Internet, typically but not exclusively video or picture files. The Mac has a built-in FTP server for giving other folks access to your machine.

To grant such access, choose ⌘⇨System Preferences, and click Sharing. Make sure the Services tab is highlighted. In the Service window, select FTP Access, shown in Figure 23-3. People on other computers can now share and copy files to and from your machine.

Don't take this step lightly. Consider the security ramifications before allowing just anyone access to your machine.

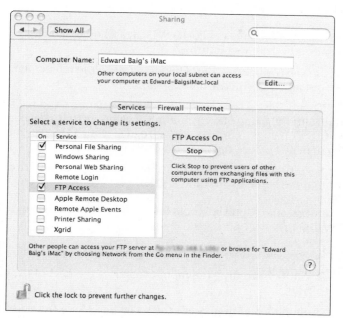

Figure 23-3:
Granting
FTP access.

Now suppose you want to access somebody else's FTP site. From the Finder Menu, choose Go⇨Connect to Server. Enter the server address in the box provided and click Connect. Depending on the server you're attempting to connect to, you'll likely have to enter a name and a password.

You may be able to drag and drop files from your machine onto that FTP server. But often you need help from outside software. I rely on a $25 shareware program called Fetch (available at www.fetchsoftworks.com) to dump files onto an FTP server. Other fine FTP choices including Transmit (www.panic.com) and RBrowser (www.rbrowser.com).

Screen Capture

Unless you're planning on writing a book similar to this one, you're probably wondering why the heck you'd ever want to take a picture of your computer screen. Let me suggest a couple of possibilities: maybe you want to take a picture of the screen for a presentation at work. Or perhaps you want to show precisely what a funky error looks like to the person who just might help you correct the problem. (Then again maybe you really are going to write a book like this.)

Regardless of motivation, if you want to grab a picture of the Mac screen (or any of its windows) it may be time to open the Grab utility. Go to Applications⇨Utilities and click Grab. Through Grab's Capture menu, you can take a picture of a full screen, window, or menu, as follows:

- ✔ Select Window (or press Shift+⌘+W), click Choose Window, then click the window to grab its picture.

- ✔ Select Screen (or press ⌘+Z). Then to capture the full screen, click anywhere outside the window that appears.

- ✔ Select Timed Screen (or press Shift+⌘+Z) to capture the full screen 10 seconds after clicking Start Timer in the window that shows up. This gives you a chance to prepare the screen to your liking (perhaps by activating a menu) before the image is captured.

- ✔ Select Selection (or Shift+cmd+A). Then use the mouse to drag over the portion of the screen you want to grab.

Still other universal system shortcuts follow, without you having to open the Grab utility:

- ✔ Press ⌘+Shift+3 to take a picture of the whole screen.

- ✔ Press ⌘+Shift+4 and drag the mouse to select the part of the screen you want to grab.

- ✔ Press ⌘+Shift+4, and then press the spacebar. Move the pointer to highlight an area you want in the picture, and then click. This is useful for taking a picture of, say, the menu bar or dock. If you press the spacebar again, you can select the area by dragging the mouse instead. Press the Escape key to cancel.

Screen shots captured in this matter are saved as files on the desktop. If you'd rather paste the captured image into a document, press the Control key when you press the other keyboard combinations, which places the picture in the Clipboard. From there, you can paste the image into your chosen document.

Watching TV on a Mac

For all its multimedia glitz, none of the Mac models, at least as of this writing, comes with a built-in television tuner. It's one of the few areas in which machines based on Microsoft's Media Center software claim bragging rights. Not only do such Media Center machines let you watch TV directly from your computer screen, but they function much like TiVo digital video recorders or DVRs. Among other stunts that means you can pause and rewind "live" TV and record shows to watch on your schedule, not the one some network programming exec has in mind.

Just because Apple hasn't gotten around to putting a TV tuner in the Mac, the same cannot be said of third-party companies. For example, Miglia's TVMini HD (about $250) is a compact HDTV tuner that plugs into a USB port. It lets you watch over-the-air digital TV and HDTV, and record high-definition programming to your hard drive. And yes, like TiVo, you can pause and rewind live TV. Go to www.miglia.com for more information or visit the online Apple store.

I also recommend checking out the various EyeTV options from Elgato Systems. To find the appropriate EyeTV product, visit www.elgatosystems.com and indicate the country you live in and the source of your television programming (standard analog cable, satellite, HDTV, digital cable, and so on). Elgato will help you find a match.

Read Magazines

The next version of OX X, dubbed Leopard, is on the way (and may have hit the market by the time you read this). It's practically a given stuff will change. By its nature, technology is a scorching hot, competitive, time-sensitive business and Apple moves more quickly than most. So while I trust the information in this book will prove useful for the foreseeable if not long-term future, I have to admit some of the info will go stale. An excellent way to stay current is to regularly peek at some of the prominent Mac-oriented magazines, including *MacAddict, MacHome,* and *Macworld.*

Would You Like to Play a Game of Chess?

Ah, the question posed by the (ultimately) defiant Hal 9000 computer in the classic film *2001: A Space Odyssey.* Turns out, your Mac can play a rather mean game of chess too, without, as HAL did, turning on its human masters. The Mac's Chess program, found in the Applications folder, lets you compete against the computer or a human partner.

What's more, by accessing Preferences under the Chess menu, you can change the board style and pieces from the wooden board shown in Figure 23-4 to grass, marble, or metal. You can also drag a slider inside Chess Preferences to make the computer play faster or stronger.

Edward Baig – Computer (2. ... e7–e5)

Figure 23-4:
Your move.

Just like HAL, your Mac can speak as it makes its moves — in about two dozen voices, no less, from Deranged (probably appropriate for HAL) to Hysterical. Then again, you can speak back, so long as Allow Player to Speak Moves is checked in Preferences. Try it out for size: "Pawn e2 to e4 to move the white king's pawn," for example.

Which leads me to the next section.

Speech Recognition

Are you the bossy type who likes to bark out orders? If so, you'll love that the Mac can respond to your spoken commands, everything from "Quit this application" to "Switch to Finder." And for people physically unable to type or handle a mouse, speech recognition may be their only avenue to getting things done on a computer.

Open System Preferences, again under the app menu, and choose Speech. Make sure the Speech Recognition pane is selected, as shown in Figure 23-5. Now, click to turn on the Speakable Items button. Figure 23-6 shows the round microphone feedback window that appears on your desktop, with the key or keyword you need to press to alert the Mac that you are about to speak. You expect the computer to respond accordingly. The Escape key handles this task by default.

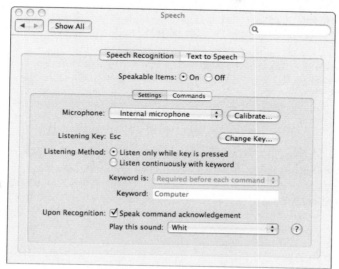

Figure 23-5:
The Mac is all about free speech.

Figure 23-6:
The speech-feedback window.

To check out a list of the commands your computer can understand, click the little triangle at the bottom of the feedback window and then click Open Speech Commands window.

Click Calibrate to improve the performance of your internal (or connected) microphone. The calibration process involves adjusting a slider (see Figure 23-7) and speaking aloud the phrases listed on the screen (such as *Open a document* and *Show me what to say*) until the computer makes these phrases blink in recognition.

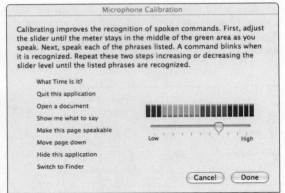

Figure 23-7:
Helping the
Mac
understand
you.

If you want to have fun with speech, ask the Mac out loud to tell you a joke. It will respond with a lame "Knock knock" joke like this one:

> "Knock knock."
>
> "Who's there?"
>
> "Thistle."
>
> "Thistle who?"
>
> "Thistle be my last knock knock joke."

Thistle, um, be my last joke too.

Index

BUSINESS, CAREERS & PERSONAL FINANCE

0-7645-5307-0

0-7645-5331-3 *†

Also available:
- Accounting For Dummies †
  0-7645-5314-3
- Business Plans Kit For Dummies †
  0-7645-5365-8
- Cover Letters For Dummies
  0-7645-5224-4
- Frugal Living For Dummies
  0-7645-5403-4
- Leadership For Dummies
  0-7645-5176-0
- Managing For Dummies
  0-7645-1771-6

- Marketing For Dummies
  0-7645-5600-2
- Personal Finance For Dummies *
  0-7645-2590-5
- Project Management For Dummies
  0-7645-5283-X
- Resumes For Dummies †
  0-7645-5471-9
- Selling For Dummies
  0-7645-5363-1
- Small Business Kit For Dummies *†
  0-7645-5093-4

HOME & BUSINESS COMPUTER BASICS

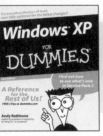

0-7645-4074-2

0-7645-3758-X

Also available:
- ACT! 6 For Dummies
  0-7645-2645-6
- iLife '04 All-in-One Desk Reference
  For Dummies
  0-7645-7347-0
- iPAQ For Dummies
  0-7645-6769-1
- Mac OS X Panther Timesaving
  Techniques For Dummies
  0-7645-5812-9
- Macs For Dummies
  0-7645-5656-8

- Microsoft Money 2004 For Dummies
  0-7645-4195-1
- Office 2003 All-in-One Desk Reference
  For Dummies
  0-7645-3883-7
- Outlook 2003 For Dummies
  0-7645-3759-8
- PCs For Dummies
  0-7645-4074-2
- TiVo For Dummies
  0-7645-6923-6
- Upgrading and Fixing PCs For Dummies
  0-7645-1665-5
- Windows XP Timesaving Techniques
  For Dummies
  0-7645-3748-2

FOOD, HOME, GARDEN, HOBBIES, MUSIC & PETS

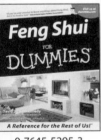

0-7645-5295-3

0-7645-5232-5

Also available:
- Bass Guitar For Dummies
  0-7645-2487-9
- Diabetes Cookbook For Dummies
  0-7645-5230-9
- Gardening For Dummies *
  0-7645-5130-2
- Guitar For Dummies
  0-7645-5106-X
- Holiday Decorating For Dummies
  0-7645-2570-0
- Home Improvement All-in-One
  For Dummies
  0-7645-5680-0

- Knitting For Dummies
  0-7645-5395-X
- Piano For Dummies
  0-7645-5105-1
- Puppies For Dummies
  0-7645-5255-4
- Scrapbooking For Dummies
  0-7645-7208-3
- Senior Dogs For Dummies
  0-7645-5818-8
- Singing For Dummies
  0-7645-2475-5
- 30-Minute Meals For Dummies
  0-7645-2589-1

INTERNET & DIGITAL MEDIA

0-7645-1664-7

0-7645-6924-4

Also available:
- 2005 Online Shopping Directory
  For Dummies
  0-7645-7495-7
- CD & DVD Recording For Dummies
  0-7645-5956-7
- eBay For Dummies
  0-7645-5654-1
- Fighting Spam For Dummies
  0-7645-5965-6
- Genealogy Online For Dummies
  0-7645-5964-8
- Google For Dummies
  0-7645-4420-9

- Home Recording For Musicians
  For Dummies
  0-7645-1634-5
- The Internet For Dummies
  0-7645-4173-0
- iPod & iTunes For Dummies
  0-7645-7772-7
- Preventing Identity Theft For Dummies
  0-7645-7336-5
- Pro Tools All-in-One Desk Reference
  For Dummies
  0-7645-5714-9
- Roxio Easy Media Creator For Dummies
  0-7645-7131-1

SPORTS, FITNESS, PARENTING, RELIGION & SPIRITUALITY

0-7645-5146-9

0-7645-5418-2

Also available:

- Adoption For Dummies
  0-7645-5488-3
- Basketball For Dummies
  0-7645-5248-1
- The Bible For Dummies
  0-7645-5296-1
- Buddhism For Dummies
  0-7645-5359-3
- Catholicism For Dummies
  0-7645-5391-7
- Hockey For Dummies
  0-7645-5228-7

- Judaism For Dummies
  0-7645-5299-6
- Martial Arts For Dummies
  0-7645-5358-5
- Pilates For Dummies
  0-7645-5397-6
- Religion For Dummies
  0-7645-5264-3
- Teaching Kids to Read For Dummies
  0-7645-4043-2
- Weight Training For Dummies
  0-7645-5168-X
- Yoga For Dummies
  0-7645-5117-5

TRAVEL

0-7645-5438-7

0-7645-5453-0

Also available:

- Alaska For Dummies
  0-7645-1761-9
- Arizona For Dummies
  0-7645-6938-4
- Cancún and the Yucatán For Dummies
  0-7645-2437-2
- Cruise Vacations For Dummies
  0-7645-6941-4
- Europe For Dummies
  0-7645-5456-5
- Ireland For Dummies
  0-7645-5455-7

- Las Vegas For Dummies
  0-7645-5448-4
- London For Dummies
  0-7645-4277-X
- New York City For Dummies
  0-7645-6945-7
- Paris For Dummies
  0-7645-5494-8
- RV Vacations For Dummies
  0-7645-5443-3
- Walt Disney World & Orlando For Dummies
  0-7645-6943-0

GRAPHICS, DESIGN & WEB DEVELOPMENT

0-7645-4345-8

0-7645-5589-8

Also available:

- Adobe Acrobat 6 PDF For Dummies
  0-7645-3760-1
- Building a Web Site For Dummies
  0-7645-7144-3
- Dreamweaver MX 2004 For Dummies
  0-7645-4342-3
- FrontPage 2003 For Dummies
  0-7645-3882-9
- HTML 4 For Dummies
  0-7645-1995-6
- Illustrator CS For Dummies
  0-7645-4084-X

- Macromedia Flash MX 2004 For Dummies
  0-7645-4358-X
- Photoshop 7 All-in-One Desk Reference For Dummies
  0-7645-1667-1
- Photoshop CS Timesaving Techniques For Dummies
  0-7645-6782-9
- PHP 5 For Dummies
  0-7645-4166-8
- PowerPoint 2003 For Dummies
  0-7645-3908-6
- QuarkXPress 6 For Dummies
  0-7645-2593-X

NETWORKING, SECURITY, PROGRAMMING & DATABASES

0-7645-6852-3

0-7645-5784-X

Also available:

- A+ Certification For Dummies
  0-7645-4187-0
- Access 2003 All-in-One Desk Reference For Dummies
  0-7645-3988-4
- Beginning Programming For Dummies
  0-7645-4997-9
- C For Dummies
  0-7645-7068-4
- Firewalls For Dummies
  0-7645-4048-3
- Home Networking For Dummies
  0-7645-42796

- Network Security For Dummies
  0-7645-1679-5
- Networking For Dummies
  0-7645-1677-9
- TCP/IP For Dummies
  0-7645-1760-0
- VBA For Dummies
  0-7645-3989-2
- Wireless All In-One Desk Reference For Dummies
  0-7645-7496-5
- Wireless Home Networking For Dummies
  0-7645-3910-8

ALTH & SELF-HELP

0-7645-6820-5 *†

0-7645-2566-2

Also available:

Alzheimer's For Dummies
0-7645-3899-3

Asthma For Dummies
0-7645-4233-8

Controlling Cholesterol For Dummies
0-7645-5440-9

Depression For Dummies
0-7645-3900-0

Dieting For Dummies
0-7645-4149-8

Fertility For Dummies
0-7645-2549-2

Fibromyalgia For Dummies
0-7645-5441-7

Improving Your Memory For Dummies
0-7645-5435-2

Pregnancy For Dummies †
0-7645-4483-7

Quitting Smoking For Dummies
0-7645-2629-4

Relationships For Dummies
0-7645-5384-4

Thyroid For Dummies
0-7645-5385-2

DUCATION, HISTORY, REFERENCE & TEST PREPARATION

0-7645-5194-9

0-7645-4186-2

Also available:

Algebra For Dummies
0-7645-5325-9

British History For Dummies
0-7645-7021-8

Calculus For Dummies
0-7645-2498-4

English Grammar For Dummies
0-7645-5322-4

Forensics For Dummies
0-7645-5580-4

The GMAT For Dummies
0-7645-5251-1

Inglés Para Dummies
0-7645-5427-1

Italian For Dummies
0-7645-5196-5

Latin For Dummies
0-7645-5431-X

Lewis & Clark For Dummies
0-7645-2545-X

Research Papers For Dummies
0-7645-5426-3

The SAT I For Dummies
0-7645-7193-1

Science Fair Projects For Dummies
0-7645-5460-3

U.S. History For Dummies
0-7645-5249-X

Get smart @ dummies.com®

- **Find a full list of Dummies titles**
- **Look into loads of FREE on-site articles**
- **Sign up for FREE eTips e-mailed to you weekly**
- **See what other products carry the Dummies name**
- **Shop directly from the Dummies bookstore**
- **Enter to win new prizes every month!**